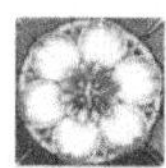

"If you think the '50s to the '70s were interesting, find out for sure, and read *Tempus Fugitive*, a true and funny history of the time."

Ian Bernard - Music Director for Laugh-In

"Dion Wright's book is a marvel. Our paths crossed in and out of one another's during the '60s, linked by people like Stewart Brand and Tim Leary, and though we might have disagreed about much "in the day" both our communities "played for keeps." This is a deep and authentic view into the life and sensibilities of a group like mine, The Diggers, but with its own, more psychedelicized orbit. Both of us were (perhaps too) fearless explorers. Both made mistakes and both he and I have lived to write about the great, late 20th-century upheaval, which changed cultural premises of our Nation. We're still dealing with those changes today. I so recognized the tone of the time in these pages and urge you to read it."

Peter Coyote - Actor, Writer, Zen Buddhist Priest

"The book *Tempus Fugitive* is a gold mine for artists and art students. Dion Wright attempted to extricate himself from the narrative and focus on the route of the specific counterculture he participated in and observed, always including artists, and from his perspective (as an artist). By not focusing on himself, he richly demonstrates the idiosyncratic, signature artists' mind, and is a touchstone for any of us struggling in the world of fine art. We will find our own idiosyncrasy has intelligent companions."

Larry Gill - Sculptor

"*Tempus Fugitive* is a crystal-clear reflection of a simpler time filled with vivid characters who would be mostly gone now if Dion hadn't put them to paper. Their voices resound with new life while the attitude and tendencies remain as before, youthful and undaunted. The stories of their art, work, and play remain fresh and relevant. Listen closely and hear Krishna's flute..."

William "Bud" Hedrick - Soldier of Fortune, Gifted Craftsman,
Philosopher, Bon Vivant, and Renaissance Man

"I was fascinated by Dion's narrative and high literary description of other characters and the important history of the time and place, being a geography south of San Francisco and the Beats a demised scene comparatively, I think. It should be taught in every school, a VERY important well-written book done by a master welder who sealed that hot seam of history."

Charley Plymell - Central Figure of The Wichita Vortex;
Poet, Printer, and Publisher

"Sharing space at the Festival of Arts in Laguna, Dion and I were disillusioned by cement and straights. I went surfing; Dion (Dionysus – god of sex and wine and patron of the arts) went seeking. In the waning Beat scene of the '50s, Wright begins an Odyssey through mind expansion and politically unsettled times. An admitted "fly on the wall" as well as participant, we're entertained by the sex and foibles of a like-minded community of artful seekers through the keen memory and acerbic wit of Mr. Wright. It is an encyclopedia of hipsters, potheads, and psychedelic voyagers.

Dion sculpts and paints (his noted Mandala at Woodstock in New York), marries a couple of times, shucks off wives and mental baggage, and is as on the road as Kerouac. Dion meets and collaborates with John Griggs and The Brotherhood of Eternal Love in Laguna, runs the Mystic Arts Gallery, takes Timothy Leary fishing, and observes in awe as Shiva does his dance—right in downtown Laguna Beach. Suggested beverage while reading: a clear blue something—I forget..."

John Severson - Maui, Hawaii - Artist, Film Maker,
Founder and Publisher of Surfer Magazine

It is quite typical of the person and artist, my good friend, Dion Wright to title his book *"A Personal History of the American Counter-Culture of the 20th Century", "Tempus Fugitive*" a punny expletive loaded version of the clichéd Latin expression 'Time Flies". And these 350 pages do fly according to his accurate description, "an historical memoir with emphasis on Art, Psychology, Philosophy, and the pursuit of expanded consciousness, via Chemistry, delivered in narrative through real stories about real people." Owing to the thirty-nine page mentions of myself and our communal group USCO, I am a totally biased and flattered commentator on Wright's flight through the druggy, sexy, "visions of truth" portrayed as Dion wandered from California's Laguna Beach through New York State's Woodstock, the San Francisco Beat Scene and always returning to Laguna portraying and characterizing along those ways in words, photographs and graphics, the times and personalities of such knowables as Aldous Huxley, Timothy Leary, Janie Chipmunk and a host of other types and artists of all genders, with a special emphasis on one of the principals of the fraternity of psychedelic buccaneers, John Griggs, who named "*The Brotherhood of Eternal Love*", and according to our author, was the "prophet" who inspired this book, writing "I am not intending to make a mythological character out of him, or even a hero, but we need him as a symbol of idealism". To close, I recommend you do your best to find "*Tempus Fugitive*" and experience these lives. A flavor of ethical, albeit controversial behaviors fill these pages depicting in toto the "ideal" meant by Wright's honoring of that meaningful Griggs association."

Gerd Stern - Poet

First, I found myself travelling West- and East- Coastally by pickup truck in artist Dion Wright's memoir *Tempus Fugitive: A Personal History of the American Counter-Culture of the 20th Century.* Then, serendipitously, I next rode pillion on Oliver Sacks' BMW R60 (and its lesser antecedents) in *On the Move: A Life*. While each of our lives involves a search for meaning, Wright's (like Sacks') peripatetic quest takes us through territory few of us have travelled and lived to tell about. Wright (like Sacks) has the literary chops to channel us with him by extensive gauntlets of modern Scyllas and Charybdises and beckoning Lotus Eaters, a truly mythic world of *"Art, Beatniks, Sex, Hippies, Art Festivals, Mind Expansion, Mortality."* Wright's completely engaging tale is rich in famous and infamous people, critical insight, irony, honesty, and laugh-out-loud turns of phrase.

George Voland - Teacher, Editor, and Valve Trombonist

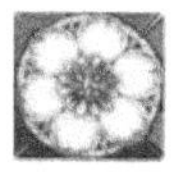

A PERSONAL HISTORY OF THE AMERICAN COUNTER-CULTURE OF THE 20TH CENTURY

TEMPUS FUGITIVE

by

Dion Wright

ART, BEATNIKS,
SEX, HIPPIES,
ART FESTIVALS,
MIND EXPANSION,
MORTALITY.

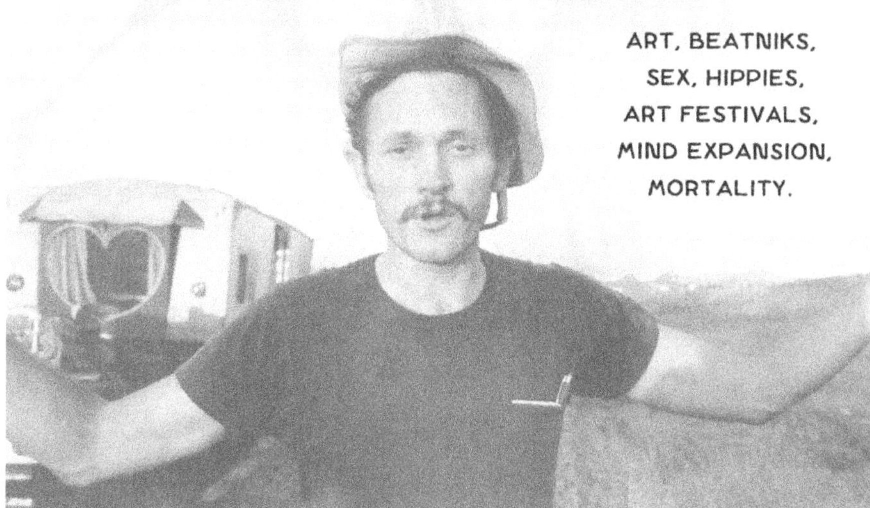

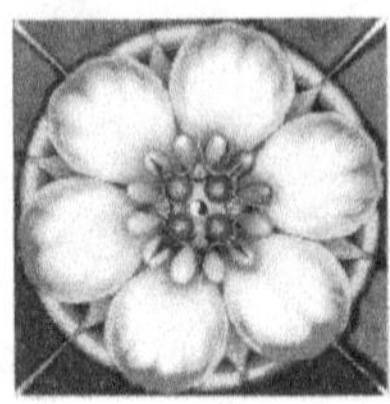

Published by Mindful Wordsmith

The author gratefully acknowledges and thanks the artists and photographers who gave permission to include their works in *Tempus Fugitive.*

Book Cover design: Starseed, by Dion Wright. Photo credit: Ruth Wright.

Printed in the United States of America

Second edition published July 2016

ISBN: 978-0-9973342-1-0 (Paperback)

dionwright.com

Acknowledgements

Thank you for the help, support and advice of Ruth Wright, Gerd Stern, Roger Taft, and most of all, the indispensable colleague, Allyn Bryan.

Dedication

To

The Spirit, the Mind, and the Memory

of

Aldous Huxley

and all other

Courageous Pioneers

everywhere

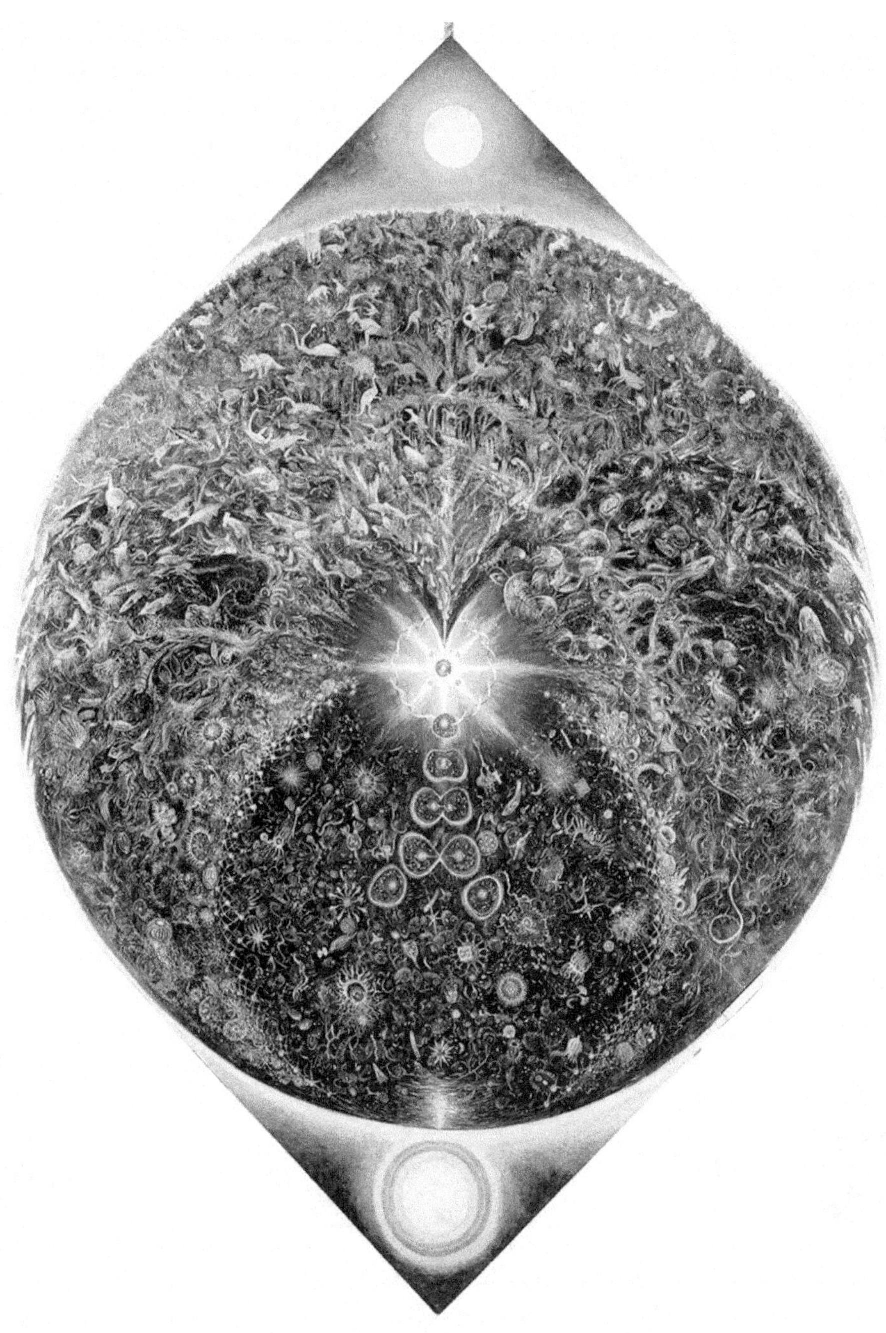

Figure 1: Frontispiece Taxonomic Mandala of Evolution
by Dion Wright. Painted in Woodstock, NY, 1965 & 1966

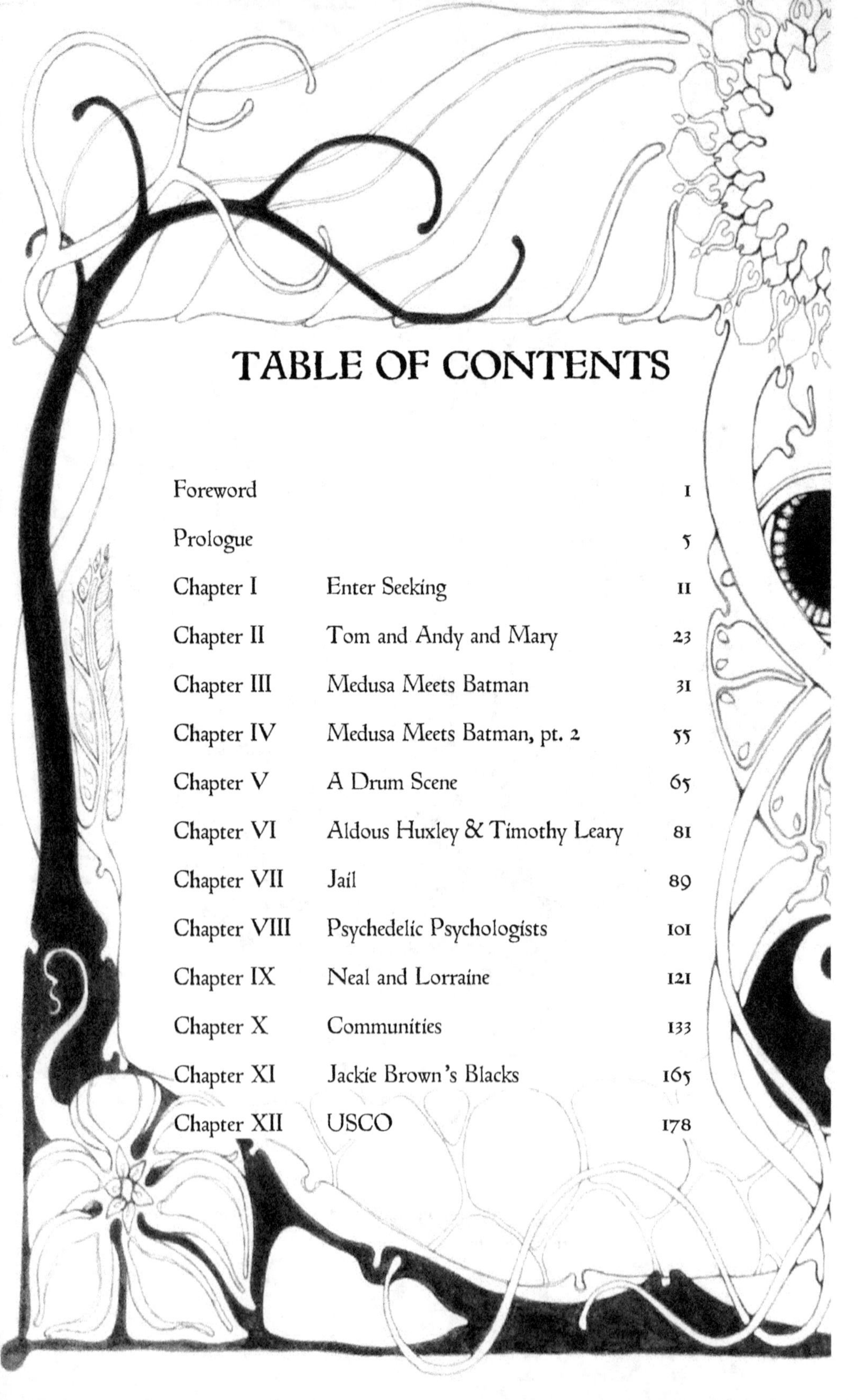

TABLE OF CONTENTS

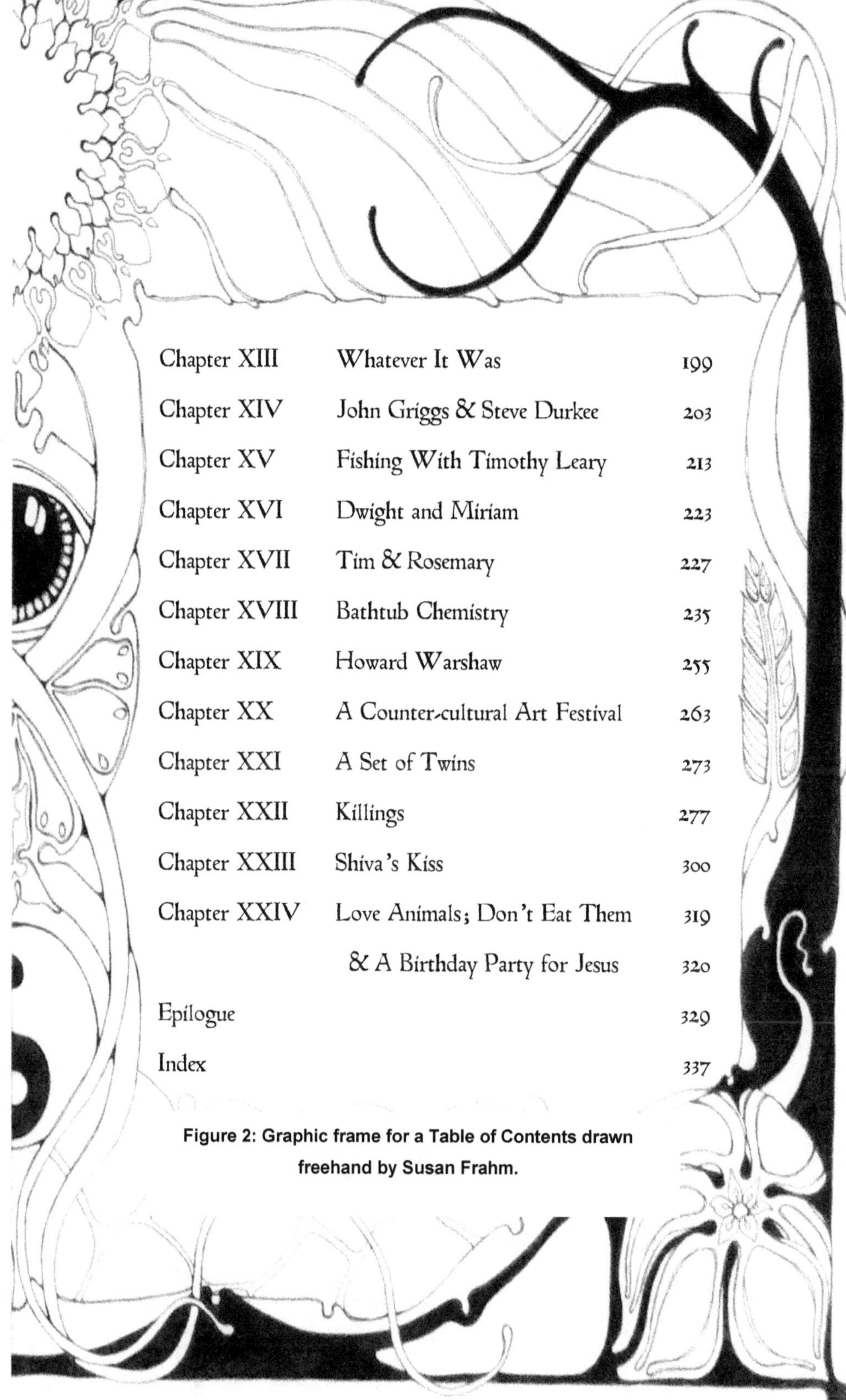

Figure 2: Graphic frame for a Table of Contents drawn freehand by Susan Frahm.

Introduction by Charley Plymell

Dion Wright's *Tempus Fugitive* is one of the best books I've read concerning the Psychedelic Hippy scene from Millbrook to Woodstock to San Miguel to Laguna Beach to San Francisco and all stops in between. A Le Corbusier of metal and philosophy, his narrative is about real characters, hilarious and insightful. The book is dedicated *to "The Spirit, the Mind, and the memory of Aldous Huxley…"* whom ironically we learn died on LSD the same date as the Kennedy assassination. This sets the tone for mind expansion and killings. I knew Dion briefly in the early '60s in San Francisco when his metal sculptures and paintings were the talk of the town. One can not only learn about the depths and downers lurking in mind expansion, one can learn a lot about morality and the law typical of Southern California in the day, and the dropout culture whose principals he knew well. There are many hippie sexual characters too, as icing on the cakes, as they say.

Kerouac stole his girlfriend but didn't steal his writing style, which, in my opinion far exceeds that of Kerouac in terms of storytelling.

He is one of the true artists coming out of that era, both formally educated and quickly learning that of the street when he was busted for a few sticks of "Indiana Roadside Weed." He spent a half-year in jail for that but LSD was legal! I think it is a very important historical book for those who really want to know what happened during those years when he literally carried his art on his back from arson fires started by the law to get rid of the undesirables when history repeats itself, reminiscent of the times the California authorities beat and killed the "Okies." It's an important document in counter-culture, as well as psychedelics. Important to us now to see how politics dictates laws which were meant to harass others' views of freedom, which lead to a conclusion of a time in history that has changed, but who knows for how long: "The flower children had gradually encountered Ultimate Reality, and discovered they were just so much meat." One will learn about the tragedies and trips in Bathtub Chemistry and Killings. The book is well illustrated with photos of the time. I can't stress enough its historical importance. To see a real artist survive to tell the tale and bring the characters to life you WILL want to meet. An amazing book, as they say in millennial speak. Seriously, this is a personal history you will cherish.

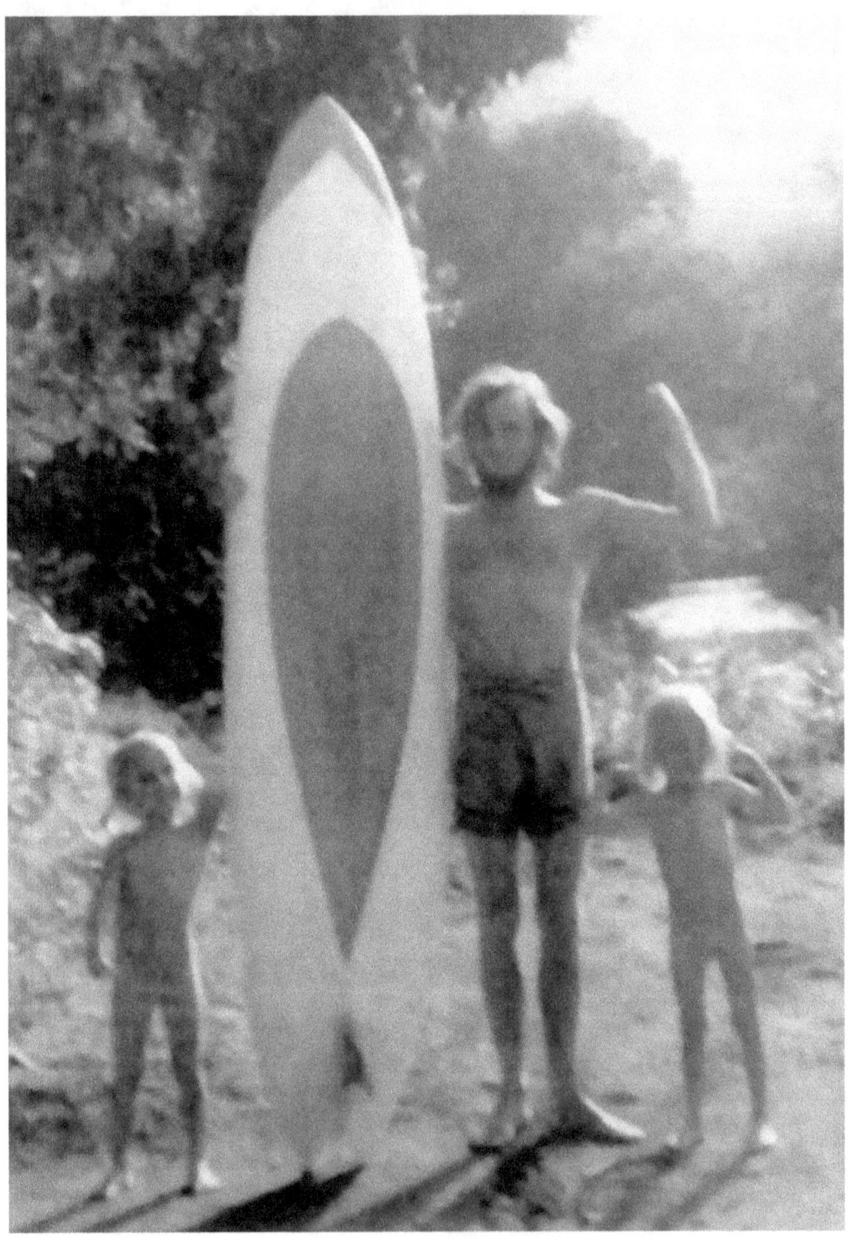

Figure 3: John Griggs in Hawaii with his children, Sissy and Jerry.

Foreword

When John Griggs, the prophet, died at 26, he left a roiling and chaotic world behind. It took me twenty-five years and more to see his life and times at least somewhat objectively. It was my conceit for years that John's shade was sitting on my shoulder, urging me, in his persuasive Okie Huckster Salesman twang to "tell the truth about it."

I think that he'd always known that I would be the one most likely to 'get it right', partly on account of my preamble experiences before I met him in 1967, and partly because he had decisive conviction, even when he was dead wrong, about who was who and what was what.

He saw me as a carrier of the story, and in this, at least, he was right. I only knew the last part of his story personally; the part where John was a testifying prophet. His earlier life as a teen-age mischief-maker was legendary, but below the horizon of my experience.

When I finally gave in to John's ghost and its persistent badgering in my inner ear, real or imagined, it took me several decades and five rewrites to get it into its present form. Once I started writing, John's wheedling spirit, real or imagined, stopped its clamoring. I could feel that he was still there, nodding in ectoplasmic approval as I trudged on.

As I approached John's story, I discovered two facts. First, that I had to go back far enough to make some kind of sense out of who he was and why he was doing what he did, and secondly, that I'd have to become a player in the saga to assert continuity, whether I wanted to or not, and I really didn't.

At first, I went all the way back to 1937, when Aldous Huxley, the gray eminence of the story, arrived in Hollywood, and more-or-less founded the Consciousness Expansion Movement along with J. Krishnamurti, Edwin Hubble, Gerald Heard and a suite of swamis and intellectuals. All the lengthy narrative of precursor events from 1937 to 1959 has been lopped off. I am now content to let the story begin with the last gasp of the Beat Generation in San Francisco, and end with the collapse of Flower Power around 1970.

When I was down in the quarry doing the first draft of this writing, I decided to be blunt about sexual matters, to put aside inhibitions that might contaminate other aspects of telling the truth. Now, I am inclined to soft-pedal such salaciousness as could be seen as sensationalistic, or pandering to prurient interests. I'm ambivalent about the subject.

Now that it has become almost de rigueur to write the word "fuck" into one's manuscript, I find that I'm leaning toward rebelling against the rebellion. I've lived through the whole arc of usage from when nobody could write those certain words, to where everyone is expected to use them.

Hemingway could not use them at all. Norman Mailer spelled it "fug" and James Jones finally just used the word freely where appropriate, in dialogue, in his case. These were the commercially narrative big guns, all of whom depended on the banned books of Henry Miller, and the courageous publishing of Henry Miller's books by Grove Press, for their liberation from censorship and proscription. But here I am, free at last, having to use my own judgment about what is apropos. So, I'll just make individual judgment calls as I go along, but I doubt if I'll add any new cussing.

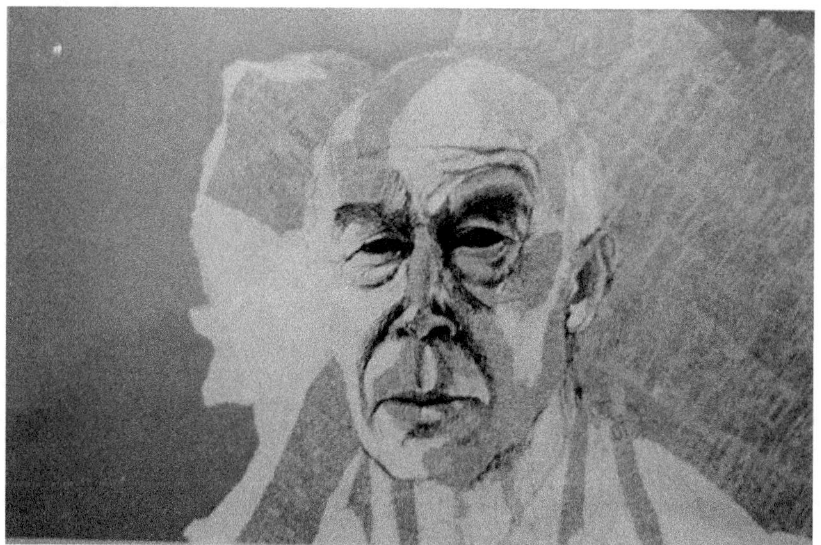

Figure 4: "Henry Miller" drawing/collage by Dion Wright ca. 1961. Cyna (Figure 5) asked so nicely for it that I gave it to her.

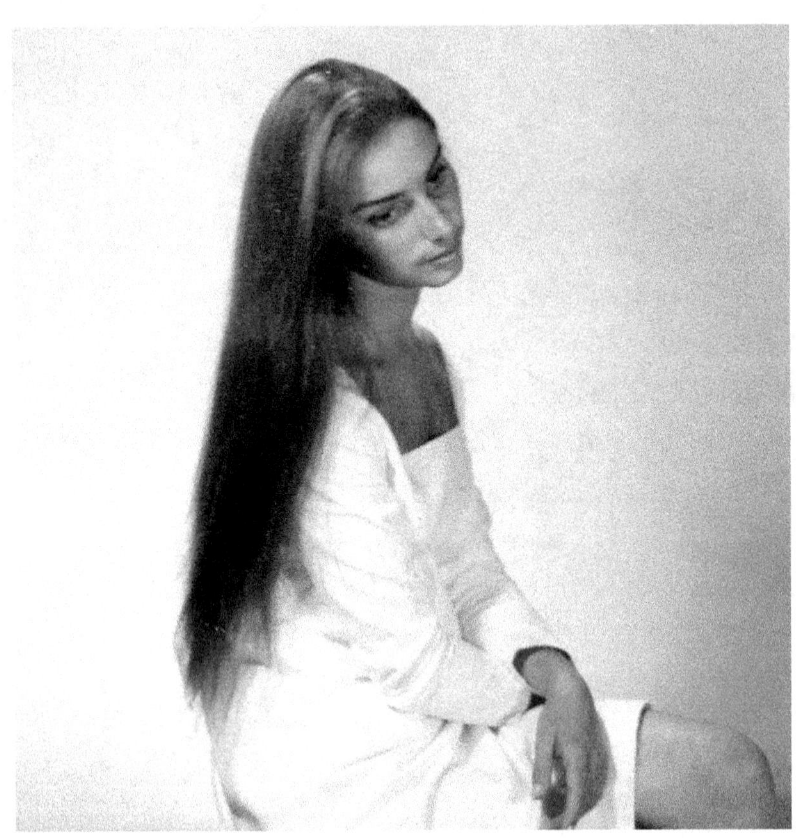

Figure 5: Cyna Stokesbary photo by Chuck Everts

Prologue

"In a democratic society the highest duty of the writer, the composer, the artist is to remain true to himself and let the chips fall where they may. In serving his vision of the truth, the artist best serves his nation."

John F. Kennedy
Amherst, Massachusetts
October 26, 1963

This is a series of stories about what happened within my sphere of observation in mid-20th Century America. The core of the narrative is about Art and how it meshed with the Consciousness Expansion Movement, sometimes called, "The Psychedelic Revolution."

It is widely asserted that a writer ought to tell The Truth. This goal might be a conceit and a folly, not that the impossibility of success should deter us. Memory is fallible, and perspectives by different people who were witnesses to this or that incident always diverge. These divergences are argued with energy and passion, both (or all) sides earnestly believing they have it right and the other guys are at least partly wrong. Everybody except a few radical philosophers can agree that *something* happened. After that, narrative splits and loses form and shape quickly, so the artist/writer has to admit that what he's yarning about is personal myth more than objective reporting, especially when telling tales of a lost world informed by substances called "hallucinogens"!

None of which relieves a writer of the responsibility of trying to be truthful and objective, even if it's a daunting challenge. One has the responsibility to be as historically accurate as possible, perhaps in direct proportion to how much love one has for the dear departed, and how exactly and precisely one wishes to evoke them. Many of these characters about to be recalled had a profound interaction with me emotionally, and one of my toughest jobs in this writing is to see them with as little prejudice as possible. Complete objectivity is a goal, but can't be an achievement. Part of the effort is to tell the facts, as best I know them, and hope they add up to The Truth.

I've been reflecting on data as knowledge and wondering at the mysteries of it. Memory in the brain seems persuasive but impenetrably occult. One thing I think about almost daily is the accumulation of knowledge and how the older we get, the more we accumulate. Where does it go when our meat vehicles fall apart? I hate to think that all this painstakingly gathered experience just disperses along with the flesh. Of course, whether I hate it or not does not matter at all, in the cosmic scheme of things.

Another amazing thing is how I seem to know more than I've learned. It's as if by absorbing part of something, I get much more of it into my consciousness to draw on, which may be an alchemical, but certainly a neurophysiological effect that feeds back to the first part of my speculation about where the knowledge goes. Getting contemplative behind such reveries is not very unattached, and bound to lead to more suffering.

I don't like the word "autobiography" or its connotations, although I suppose it qualifies, at least partly, to define this book.

I like "memoir" better, but even that noun is conditional. It has become the era itself, which is central. I would prefer to stay out of the narrative altogether. Now, I've given up on anonymity, but with regret.

Full of profiles and sketches as this book is, it seems to come up short as self-definition. That's OK with me. I, as a personality, am beside the point. I started out trying to write this leaving myself out completely, but the narrative had no rudder that way. Many times, I've marveled at having been the fly-on-the-wall in lots of colorful situations. I suppose that could be called "karma" by some. So, as a personality within these pages, I see myself as a camera and bend my efforts toward minimizing distortion.

Presenting patterns and appearances, which are not what they seem, is one of nature's oldest gambits among creatures. It allows some of them to remain undetected, either for their own survival or so that they can ambush others, as more successful predators. Human beings also dissemble, usually on purpose. Some people have quality, and some pretend to it.

In the era that centered in the '60s, it often seemed as if the subjective and the irrational might be likely, while the objective and the prosaic often came to seem false. The nature of perception itself was warping daily under the media manipulations of a government that seemed ever less trustworthy and also under the persuasion of mind-expanding chemicals. In such a time of shifting bearings and changing appearances, the 'doors of perception' swung open wider than they ever had before, and in such a general and pervasive way as to clear the stage for many rampaging egos to prance forth; sometimes real geniuses, sometimes base charlatans, and sometimes both wrapped up within a single skin.

This was an incredibly complex situation to see into with clarity. The problem right now is to decide whom, within the intersection of Art with Consciousness Expansion; best reflected the split between the genuine and the bogus. You'll have to take my word for it. It is the most subjective of perceptions.

May a person be a true genius who has a deplorable character? I'm afraid so. Especially among artists, the "genius" appellation is very loosely assigned to people who have one brilliant vein, of, say, painting, or writing, or performing, but who may have almost nothing else to recommend them as excellent specimens of humanity. We ought to get over this tendency to give adulation to monsters, just because they can splatter or warble pleasantly.

A word on narrative organization and structure: Each chapter is concocted to be a complete unit with a beginning, middle and an end. The units follow a loose chronology and overlap in particulars. The intent is kaleidoscopic, but not random.

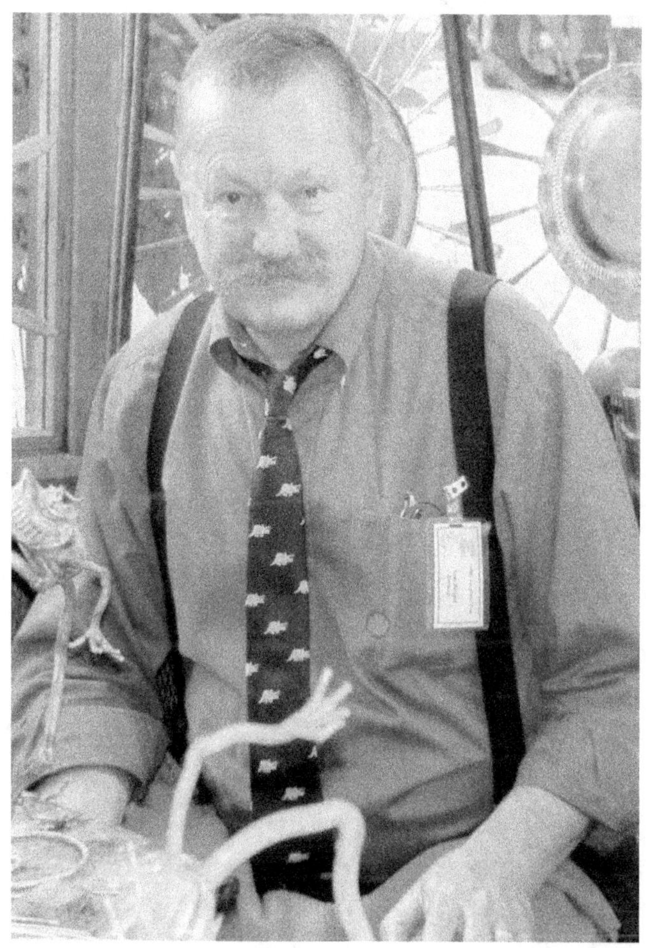

Figure 6: The Whimsical Old Fart

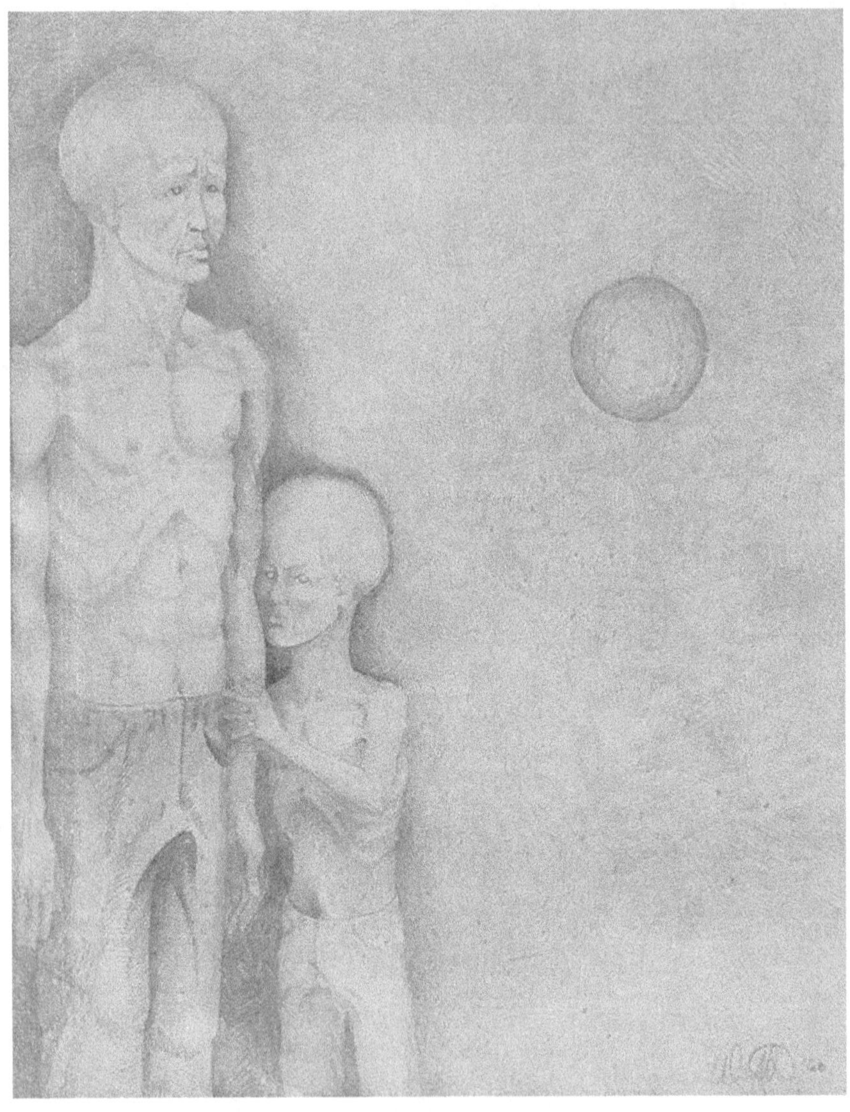

Figure 7: The author has a jaundiced view of the future as early as 1960.

Chapter I

Enter Seeking

When World War II ended, Americans seemed to think that Evil was conquered. It was never as blatantly obvious again, who the good guys were, and who were the bad, but the struggle continued.

By the end of the Eisenhower years, in 1959, my UCSB Art degree in hand, I had a head full of fervent idealism. I juried into *The Festival of Arts* in Laguna Beach, California for my first season of engaging the public.

The Festival of Arts was the sacred cow of the town. Outside of the town, it had a reputation among the Art intelligentsia as a provincial gathering of calendar painters who were a sideshow for the real production, *The Pageant of the Masters.* This Pageant was, and is, a high-quality professional theater presentation of tableau vivant, "living pictures," as they described it. Famous paintings and sculptures from the History of Art are recreated in life size, with living people.

The exhibiting artists living in the little resort town invented the Pageant back in the '30s to attract an audience to look at, and hopefully buy, their paintings. But by 1959, the tail was wagging the dog. The artists had become secondary to the theatrical presentation but tolerated as a necessity that gave the Pageant its authenticity. Into this circumstance, I stumbled, slightly cynical and exceedingly ignorant of the nuts and bolts reality of Art in the street, but with a head full of high-minded idealism.

Al DuPont, the extroverted seascape painter, was a man of many parts. He was my immediate neighbor at the 1959 Festival of Arts. In appearance, Al was a spare, tall, balding guy of wily expression, who talked in clipped New Yorkese. He wiseacred and joked all the time when he wasn't trying to sell something. Al had been a sailor-man with all the characteristics associated with that pungent group, plus more.

During World War II, there was a naval coast-watching station on the very end of Dana Point. A half-dozen acres make up the level area on top of the point. From here, Richard Henry Dana, on the brig *Pilgrim*, retrieved the thrown-down dried ox hides, the main California export, processed in San Juan Capistrano in the 1830s.

Dana Point is surrounded on three sides by steep, high cliffs with no convenient way down, except for the occasional plunges taken over the years by various luckless souls. It was a great vantage point to survey the coast, with unobstructed views to Point Loma in the south and to Point Fermin in the north. A constant breeze blows in off the Pacific Ocean. In the center of those six flat acres on the end of Dana Point, the U.S. Navy had built an H-shaped structure of two parallel barracks buildings of about twenty by forty feet each. They were connected in the middle by an enclosed hallway. A tall radio-transmitting tower rose next to the buildings. These communicated with the coastal guns in the naval artillery bunkers above Laguna Beach to the north, and Camp Joseph H. Pendleton, USMC, to the south.

When WWII ended, the official mission of the coast-watching installation ended. Some sailors and some of the locals took up the abandoned premises as a party pad. It was a remote site in

1947, no longer monitored by the Navy. Al DuPont had been a regular on that scene. My parents rented a house in Dana Point at the same time. I had my ninth birthday there in 1946.

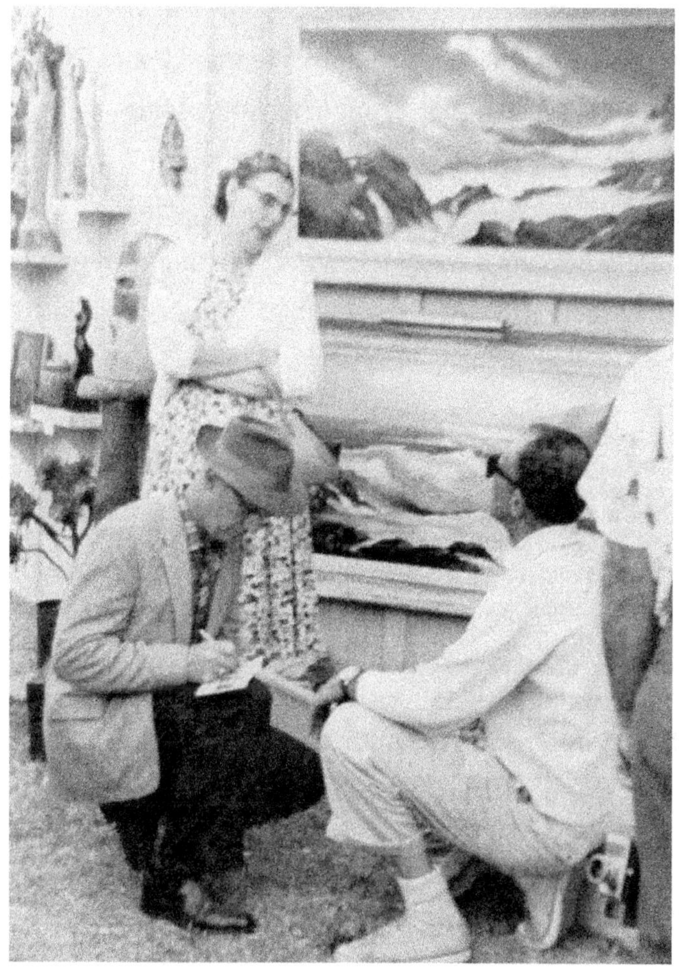

Figure 8: Al DuPont making a sale.

Al DuPont was assigned to the coast-watching station during the war, where he painted stirring naval warfare murals on the barracks walls. They featured the tigerish exploits of the "Tin Can" destroyers and the destruction of Japanese foe. The paintings were probably fictional as historical documents, but bang-up as melodrama. I used to look at them as a kid when I often went onto the Point investigating natural history.

By the early '50s, the barracks were dilapidated and woebegone relics, falling apart and untended, but Al DuPont's art survived. It stirred a boy's imagination, seeing these violent scenes of naval warfare rendered on the walls of a falling-down barracks building, with the wind perpetually blowing in through broken windows and gaping doorways. The murals were very well painted; far better than the commercial work Al did in later life as a Festival of Arts seascapist.

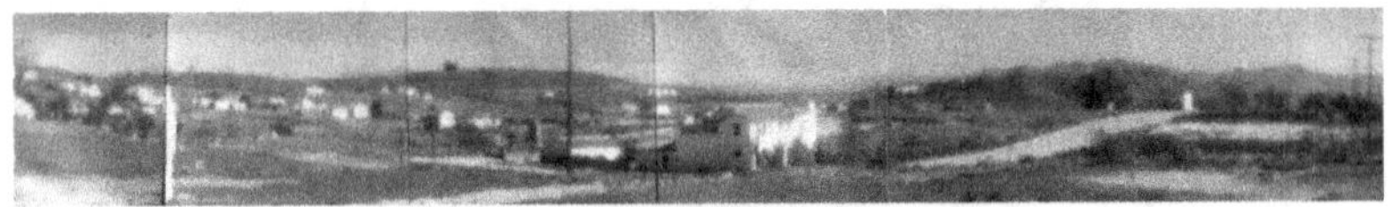

Figure 9: Panorama of Dana Point California looking NE in 1947. Edited from 8mm film shot by Bruce Wright.

So, I was taken to live in Dana Point in 1946 because my parents regarded the tiny and half-defunct town as desirable, despite its being equally far from Los Angeles and San Diego. It was centrally convenient to my Old Man's circuit of customers, who hired him to service their analytical balances.

There were less than three hundred residents in Dana Point then. The dead-on-the-vine planned community had gone broke, half-completed, after the Crash of 1929. It was a great place to be a kid during the late '40s when everybody in the town knew everybody else. The remoteness was hard on my mom, though, who was a dyed-in-the-wool transplanted New Yorker. She longed for whatever sophisticated society might be found in such a provincial place, and the most civilized person she found was the vibrant divorcee, Carla Penney.

Carla was an elegant woman. She was a long-necked, long-legged brunette with perfect features and what I was as yet unprepared to fully appreciate a terrific figure. She was always dressed and made up as if she were in Brentwood or Pasadena, rather than in the boondocks of Dana Point. She was also well off. She was only living in the Dana Point backwater while she recovered her bearings after a messy divorce from her playboy spouse.

Carla had redheaded twin boys, Biff and Ben, who, at eight, were a year or so younger than I. They looked up to me, an unworthy surrogate, as an older brother. When they asked, "Dion, why do our peckers get stiff?", I was forced to admit that I didn't know.

We three boys were about the only kids in Dana Point at all close to each other in age. We spent the golden days exploring the concrete architectural ruins of the unfinished planned community, emerging from the grassy, clifftop landscape like the antediluvian bones of a lost civilization.

The streets were named Street of the Blue Lantern, Street of the Golden Lantern, Street of the Silver Lantern, and so forth. At one time, there were appropriately colored lanterns along Pacific Coast Highway to designate each street, but they had disappeared, along with the mission bells that once punctuated Highway 101, on the old Mission Trail. In 1946 there were few houses yet built on any of these romantically named streets.

There were fascinating places for boys to explore: the vacant concrete shell of an incomplete hotel perched mid-town on the cliff; the estuary of San Juan Creek; tide pools full of exotic creatures at Doheny Beach; and a labyrinth of cement tunnels for run-off, which ran in a grid throughout the town.

The tunnels were a hundred feet down, interconnected and accessible at every street corner via concrete lids with recessed steel handles that allowed a little boy to lift them up, with effort. Vertical shafts went down to the tunnels, accessed by steel ladder rungs set into the cement. It took bravery for little kids to enter such precincts, but Biff and Ben were nothing if not daredevils. As the elder boy, I was obliged to lead the way into the daunting subterranean abyss, candles or flashlights in hand. If our parents had realized we were plumbing such depths, there would have been hell to pay.

They never found out. Cliffs, sloughs, rattlesnakes, and an abyss; there were many ways for a boy to get killed in Dana Point, but whoever died, it wasn't us.

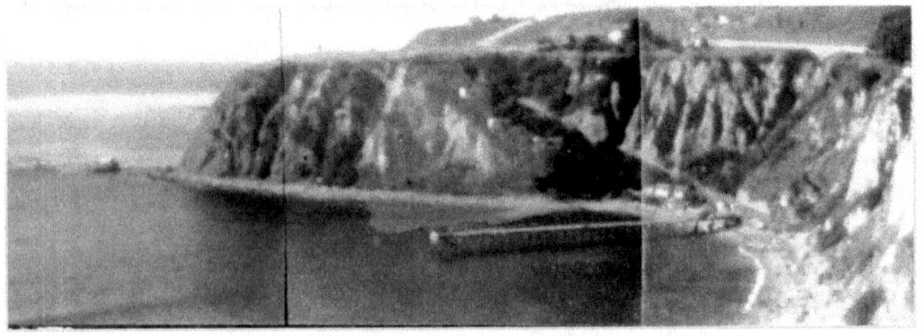

Figure 10: Killer (?) Dana Point in 1947, looking NW. From 8mm film shot by Bruce Wright.

My mom, Helen, was sometimes pressed into service as a babysitter for Biff and Ben. She didn't mind and enjoyed her daily jawing sessions with Carla. Though a decade younger, Carla was at home with the political and cultural themes that made up Helen's interests. It was a mild mystery where Carla might go at night in that provincial place, until one day, I heard Helen whispering to my Old Man that, "Carla is going out to raise hell with those sailors on the Point."

I didn't altogether get the drift of this eavesdropped tidbit until 1959, when, as a new artist at the Festival of Arts, I found myself situated across the aisle from Al DuPont. I was amazed when I learned that Al had been involved in those drunken orgies with Carla Penney. Carla had a lot of class, which is more than anybody would ever say about Al, but Carla had the soul of a party girl and enjoyed indulging it.

Al took a fancy to me and commenced to mentor me in the manner that he regarded as good. He recreated himself as a successful purveyor of formulaic seascapes, cranked out by the dozen. Not scorning the use of rollers to lay them out, he painted them in a line of half a dozen or more at once. This was production painting, offered up to the public as inspired genius. He may have been a vulgar, if entertaining, specimen, in and of himself, but he knew how to present his concoctions with elegance. He had the most sophisticated and cultured European woman in town running his gallery.

She was a bit faded, but the genuine article. This woman, Marta Mitrovich, was so high-class that the tourists fell to their knees upon encountering her, and bought many paintings they really didn't need because they wanted Marta to think well of them. At the Festival of Arts, Al did his own selling and he was a spellbinder to watch.

"Marta Mitrovich reminds me of a lady I used to know in Dana Point," I said to Al one day.

"Oh? Who was that?" asked Al.

When I said, "Carla Penney," Al, with his customary blasé insouciance, said, "Oh yes, I knew Carla."

Remembering the stirring paintings in the abandoned barracks on Dana Point, I began to add it up. "Say, Al, I think I saw some murals you painted in the old coastwatcher's station on the Point. They were of naval war scenes. Were they yours?" Al said they were indeed his, and then launched into heady reminiscences about the wild parties out there after the war. Al was given to nostalgia, and as a sailor, he was uninhibited in his expression. My imagination ran wild as he talked, and I recalled the trailing history of my relationship with the Penney Clan.

Contacts with Carla and Biff and Ben had been infrequent in the years after we all left Dana Point. One time, our two families spent a sunny day together in Carla's upscale La Jolla home. At twelve or so, the twins were still friendly. The adults tossed back some highballs, and the gorgeous boxer dog, Buddy, ran around in an ecstasy of excitement over the visitors.

I never saw them again until 1956, when I was in college at UCSB and found out that the Penneys were now also located in Santa Barbara. I called to say hello. Carla was happy to hear from me and graciously invited me over for an excellent meal, where the twins and I looked each other over as novel souvenirs of the past. The twins were now robust young men of barely contained animal energy, while I had developed along less athletic and more aesthetic lines. We all parted warmly, but that was the last time we met.

Five years later, Mom told me that she heard from Carla that Biff and Ben had both run away with the circus. In the circus, they had both fallen in love with the same bareback rider, and in a fit of jealousy, Ben killed Biff. Ben went to prison for life, and we never knew what became of Carla. It was difficult to fit this Cain and Abel story into my developing worldview.

As for Al DuPont, he died in 1985 while riding his Indian Motorcycle to Oakland to visit his 104-year-old mother. He had a heart attack on the freeway.

In 2005, I ventured out onto Dana Point at midnight, squeezing through the sagging chain link barrier, and pushing through the brush onto the high plateau. There was nothing left to show that the coast-watching station had ever existed. The area has lately become a nature reserve.

It's only a few acres, but enough to allow a marginal ecological remnant to survive.

Al was a huckster, but he was no fool, and as a mentor, he gave me the best piece of advice I ever had. He said, when he observed a certain nymphet spending time at my booth, "Stay away from San Quentin quail." For the time being, I paid attention, went off into Mexico for Art school, and then up to San Francisco to see what the Beat Generation might have to offer.

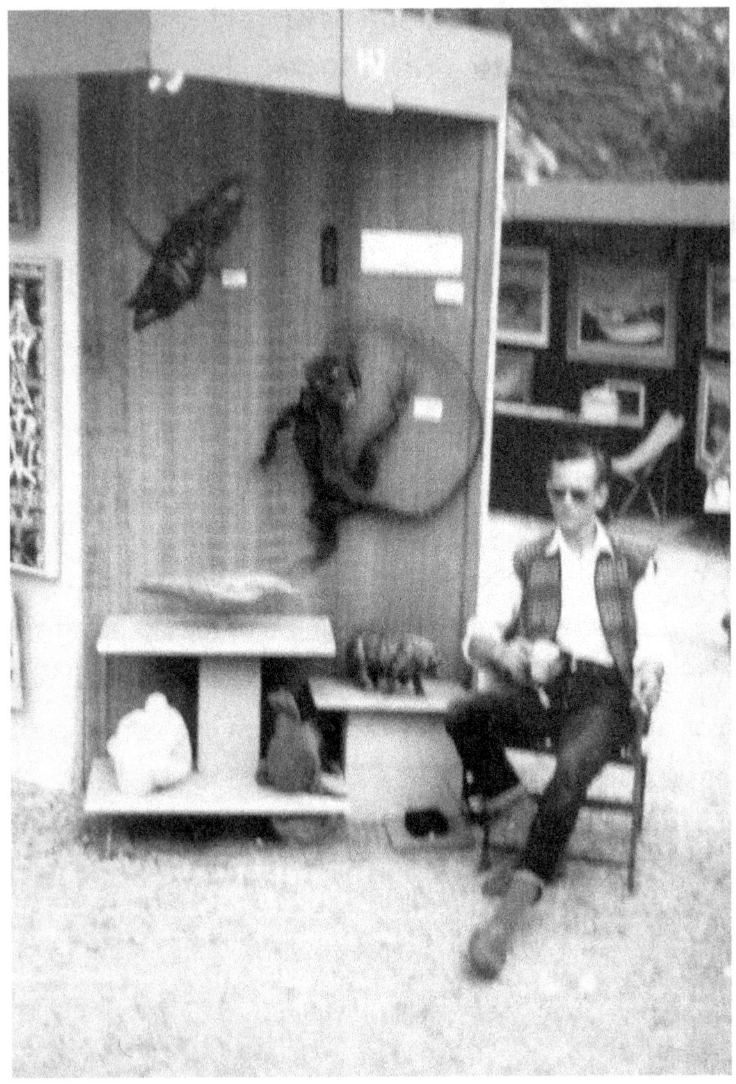

Figure 11: The author in his first Festival of Arts booth, 1959.

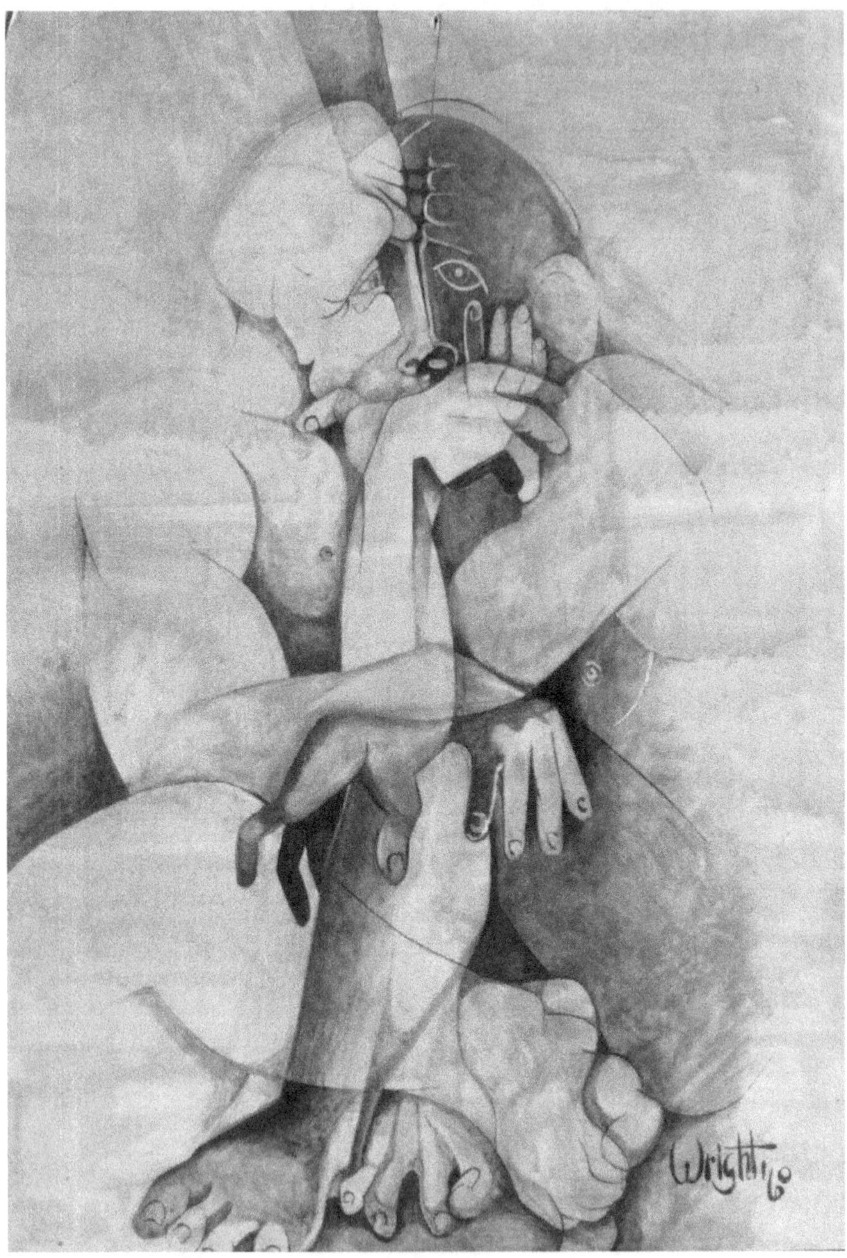

Figure 12: Author's 1960 image in oil on canvas of the revelation that the dualism of the Universe has a personal dimension.

Chapter II

Tom and Andy and Mary

On the first day of my first year at the *Festival of Arts* in 1959, I walked in at dusk to find two remarkable men painting like beings possessed. They were on opposite sides of a four by eight panel, set up on the sidewalk near the entrance.

In those days of yore, when facial hair was looked upon in Orange County as a sign of moral turpitude if not an outright perversion, here were two of the hairiest wild men I'd ever seen. They were positively bushy in their hirsute abandon, painting more frantically than the most exaggerated cartoon. The physiognomies that lurked beneath the hair were remarkable enough, without the added bushiness.

The red-haired one was small and bouncy. The comedic nature of his red nose was offset by the scowling seriousness of his penetrating blue eyes, somewhat sunk in their sockets, and darkly shadowed below. This was Tom Blackwell. Paint was flying from his brushes in an extravaganza of brilliant effect, somewhat confounded by the image he was concocting. It was a sort of Toonerville Trolley train with yellow windows rocketing across the surface of his picture. He looked as if he thought he was painting an El Greco, rather than a sketch.

On the side of the panel opposite, was Andy Wing. Andy looked like a man who actually *had* stepped right out of an El Greco painting. I later heard it said that Andy had Marfan's syndrome, like Abraham Lincoln. The syndrome causes the person to appear knobby and elongated, like El Greco's figures always were. Andy was extremely tall and large-jointed, with thick glasses set somewhat askew against his watery eyes. He too, was action painting as if he were in a war zone. His splattering technical approach reminded me of Jackson Pollock, the founder of modern American abstract Art whose work had been held up to corrosive derision by the greatest Art teacher I ever had.

The contrast of the exertions of these two remarkable painters, with the bovine lethargy of the patrons of the *Festival of Arts* as they shuffled past, incomprehension writ large upon their well-scrubbed faces, was tremendous.

I still wonder how such an unconventional and atypical thing could have happened right on the sidewalk outside of the staid and conservative *Festival of Arts*. It was likely cooked up by the charming and curly-headed grounds manager of that day, Mogens Abel, of the Danish woodcarving and architect family. Mogens never stopped smiling and was always open to novelties.

On the basis of over fifty years tracking Andy Wing and Tom Blackwell, I believe that they were, indeed, both brilliant, but that neither of them quite realized his full potential, but for different reasons. But then, who does?

At the moment of their joint painting exercise, Tom and Andy were as close as Mediterranean brothers, but their drift into separate lives was already underway. Part of what sent these quixotic wild men off on separate paths was the arrival on the scene of a world-class charlatan. One of these painters was absorbed by the charlatan's blandishments and the other was not.

Tom and Andy's joint gallery down on Cleo Street was in an ancient frame building slated for destruction to make way for an

Albertson's supermarket, so the friends were also experiencing a physical dislocation of domicile. I must add that my phrase "joint gallery" was also descriptive, in that they both smoked grass like smudge pots.

Stumbling upon the kinetic painting demonstration in front of the Festival by Andy and Tom was a bravura introduction (which was the exception proving the rule) to the dispassionate mediocrity and calculated effect that characterized most of the work in the *Festival of Arts.* Such eccentrics as Tom Blackwell and Andy Wing were relegated by administrative fiat, along with other abstract artists, Jews, and Italians (often overlapping categories), to a single aisle within the show known as "Red Alley". The presumption, one supposes, was that such work was too radical to be Democrat, much less Republican. The best conversation was found on this aisle at all hours. The aisles in those days were lanes of sawdust, and would be for the next few years until the grounds became a grid of permanent cement pathways.

Among us bright young artists groping for a shtick, there appeared this magnum charlatan, loaded for bear. She was as relentless as a labor leader, which she actually had been in NYC. Her name was Mary Marx, older sister of David Rosen, one of the Red Alley painters. She appeared in Laguna Beach in the wake of her divorce from Mr. Marx, poor man, whoever he was.

Mary Marx was one smart cookie, and tough as an anchor chain. She became active simultaneously in the lives of Tom Blackwell, Andy Wing, and me (as well as numerous other artists). She especially targeted us because we were young, open, trying to figure out the truth and nature of existence, impressionable and…the most vulnerable specimens in the lot.

Her intention, I discovered, was to insinuate herself into artists' relationships, manipulate the constellations of their relatives and friends, and gradually become the primary focus of their lives. She was a megalomaniac swiftly emerging, with a terrific intellect used as unsparingly as a peacock uses its tail (or a woodpecker its beak). If her target of opportunity demurred too much, she had a hoarse, cracking, sneering voice to batter with, which also knew no restraint.

As the oldest of nine siblings from the Bronx, she was a forceful character. When Mary Marx commenced her efforts to become queen bee among artists, she presented herself as a professorial type, using her wide knowledge of psychology to explicate, elucidate and convince. The subtext of her expositions was that we were all sick, broken, neurotic, and desperately in need of...her.

Fascinating to listen to, her karmic timing was inept, so she set off alarms in me and in Tom Blackwell too. We soon put some distance between ourselves and the doyen, but Andy Wing, for reasons of character and psychology beyond my intention to explore, fell for her act. He became her primary acolyte and remained so for the many long years until her death.

She filled his horizons and squelched his romantic possibilities, becoming weirder and weirder in the process. Her initial "Mary Marx the Enlightened Psychologist" act began to morph when she was turned on to LSD by the first, and most spectacularly dramatic, psychedelic psychiatrist in Laguna Beach, Dr. Frank Dunne.

Dr. Dunne turned on everyone he could, especially favoring the Arty set, for $100 a dose. It was completely legal at the time. I steered well clear of this large satyr, having been alerted to the type already through my San Francisco experiences.

We all know that LSD is a very potent substance, and we also know that a native's response/reaction to it is unpredictable. In

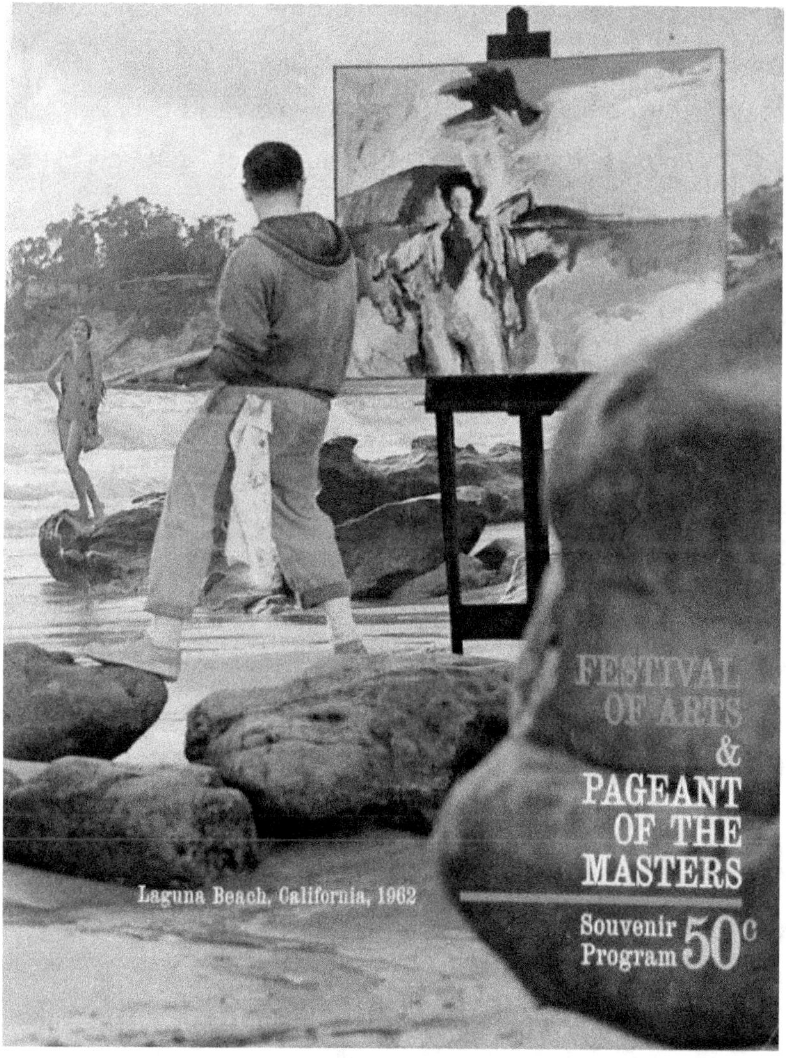

Figure 13: Frank Interlandi of "Red Alley" painting Miss Laguna on the beach in 1962.

the instance of Mary Marx, she instantly tumbled headfirst into the irrational and the absurd, changing her name to "Mirkla," and assuming the mantle of a gifted Bruja/medicine-woman/witch.

Her tools of persuasion shifted from citing of theories of Abraham Mazlow, John Cowper Powys, Otto Rank and many others, to reading tarot cards, casting horoscopes and other such medieval and occult folderol. She became madder and madder over the years, and frowzier and frowzier. At last, she was the Crazy Old Woman in Laguna Canyon who ruled over her Igor, Andy Wing, and had a soft gaggle of semi-convinced disciples...and a filthy cottage full of rats.

Before she infested the cottage, she lived in a house on Roosevelt Lane that Andy Wing bought from Art Risley. It was Andy's house, but Mirkla made him move out of it to go live in the little detached cottage, a sort of second building/shed on the lot. She soon burned Andy's house down by piling his paintings over the heat register in the floor and then forgetting about them. When the house went up, so did the bulk of Andy's work up to that time.

After the fire, Mirkla kicked Andy out of the cabin too and moved into it herself, where she lived out the rest of her life. Andy camped under some tarps in the yard for a few years until he started building another, larger house. This was less awful than it would have been for most people because Andy and his works were part and parcel of the environment where he worked. His Art works were at home out in the elements, and so was he, like a sort of exaggerated Scandinavian wood spirit.

Andy would never have admitted any of this because Mirkla could do no wrong in his view. He bought her line that she was a gifted mystic, when in fact, she was a low-rent dominatrix, canny and clever as a wily peasant, but as déclassé as clashing stripes and checks. She was his surrogate mom and made him cease relating to his real parents. She sabotaged every relationship with women he ever had.

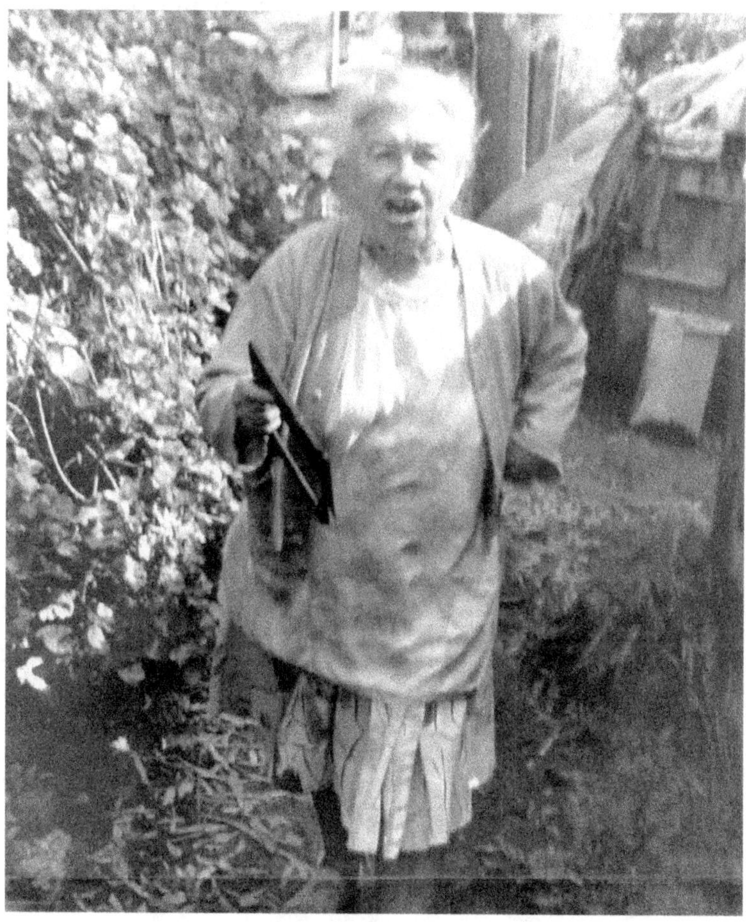

Figure 14: Mary "Mirkla" Marx, under a full head of spleen. Photo by Art Risley.

There was always some bad blood between Bob Young and Andy Wing, who were as contrasting persons as can be imagined. They were equally seminal and somewhat similar, painters. Andy used to complain that Bob Young's house across Roosevelt Lane was too tall for code until he built his own house, six inches taller than Bob's.

Why do I assert that this Mary/Mirkla character was a pure charlatan? Because in the first place she was not really an academic and she was not really a gifted mystic in the second place. She never claimed to be a raving megalomaniac, but that was the actual truth. To mention her at all can't be avoided, and once mentioned, she commands too many words.

"Mirkla" was an invaluable lesson for me in the nature of recognizing mental gamesmanship and how to see into and through ploys to motives. Avoiding the dragon of Mirkla, whom Mary Marx became, armed me well for coping with later mental manipulators (who were never what they seemed), including Dr. Timothy Leary.

Chapter III

Medusa Meets Batman

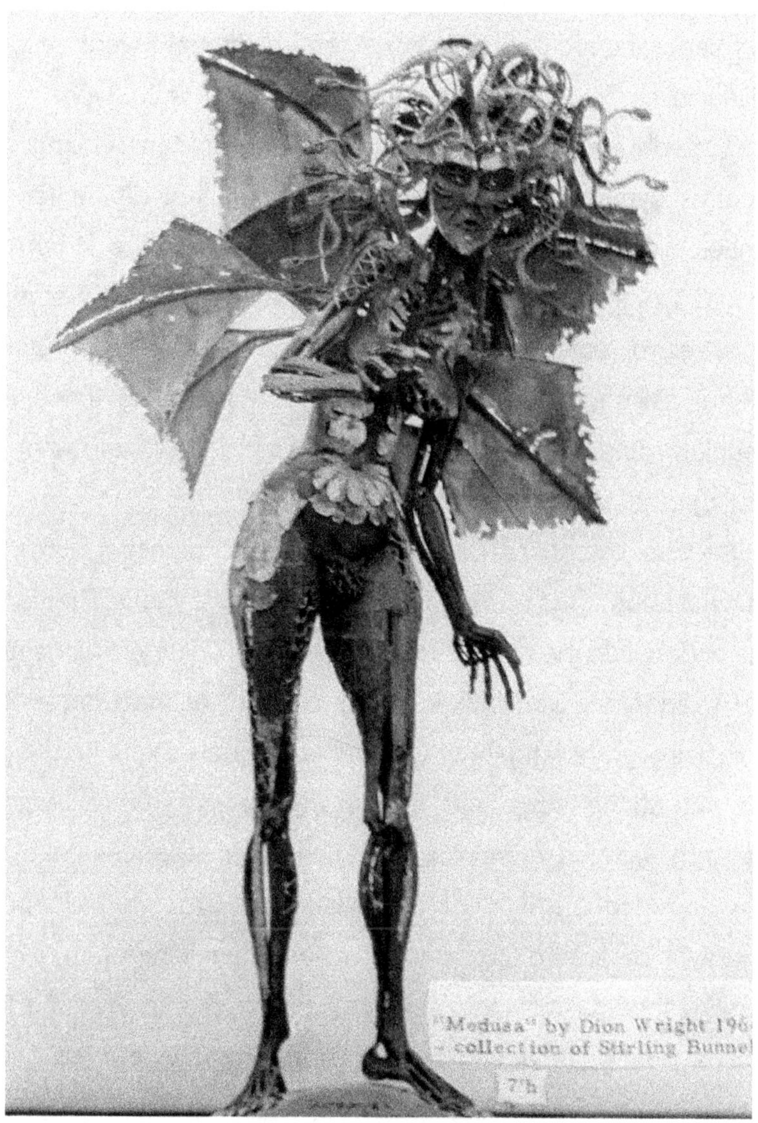

Figure 15: "Medusa" by Dion Wright. Welded metal, 7' high, 1964. Photo by Neal Wolfe.

Batman overtly entered this story first, but I admit that Medusa was always there, lurking down in my subconscious, just as she is in everybodys. It took Art fueled by historical tragedy to manifest her to where she could be seen.

Back in the caves, the essences that refined out contemporaneously as "Medusa" and "Batman" were already solidly in place, long before those particular archetypes were formulated. Medusa stirred earlier in awareness, being the negative symbolic face of Mother. That aspect of the female gender predates language. Who can tell, about the *Willendorf Venus*? So, then, can Batman be seen as a symbol of Father? I suppose so, but he took longer getting onstage. The Gothic cultural elements of him emerged from medieval times and Freudian roots, which didn't coalesce solidly until the day of the printing press and comic books.

Serious intentional Art comes out of plunging into the subconscious in the hope of emerging again with gold. That factor was endemic in the act of Art done by the Wichita Vortex painter, Bob Branaman. Bob lacked many aspects of the mature and socially integrated artist but was hell-on-wheels about jumping in and out of the soup that makes mythology. Confronting the unknown, with the intent of dragging chthonal essences out of the dark and into the light of day was what Bob was all about. Whatever other shortcomings may have diminished him, it was scary. Nobody at all within academic precincts had revealed that seminal approach. I intuitively "got it," immediately, so I dug deeper into my own psyche and sought to be brave in wrestling with what was down there, cloaked in the Unknown.

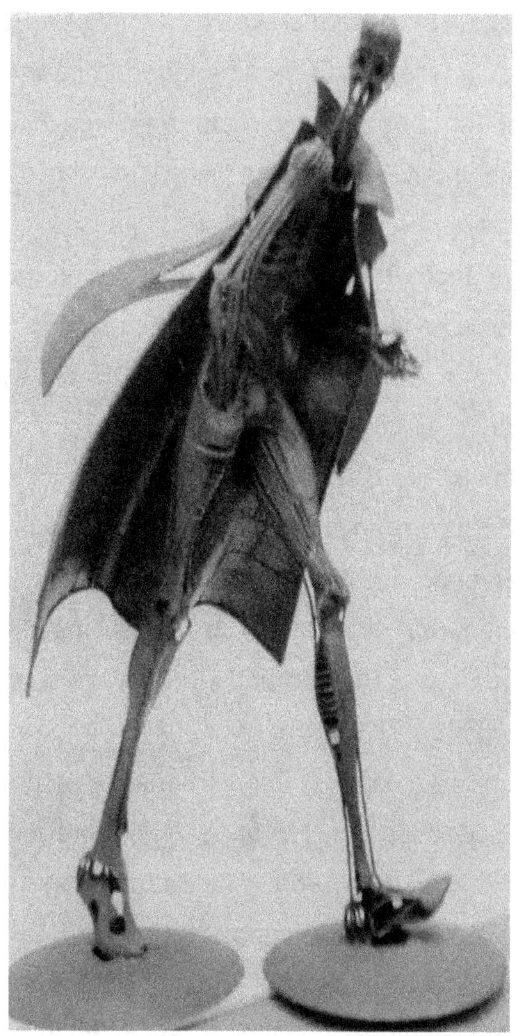

Figure 16: Bob Branaman rendered in welded steel by Dion Wright.

Making *Medusa,* the sculpture, was an achievement resulting from some hard digging and some accumulated experience. I had to grope in the arena, which I had widened for some bearings. Probably my first success at that sort of wrestling with indefinite essences was the semi-portrait sculpture I welded in black steel of Bob Branaman, himself. The sculpture depicted him striding darkly and hopelessly with his overcoat across his shoulders, billowing behind him in a cape-like way (worthy of Batman, as a matter of fact). It was a stop-frame image of him that I saw one day when he strode into my room on Page Street in San Francisco. Everybody who saw the piece knew that this sculptural item had chops.

There was another entire world of perception growing out of the ancient apprehension of Nature and its mythic spirits, as first revealed on cave walls, which in mid-20th century rigorously asserted itself as Biology. Biology itself was on the cusp of a unifying catharsis, the discovery of DNA. This discovery played into my hands as an artist but came somewhat later than the marriage of Batman and Medusa. We might justly suppose that DNA and the matrix wherein it was discovered are in the province of the cerebrum, while Batman and Medusa are entities from the medulla oblongata.

For the purposes of this story, Batman entered the flow of events before Medusa did. He appeared in the form of an Art gallery in San Francisco in 1960: "The Batman Gallery." I returned from Art school in Mexico (at the Instituto Allende at San Miguel de Allende) in the state of Guanajuato and went to San Francisco to see Mike and Jane Lewis on Oak Street in the Fillmore District. We had been together at UCSB, and now Mike was writing for *Newsweek* and supporting an extended group of bohemians, including his sister. Mike and Jane's father, Herbert Lewis, was one of the blackballed screenwriters of the Hollywood '50s.

Consciousness itself was the subject, via such chemicals as presented themselves, and particularly through peyote. Peyote was the catalyst of a warty little cactus, regarded as holy God's flesh by all the Amerindians who ever had contact with it. We had an address in Texas, "Moore's Orchids," from which we ordered boxes of the sinister-looking little succulents at ten cents a button. Once we started to get into this, our first mind-expanding psychedelic substance, we ordered plenty. We experienced many mind-boggling revelations drifting around San Francisco and feeling the emergent essences of things. Peyote makes most people violently ill upon ingestion. Mike Lewis reflected that "With peyote, you pay for everything you get."

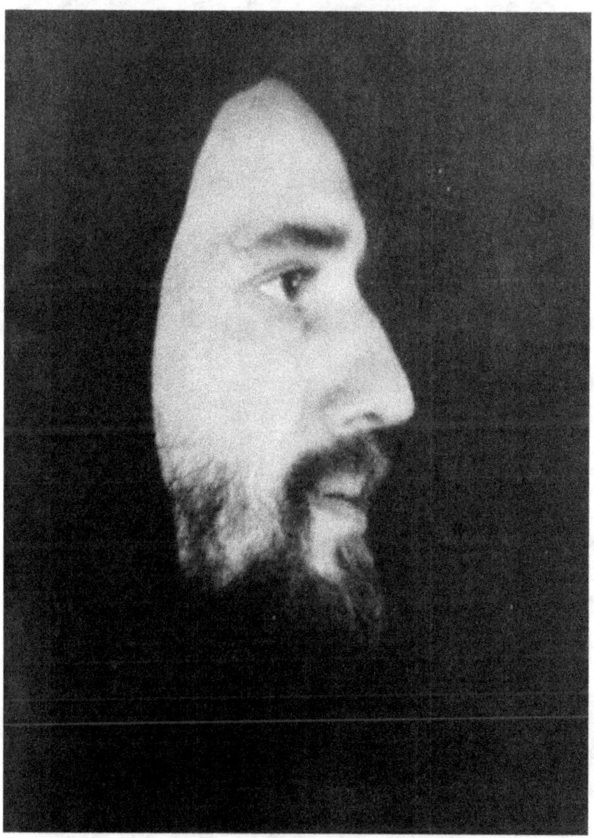

Figure 17: Bob Branaman, painter, magus, warlock, intrepid explorer on the frontier of consciousness. Photo-profile from brochure ca. 1965. Photographer unknown.

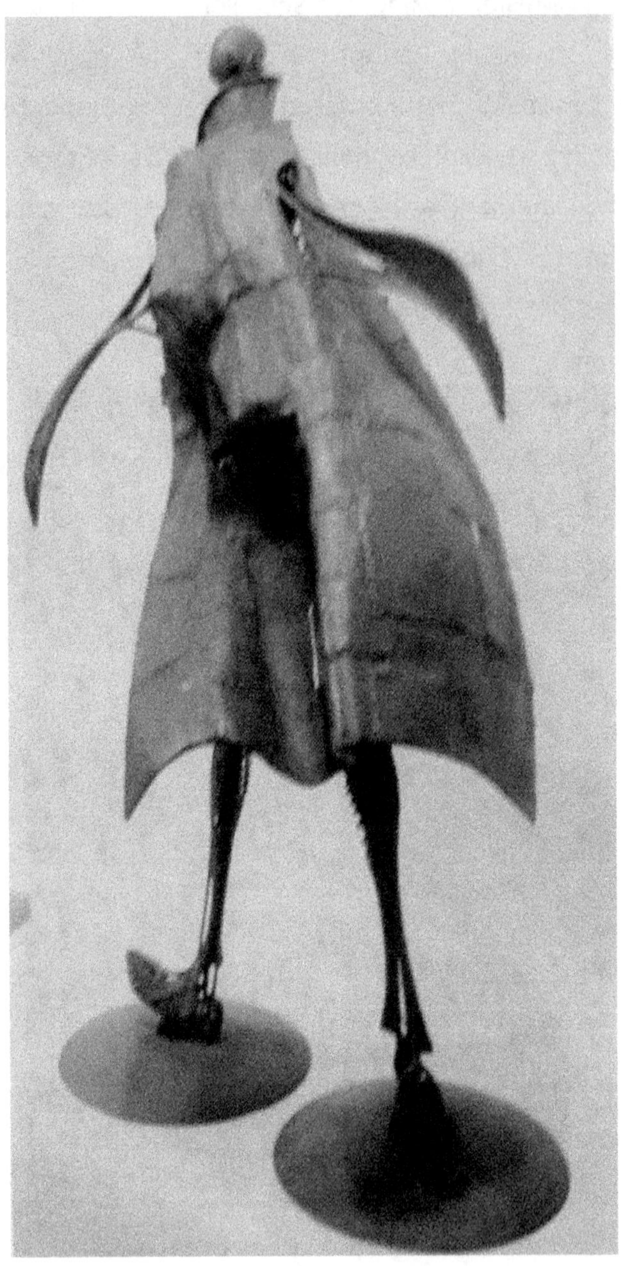

Figure 18: Another view of the Bob Branaman sculpture by Dion Wright.

Oak Street became the center of a sort of peyote summit, as a nexus of hitherto unacquainted "old souls" started investigating the nature of what it actually was to be "aware".

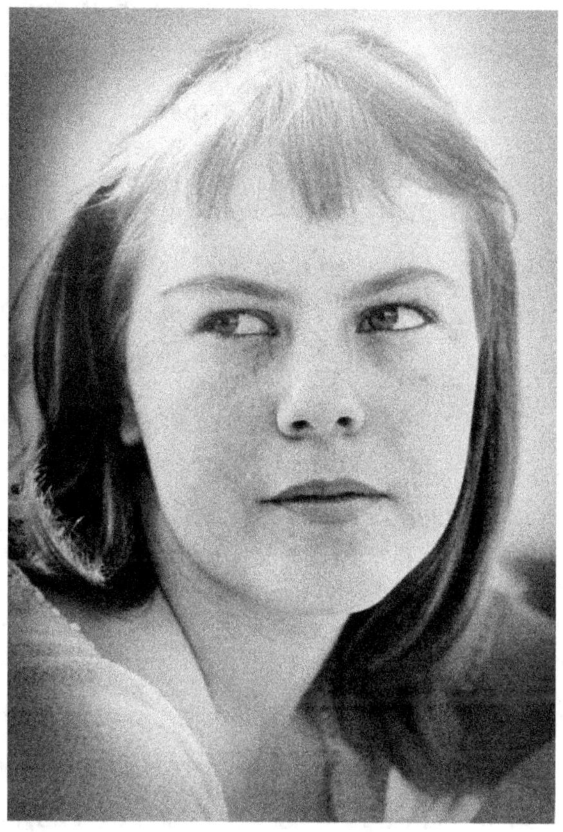

Figure 19: Jane "Chipmunk" Lewis, photographed in 1959, in her healthy mode. Photo attributed to Wynn Bullock.

Beth Branaman, recently separated from her husband, Bob, was one of the few who held a regular job. She helped to keep us residents alive with regular offerings of peanut butter and Wonder Bread. Beth entered the pantheon of the Heroic by barfing peyote into a saucepan, holding her nose, and chugging it back down again.

Mike and Jane were friendly with artists from the group that the Beat poet Allen Ginsberg had named "The Wichita Vortex". The Wichita Vortex was a loose association of writers and artists from Kansas who got there by following their dean, Michael McClure, one of the original Beats. McClure was inspired, but a couple of his acolytes were more inspired still, although they reaped no fame.

Among these Wichita émigrés were the artists, Bruce Conner, and Bob Branaman. I first saw their startling works on the walls of Dave Haselwood's Auerhahn Press, a publisher of fine poetry editions, especially works by William Burroughs and Michael McClure. The "Auerhahn" publishing house was named for a huge and secretive grouse that screams eerily in the Black Forest. As a symbol of the place and times, it was emblematic. I drew the logo of it for Dave.

Bruce Conner was a tall enigmatic kid with a red buzz-cut and buckteeth. He had a great knack with various materials. Whatever he put together from a teeny drawing to a large assemblage of wax, dolls, costume jewelry and torn nylon, had a freshness to it.

When I arrived in San Francisco, Bruce was having a show on the walls of Mike Lewis' bedroom at Oak Street, and soon became a pioneer member of the stable of artists at the newly hatching Batman Gallery.

Within a couple of weeks of my arrival in San Francisco, the House Un-American Activities Committee was having their final meeting of all time at City Hall. This was the last gasp of McCarthyism, meaningful at Oak Street, because Mike and Jane's father, the screenwriter of *It Happened on 5th Avenue*, among other films, had been one of those hounded to destruction by the Red-baiters in the '50s.

There was a big protest on the steps of City Hall when HUAC was in session, broken up by police, hurling us down the steps and onto the mall. Bruce Conner was there with one of his most daunting works, a dead baby (doll) in a high chair, nearly obscured by black nylon cobwebs.

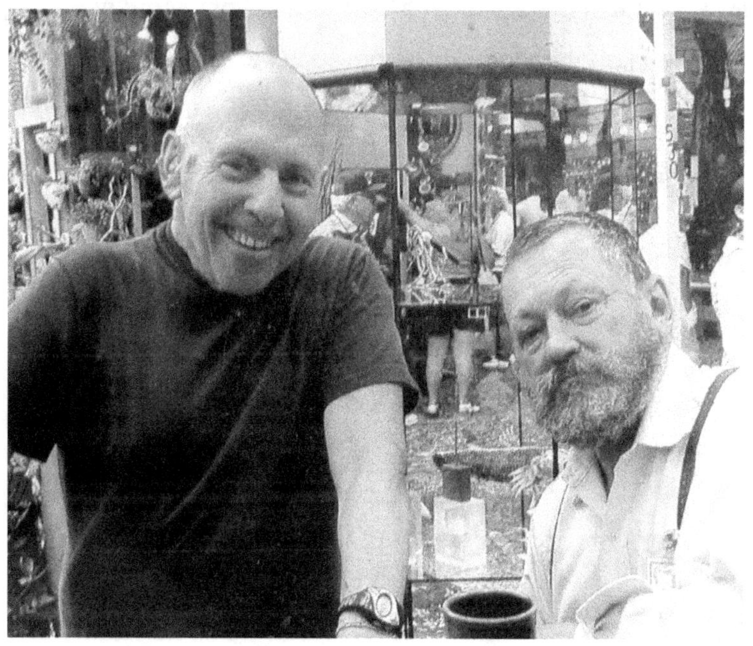

Figure 20: Mike Lewis and Dion Wright at the Sawdust Festival, half a century after Oak Street. Photo by Ruth Wright

2222 Fillmore Street was the address of the store that eventually became the Batman Gallery in 1960. It was at the north end of Fillmore Street, the main thoroughfare of 'black' San Francisco, where it morphed into upscale galleries and mixed residential. The address seemed meaningful to me because of its symbolic relationship to the higher arcana of the standard Tarot deck of divination cards.

During that period, I was busy reading all the esoteric literature I could find that I'd never been exposed to at the University of California. One book was about Tarot and the inner meaning of the cards, as psychology, as divination and as symbols of general principles, particularly the implications of numbers. In the Tarot deck, there are four suits: earth/pentacles/spades, air/wands/clubs, fire/swords/diamonds, and water/cups/hearts. Above these is a set of twenty-two images called "the Higher Arcana," numbered zero through twenty-one.

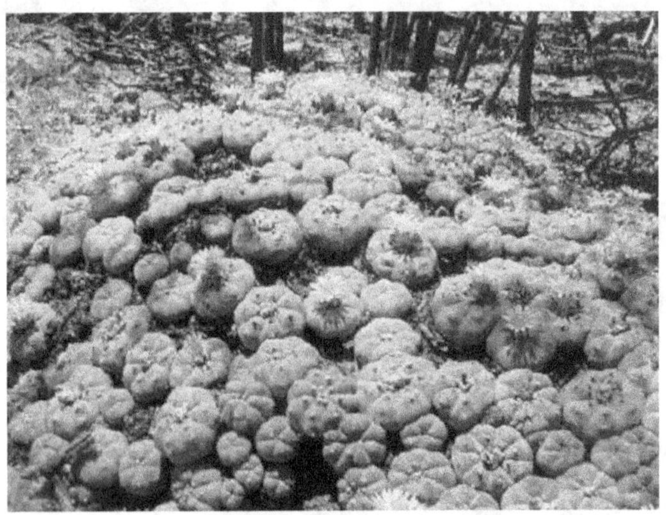

Figure 21: A garden of peyote cactus, probably a cultivated colony.

These cards are symbolic in nature and refer to over-arching universal qualities that determine what happens within the suits. The first card, the zero card, is also the last, or twenty-second card, and has a dual meaning. They all have dual meanings, but the zero card, called "The Fool", is the most profound. It illustrates a happy vagabond with a rose in his hand, about to step off a cliff.

The figure can be interpreted either as the spontaneous artist or as the victim of self-inflicted failure and folly. It can mean either transcendence or crucifixion. Knowing this, I imagined how swiftly Billy Jahrmarkt must have acted to acquire the building at 2222 Fillmore Street in San Francisco, the twenty-second card doubled; An Art site on steroids.

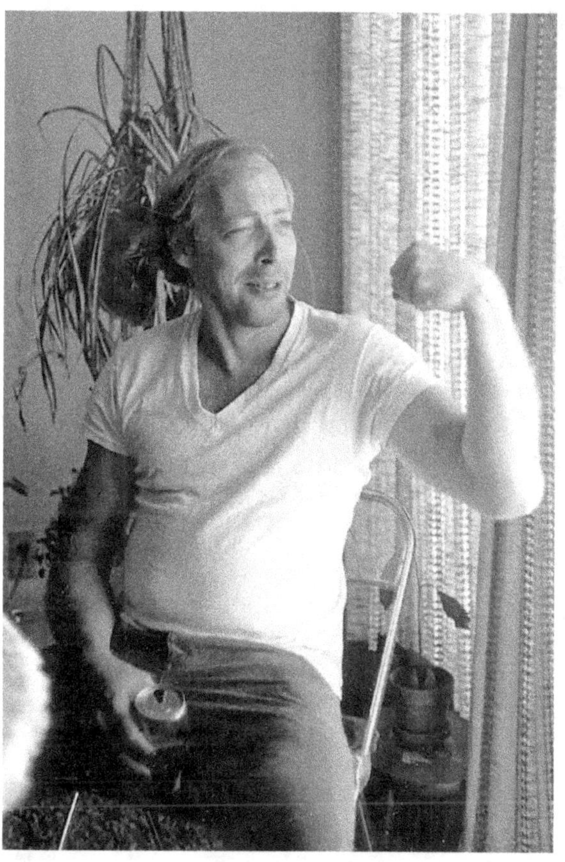

Figure 22: The poet, Alan Russo. A tortured artist suffering at least half from self-inflicted pain. Photo by James Bearden.

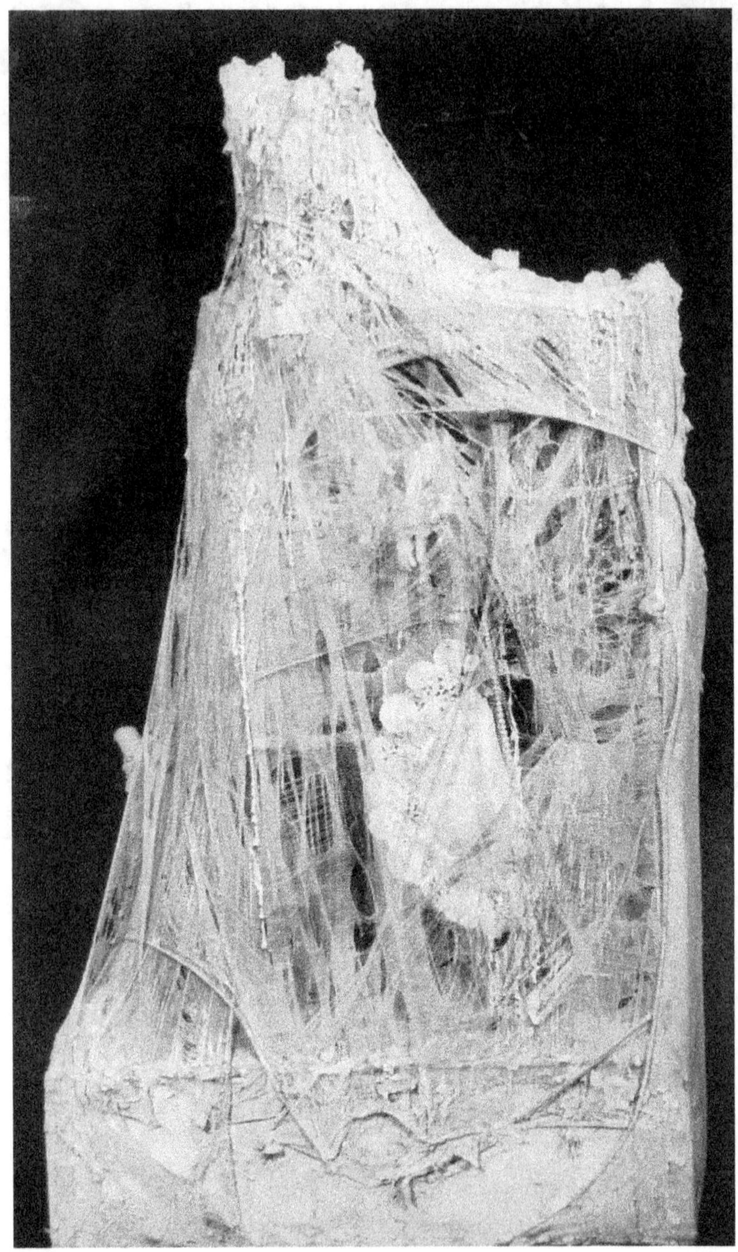

Figure 23: The Bride. One of Bruce Conner's' ominous wax and nylon assemblages at the Batman Gallery. 1960. Photo courtesy of Bruce Conner.

Billy Jahrmarkt seemed at first sight to be a wounded creature. He was a slender youth with a great shock of dark hair, pale skin, long aesthetic fingers, and large brown eyes that had a vulnerable look, but also a distracted and preoccupied expression as if he were peering out from a state of being half-lodged in another dimension. His body language was folded up, and he always wore black.

The grapevine had been buzzing about a young jazz drummer from New York who was arriving in San Francisco with the wherewithal to open a new gallery. Billy Jahrmarkt was, the rumor-mill said, going to have the hippest, most avant-garde Art venue ever seen in San Francisco.

Jane Lewis and Bob Branaman ferreted-out Billy and his wife Joan while the gallery was still in the formative stages. They found them the way iron filings find a magnet, and that magnet was heroin. The drug was so hip in Batman that you could swim through it. I, however, was not hip and knew it. But I was still attached, after all, to my junkie buddies, Bob Branaman and Jane Lewis, whom Bob had taken to calling "Chipmunk".

I followed them around, somewhat haplessly and certainly harmlessly, and was therefore tolerated. I had that passion for finding out what Art was about at its best, and was content to be quiet and watch from the wings as these indescribably charismatic and beautiful people cleaved a sure course of Cool through every scene.

When asked by Herb Caen why he named the place "Batman," Billy Jahrmarkt responded, "I had to call it something."

Of course.

That begged the nature of Billy, who was, indeed, a very bat-like creature, or at least had adopted the overtones of one. Frank Langella had nothing on Billy, the way he folded himself up like a drowsy fruit bat, blinking and murmuring sleepily from his cocoon of heroin insulation. He usually had good smack, so Janie Chipmunk said. That distinction put a certain paranormal atmosphere on the place and attracted various other junkies to the scene.

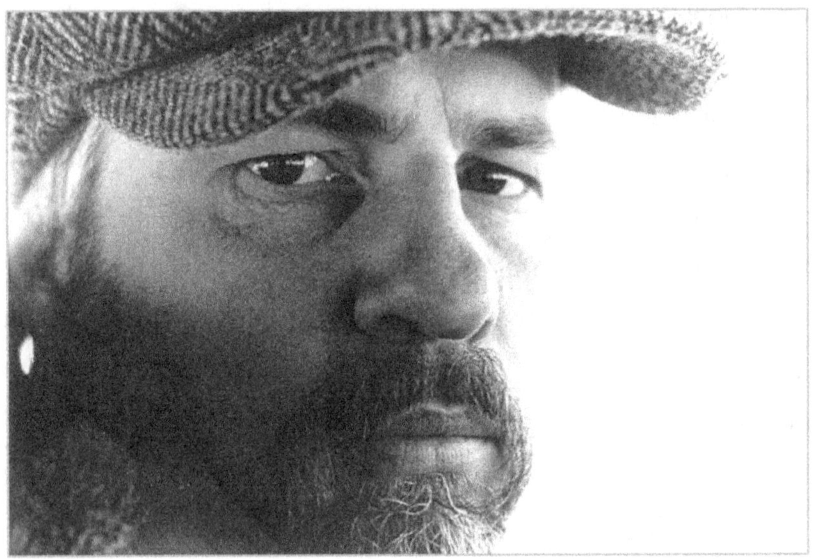

Figure 24: The poet, David Omer Bearden. Brilliance with suffering, tempered by social responsibility. Photo courtesy James Bearden.

Billy's nurturing wife, Joan, was soulful and Madonna-like, and as open and friendly as Billy was folded-up and guarded. She had a depth of compassion that acted as the wellspring of support on which Billy floated his act. She also wore black all the time, but her eyes told a different story from the wounded despair seen in Billy. Joan seemed saintly.

The Batman Gallery was the most Beat scene that can have existed anywhere in America at the time. Besides Billy and Joan always being dressed in black, the entire interior of the gallery was painted black. The opening show of Art there leaned toward black. Billy's own entry was a large canvas complete with an attached baby stroller sticking out into the room, all painted thickly black.

Art Grant had a strange black assemblaged box cum mirrors, giving the impression, through reflections, that one was looking at oneself from somewhere behind the surface of the wall. Bruce Conner had a piece of his black wax and torn nylon cobwebbery in there, and Bob Branaman (who loved having a prosperous junkie Art dealer on the scene) had concocted a black monstrosity, harrowing in its dark power. Michael McClure smeared his infant daughter's first bowel movement across a canvas and framed it. George Herms' offering in the first Batman show was the afterbirth of his infant daughter, Nalota, sealed in a jar. Naturally, it decayed, and gasses built up inside the jar until it exploded. It was the perfect piéce de resistánce of Beat anti-culture.

Looking at all of this, it was hard to see how it connected to the word "beatitude" or "state of being blessed", as Jack Kerouac had cited as the origin of the name "Beat". I was too lame, and couldn't penetrate the essence of it, not realizing then the political nature of what was happening.

Did the creative virility of post-Beat Art derive from opiate addiction, or flourish in spite of it? Was it even real, or just a public relations triumph? This was not a question I dared ask of the principals, who would have responded by regarding me as square, at best, or some kind of agent, at worst. This left me anxious in my naiveté that my own merits, whatever they might be, were compromised by my disinclination to get hooked on junk.

It was a social assumption, almost a political principle that junk was at the heart of the hippest and most seminal creativity. To question that assumption too closely or anything like analytically would be a fast-track ticket to excommunication. The heroes of the Beats were William Burroughs and Charlie Parker, both junkies, and a host of lesser-addicted personalities. They were undoubted geniuses, but was their genius the result of "chasing the dragon," or despite it? Either way, I thought that seeking to get hooked was unlikely to make an uncreative person into an artist, no matter how closely the person aped the heroes.

One time Charlie "Bird" Parker, the founder of bebop jazz, had been wearing a red kerchief around his neck. He looked into an audience one evening to see many red scarves around many necks, much to his disgust. "They thought," remarked Bird sarcastically, "that a scarf would help them more than chops would."

Charlie Parker and William Burroughs were both thoroughly immoral people who would blithely cheat, steal and lie when it suited them, bad behavior that beatniks not only excused or overlooked but tried to copy. It was awful, especially for me, to watch some of my dear friends single-mindedly setting out to become junkies. In retrospect, the nature of the interface between drugs and creativity became the deepest conundrum of the 20th Century; a puzzle that vexes us all right up to the present.

Society, per se, has tended to lump all the different chemicals together under the umbrella of "drugs," and treated them all the same. They could hardly be more different, than say, junk and peyote are from each other. This distinction, while clear among the experiencers on the "lunatic fringe", was opaque to the agency functionaries in the establishment trying to control it while not understanding it. Nobody on the inside seemed to understand it much, either, rather like the man who had the tiger by the tail. I never unraveled this mystery but never regretted passing up on junk addiction either.

People normally are stiff and ill at ease at any Art opening. They are there to be seen as much as to see, most of them hoping they won't be called upon to say anything intelligent about the Art, much less to assess their feelings about it. That's the way it is at a normal opening.

At the opening of the Batman Gallery (anything but normal by any standard measure), the attendees seemed petrified by self-consciousness. They had to be there to be hip but didn't know what was going on, whatever their inarticulate aesthetic leanings and longings may have been. "Something is happening here, but you don't know what it is, do you, Mr. Jones?" was the Bob Dylan lyric that a few years later described the mystery of this sort of environment. Establishing an uncomfortable situation for the viewers may have been just what Billy Jahrmarkt had in mind.

The senior poet Beat statesman from Wichita, Michael McClure, had been writing some plays. His avant-garde production of *The Beard,* ostensibly about a relationship between Billy the Kid and Jean Harlow, had received positive notice and good reviews, so he followed it up with *The Feast. The Feast* opened in the theatrically cramped precincts of the Batman Gallery. The play had the additional oddness of being a sort of commentary on Art openings in particular, if not on social gatherings in general. In this play, weirdly made-up characters mill around and have dialog in which they announce their names to each other: "I am Yee-Org!" "I am Re-Torp!" There was no denouement I could see, and the meaning of it seemed to be the ignorant posturing of individuals within social settings.

The entire aesthetic of the Batman Gallery was seen as pure Art, which could only exist because Billy Jahrmarkt could afford to present it. It had little or no commercial potential. I never heard that Billy sold anything during his tenure running Batman. With or without commerce, however, the Batman Gallery became the seminal hub of Art in San Francisco. Herb Caen and Kenneth Rexroth touted it. The philosophy of the gallery seemed cryptic, implying unstated meaning and appalling viewers. The Artworks in there showed the squares just how un-hip they truly were if they could only understand it. They couldn't. They *could* get outraged and confused, though, the very few visitors who ever found their way in there.

Mostly, the clientele were the intellectual elite. Billy succeeded in distilling an almost completely nihilistic aesthetic that summed up Beat rejection of square society and pushed the idea of Beauty to a nadir of apogee. Within his brilliant apocalyptic poem, "Poisoned Wheat," Michael McClure, the crown prince of San Francisco poets, summed it up in one line: "Beauty IS hideous!"

Bob Branaman and Janie Chipmunk were part of the inner circle at the Batman Gallery because of their commitment to junk. Billy seemed to dislike me, despite my friendship with Janie and Bob. I may have imagined Billy's unfriendliness, but I had an acute sense of psychological nuance, and I trusted it. The looks Billy threw at me usually seemed either fearful or hateful, sometimes being merely suspicious. There was nothing I could have done about this, other than to become a junkie myself, I supposed. So, I just stayed out of the Batman Gallery, save for openings or when it was necessary to go there on some errand with Branaman or Janie.

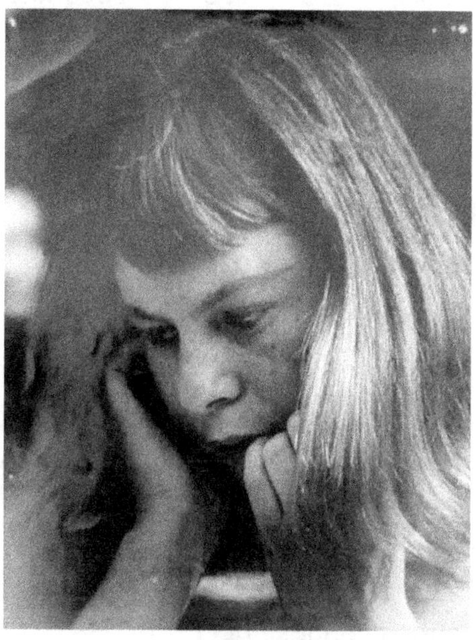

Figure 25: Jane "Chipmunk" Lewis ca 1959, in her self-destructive mode, the mode of nail biting. Photographer unknown.

After breaking up with me, things had inevitably gone badly for Janie Chipmunk in her unwholesome imbroglio with a self-destructive Wichita junkie-poet, infamous within Vortex circles for feeding used sanitary napkins to his dachshund (Nietzsche by name). When that radical poet had spun off back to Wichita again leaving Janie in the lurch, she moved in across Fillmore Street and down a block from the Batman Gallery with Billy Jahrmarkt's sister, Suzie, and her boyfriend, the painter Joe Goff.

Here was yet another extra-Beat living situation in which Jane was single again. Suzie was a cheery and plump ingénue-type, as much as a girl could be that within the Beat Generation, while her lover, Joe Goff, was a sullen, mustachioed introvert who seemed to be resentful of the fact that Billy wouldn't show his work in the Batman Gallery. I could see why because I also thought that Joe's work was behind the curve, but I wasn't able to get my own work into the Batman, either, and I thought that my work was great!

I was living on Page Street then, renting a room from an old Spanish Civil War vet of the Lincoln Brigade named Neal Hoskins. I had a furnished room, and it was difficult to get any serious Art done in such cramped quarters. Neal was a hapless sort of angular and gawky scarecrow of a man who was also a painter. He tried to ape the Beats with the black interior of his apartment, but he was such a sunny person by nature, that Beat was simply outside his potential. He wrecked the effect by painting the ornate wide moldings in the old house gold.

The FBI came checking up on this poor schlemiel every few months, to see if he was still a threat to the American Dream. Neal's best friend was an ominous force of nature named Joe Trujillo. Neal and Joe had been in the Spanish Civil War together and were later cellmates in San Quentin on charges I never learned.

Joe Trujillo was a top-coated and fedoraed dark mass of a man, with razor-creases in his slacks and gleaming patent-leather shoes. He never took his hat off nor stopped smoking. His eyes were as opaque as marbles, and his eyebrows and mustache were as thick and black as Ernie Kovacs'. He stood under the streetlight in the swirling fog, feet wide apart and hands jammed into the pockets of his overcoat, cigarette smoke curling up from under his hat brim as he spoke softly, in a whispering rumble. Joe always called everybody, male or female, "Cat." There was an air of imminent danger and the possibility of hair-trigger violence of an ungovernable sort in Joe Trujillo's looming body language. He liked me, for whatever reason. He was one of a primitive type that often made friends with me throughout my life. I speculated about this recurring phenomenon from time to time, but never could imagine why there was usually one of this sort of monster hanging around me. I was glad enough to be turning up on their good side. Joe Trujillo was full of pithy aphorisms and cautions that I took seriously. I wished that Joe might assess the Batman Gallery for me from a sort of Neanderthal perspective, but the Art scene was the last place one could expect to see Joe Trujillo. Neal Hoskins never went there either.

The Batman Gallery continued to accrue repute and press coverage as the months rolled on. At the behest of Kenneth Rexroth, Billy Jahrmarkt agreed to stage a benefit Art auction at the Batman for the old and ill poet, Kenneth Patchen, who was languishing destitute in the hospital. All sorts of artists donated works to the auction to help Patchen. The auction received much PR via Rexroth and his media friends. The night of the event the Batman was packed with people, including me. Despite the glowering glances I sometimes got from Billy, I wasn't about to miss such a seminal occasion as this promised to be.

I had no car, so on the eve of the auction, I strolled all the way down Fillmore Street from Page Street to the Batman Gallery, taking in the twilight scene all along the swinging thoroughfare.

As I neared the Batman, I noticed some burning curtains flapping out of a second story window. I realized with a jolt that it was Janie Chipmunk's apartment. I rushed the next hundred yards to the Batman Gallery and burst into a standard opening scene where everyone was standing around as cool as jazz musicians, or as stiff as a bunch of cold-war diplomats.

Spotting Janie standing right next to Billy Jahrmarkt, I hurried up to her and hissed, in a stage whisper, "Your pad is on fire!" Billy recoiled like a startled rattlesnake and looked at me as if I had just farted loudly. Was this a crude attempt to screw up his opening?

It was no joke. Janie ran out and missed the auction. I stayed, despite the dire looks I was getting from Billy. The auction proceeded, and it was SLOW. Nobody was spending squat. Some great Artwork was being picked up for nickels. Finally, the red-haired and volatile poet, Lew Welch, leaped onto the podium and grabbed the mic. "What's the matter with you people?" he yelled into the faces of the San Francisco elite, "These fucking things are beautiful!" It did not do much good. The receipts were slight.

After the auction, I went over and found Janie Chipmunk standing in the middle of her soaked and trashed room. The fire had been squelched by the SFFD, but Jane said that they had gone out of their way, when they realized that beatnik artists lived there, to tear it apart far more completely than they needed to. "They gave me sly looks and evil smiles," she said. And so it went.

Beth and Bob Branaman were playing out the end of their marriage. Bob went off to Guadalajara, presumably to study Art, but everybody who knew Bob realized that academic endeavor of any kind was as far as it could be from who he was and what he believed. Whatever it was that propelled him there, he did get inside of Mexican classrooms enough to manage to meet a sweet young thing. Manipulator of women that he was, when Bob found out that this girl was the heiress to the Mack Truck fortune, he caused her to fall in love with him. She was head over heels and stayed that way. Susan was a pretty enough girl, who looked stoned and happy all the time. She willingly followed Bob back to San Francisco and agreed to marry him. The marriage took place in the Batman Gallery. It struck me as a somber event because it was colored by Mr. Mack's strenuous and futile efforts to keep the wedding from happening. He failed. I would always remember the attitude of despair that Old Man Mack's slumped shoulders radiated as he walked off, crushed and defeated, down Fillmore Street.

The pertinent threads of karma were played out, the summer of 1960 was nigh, and it was time to go back to Laguna to mine the Festival of Arts for money. Packing my meager possessions in a portfolio and a couple of rucksacks, I said goodbye to Neal Hoskins and went down to the Greyhound terminal on Mission Street. I appeared more like a refugee than anything else in that cheesy environment, which may have been why the baggage check guy, who looked a lot like Jimmy Rushing, gave me the fishy eyeball. He refused to allow my portfolio on the bus.

"I know what you've got in there," said the man. Stopped flat, I thought it over and assessed what I had, which included a small portable record player. I asked the man, "You got kids?" He allowed himself a nod. I handed over the record player. "Give them this," I said. The man broke into a wide smile and accepted the "gift," and then received the portfolio.

The funny thing is, he was right in his assumption. The portfolio was full of seditious imagery and a matchbox of pot I got for five bucks from Bob Branaman, the matchbox that eventually led to my bust in San Clemente. I could have snitched Bob off and got a lighter sentence, or maybe no jail time at all, but I held my mud, perhaps foolishly, as I'm certain that if the situation were reversed, Bob would have thrown me under the wheels without hesitation. But, maybe I do him an injustice. Anyway, it was lousy grass, and hardly worth doing time for, much less the six months I got. We have to adhere to our principles whenever we can own some, even if they are follies.

All the circumstances of jail, probation, the doorknob factory, the parade of girls, and finally my first marriage, unfolded until the day when our libertine joint studio, "Little Rome," perished in a flood of mud and my new wife and I were home at 703 Browncroft in Laguna Beach.

Then one morning, we turned on the TV to learn that John F. Kennedy had just been assassinated.

Chapter IV

Medusa Meets Batman, pt. 2

We moved out to Laguna Canyon on the Big Bend. Thanks to smiling Bill Baldwin, the local purveyor of fine psychedelics (which were still legal), we had a period of dense LSD experiencing. The place we rented was the top story of a series of gimcrack additions behind and above a rambling old two-story frame house. The additions were built up against the canyon hillside, which was bulging with huge sandstone outcrops, riddled with caves, thick with poison oak, and rife with a wide variety of feral creatures, among whom we were pleased to number ourselves. We acquired a pet barn owl.

The landlord of this establishment, an old duffer named Dick Sortomme, was one of the calendar painters who gave the Laguna Art scene its questionable reputation. Dick was white-haired, crew-cutted, thick-lensed, snaggle-toothed, long-winded, medium-sized, and in his sixties. He was a sentimental and nostalgic raconteur full of non-sequitur anecdotes about the Harding Administration, the form and function of the magneto, the habits of Trobriand Islanders, and other abstruse topics, all delivered in avuncular style. Dick stayed robust and fit by running the couple of miles down the canyon to the Main Beach every morning, donning his rubber swim cap, stroking a mile out to sea and back, and then running home to Sally, his fat bride who was half his age and twice his size. In her fertile expanse, he generated one baby after another, three on the ground and a fourth in the oven at the time we lived there, up behind the main house, among the oak branches and the lizards.

Janie Chipmunk arrived in this bucolic scene, having left her lodgings at her unappreciative mom's house at Ojai, and came to live downstairs from us in a ramshackle studio apartment cum cavern that suited her just fine. She reprised her den mother act, honed at Little Rome by being auntie to the plethora of children on the premises, including four more next door at the neighbor's.

Over five years she had morphed from an ingénue hungry for experience into a wise old Bruja who was full-up with world-weariness, but kind and gentle, and, let's face it, resigned to an indeterminate but inescapable future on which the bloom of possibility had been tarnished by junk.

Janie had a TV set, which she draped with gauzy fabric and kept turned on with the volume at zero. She liked the shifting and indefinite colors of light that filtered into her dark premises and was disinterested in the content. It was quite idyllic out there in the crackling bosom of nature, smoking joints, making Art, and just far enough off the Canyon Road that we heard no traffic, except for the frequent crashes on the Big Bend.

The JFK post-assassination national mood was ominous and confused and stayed that way. One dark night as I was picking my way up the long driveway to the rickety flights that led up to our tree house aerie, I was assailed in the dense darkness by a palpable menace. Seeing nothing with my outer eyes, my inner ones were confronted by the apparition of Medusa.

Stumbling up into our tree house, my hair on end, I sketched the essence of my revelation on paper. The next day I started work on the sculpture, framing it at eight feet tall. It was daunting.

It was a thing released by the horror of the JFK assassination. It was also Mom, but that revelation didn't crash onto the surface of my brain until after the sculpture was finished, and a good thing, too. If I'd understood that symbolism before making the sculpture, I would have failed at it. In any event, the object caused lot of trouble.

That was my sixth year as an exhibitor in *The Festival of Arts*, and into that 1964 exhibition forum, I injected *Medusa*. By then, the grounds had evolved from pegboard panels on sawdust-covered dirt, to concrete terrazzo paths through green swards, with cast-cement columns growing from them into geometric overhead roofs.

It was all permanent and well-designed but had lost its organic folksiness in the process of upgrading. Some artists claimed that the grounds had been sterilized. This new structural presentation suited management well enough, though management included no more than a token artist or two. To be one of these token artists required a marked ability to go along with the entrenched interests that husbanded the Golden Goose, *The Pageant of the Masters.*

The *Medusa* did not exactly fit in with the aesthetic overview endorsed by the Board of Directors of the *Festival of Arts*, who were largely indistinguishable from the City Fathers. All of which is neither here nor there as to quality, except that censorship came into the situation as soon as *Medusa* did. Probably the part of the sculpture that raised the most hackles was not the writhing vipers for tresses, but the wiggling worm snakes in its pubic region. This seemed logical and reasonable to me, but it caused a furor among the more conservative viewers, including quite a number of so-called artists.

When consternation over *Medusa* hit the papers, they put a diaper on her. Stressed to the max already, I snapped and left town, taking *Medusa* with me. We hit it north to San Francisco, *Medusa* standing in a U-Haul trailer pulled along behind my VW microbus, gesturing malevolently at the traffic.

Janie Chipmunk left Laguna Beach a month or so earlier to go back to San Francisco, where she moved into a flat on Golden Gate Street with poets Charley Plymell and Anne Buchanan. I headed for that place as a destination, with no further plan beyond getting there.

We washed up on Charlie's beach, at the place he referred to as "...that piss-hole on Golden Gate." He was hospitable and laconic, his thumbs in his jeans, doing his habitual act of a slightly injured and misunderstood Will Rogers. Anne Buchanan was hot stuff. Our sudden appearance was either timely or untimely, depending on your viewpoint.

As we arrived, Anne, Charlie, and Chipmunk were literally on their way out the door. Bruce Conner was having an opening at the Batman Gallery, and it was about to start. We didn't even catch our breath from the freeway grind before tagging along behind Ann and Charlie for the short drive between Golden Gate and 2222 Fillmore Street, still in the same ghetto, in fact.

In the four or so years since its inception, Billy and Joan Jahrmarkt had developed the Batman Gallery into a serious establishment, and sold it to Beth Branaman's LSD psychiatrist, Mike Agron. He was a slight man, bushy-haired, bespectacled, and friendly. Bob Branaman was terrified of him. "I know all I need to know about that guy from his name," said Bob. Mike Agron was already the shrink for most of the artists in the Batman stable, or well known to them, so there was no sea change in the aesthetic direction of the place.

Bruce Conner had been in the Batman Gallery since the beginning. We pulled up and parked on Fillmore a block or so north of the gallery, and made our way in.

The atmosphere was as stilted and wooden among many of the attendees, as it always was at openings. Charlie, Chipmunk and I were as garrulous as could be among the quasi-taxidermied patrons of the arts. We greeted this and that old colleague that we hadn't seen for a while, with a certain amount of Byzantine intricacy of relating, due to the convoluted nature of the checkered history between many of the principals. It was stimulating and it was nostalgic and it was dripping with intelligent awareness, but nobody could think it was free flowing and natural.

Bruce Conner was mounting a concept show, which was riveting, but had no commercial potential. He hadn't arrived yet. We entered the Batman Gallery, already full of people. The artwork was on the walls, which were still painted black. Right inside the door was an old-fashioned department store glass-topped display case with nothing in it. Around the walls were twenty framed white canvases of equal size, about two by three feet, equally spaced.

They were all blank except for small block letters at the center of each one, all saying the same thing: DO NOT TOUCH. They were without glass, but on a panel just behind the empty display case, was a twenty-first identical canvas hung, covered with glass. It bore a different printed message in the middle of it: TOUCH.

It was all mind-bendingly enigmatic, and the performance nature of the event, equally cryptic, began when Bruce Conner entered. Looking as divinely goofy as ever, and dragging two heavy leather suitcases, he schlepped the suitcases behind the empty display case and opened them, revealing them to be full of ordinary children's marbles.

With deliberation and no expression, Bruce began to scoop out the marbles and pour them into the display case. He proceeded until all marbles were in there, making a layer a few inches deep. Then he climbed in with them, and lay upon them, where the patrons of the arts might gaze down upon him through the glass top.

At this exact moment, a markedly informal man in a Burberry topcoat burst through the front door shouting, "Who made that *Medusa* out in the street?"

It was Sterling Bunnell, LSD psychiatrist colleague of Mike Agron, looking like a disheveled doppelganger of young Clarence Darrow. His loud words were like a pinprick to a balloon, and all the people in the Batman Gallery immediately rushed into the street to look at *Medusa*, leaving poor Bruce Conner lying non-plussed on his marbles.

Flabbergasted with remorse and confusion, I felt that if there were any blame in this, it had to belong to Sterling. He'd come on like a china shop bull, insensitive and oblivious to the circumstances; while all I'd done was park my microbus. I had forgotten all about the presence of *Medusa* trailing along behind. It got worse. Sterling Bunnell bought the *Medusa* from me, and prevailed on his colleague, Mike Agron, to put the bitch in Batman until he could move it. And that's how it happened.

To add further discomfort, the featured artist at the Batman shows was responsible for the gallery sitting. Bruce had to fume in there at his own show, with the malignant Gorgon attending, for a few days anyway. It was all good for me, although I never again had a good rapport with Bruce, who could only be soured on me.

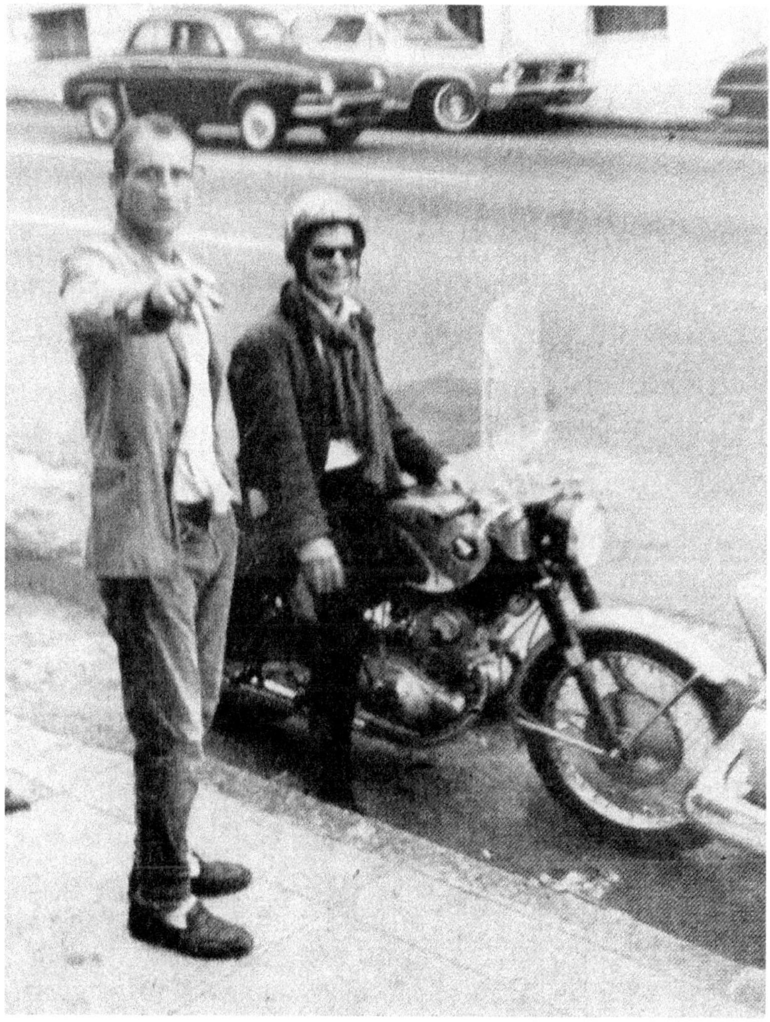

Figure 26: Neal Cassady and Charley Plymell at 1403 Gough Street, San Francisco, ca. 1965.

Getting to know Sterling Bunnell better and better, I was thoroughly pleased by his domestic environment, including an aquarium full of green algae that Sterling found to be as nice to look at as some fish, and a room containing ferrets, all running around, and around, and around the perimeter baseboards. He also had an insane coyote living in his back yard, and another room containing hawks and falcons, which he flew to get pheasants on the Richmond tidal flats.

Part of my payment from him for *Medusa* was in the form of rent for a house he owned on Twin Peaks, an elegant place for us to live until the day my wife told me, in one sentence, "I'm pregnant and I'm leaving you." I suppose I deserved it, but it was painful when she ran off to Mexico with...Bob Branaman. Who's writing this screenplay of life, anyway?

Sterling Bunnell, among his many other Renaissance Man qualities, was an astute compendium of biological knowledge. We had a rapport on the subject, and he poured much evolutionary information into my ready ear. Sterling helped to float the boat that would carry me onto the shores of Mandala-making a year later at Woodstock, NY, right in the lap of USCO, in yet another unanticipated karmic wrinkle.

Three years later, I ran into Billy Jahrmarkt one more time. It was 1967, outside the offices of *The San Francisco Oracle*, during the "Summer of Love." Billy had morphed from Nosferatu into Saint Francis. His hair hung long and Christ-like down across his shoulders, his eyes as limpid and loving as Sri Ramakrishna's (or a spaniel's, whichever metaphor you prefer). Nothing could have surprised me more than to have Billy embrace me with sincerity, gazing into my face with the genuine love that was the subtext to everything psychedelic in that year of the Summer of Love. It was early in the summer, and the bloom was still on the rose. We exchanged a few words and parted. I never saw him again.

A few years later, after the demise of the Batman Gallery, after the Summer of Love, even after the coming of Timothy Leary to Laguna Beach, Billy Jahrmarkt had his final intersection with number 22. This time, it was crucifixion rather than transcendence. In Kabul, Afghanistan, a gun dropped out of Billy's clothing and discharged when it hit the street, shooting him in the thigh. It nicked his femoral artery, and Billy bled to death in bed that night. The gun was a .45, but Billy had modified it with an insert-barrel and modified clip to change the caliber to...22.

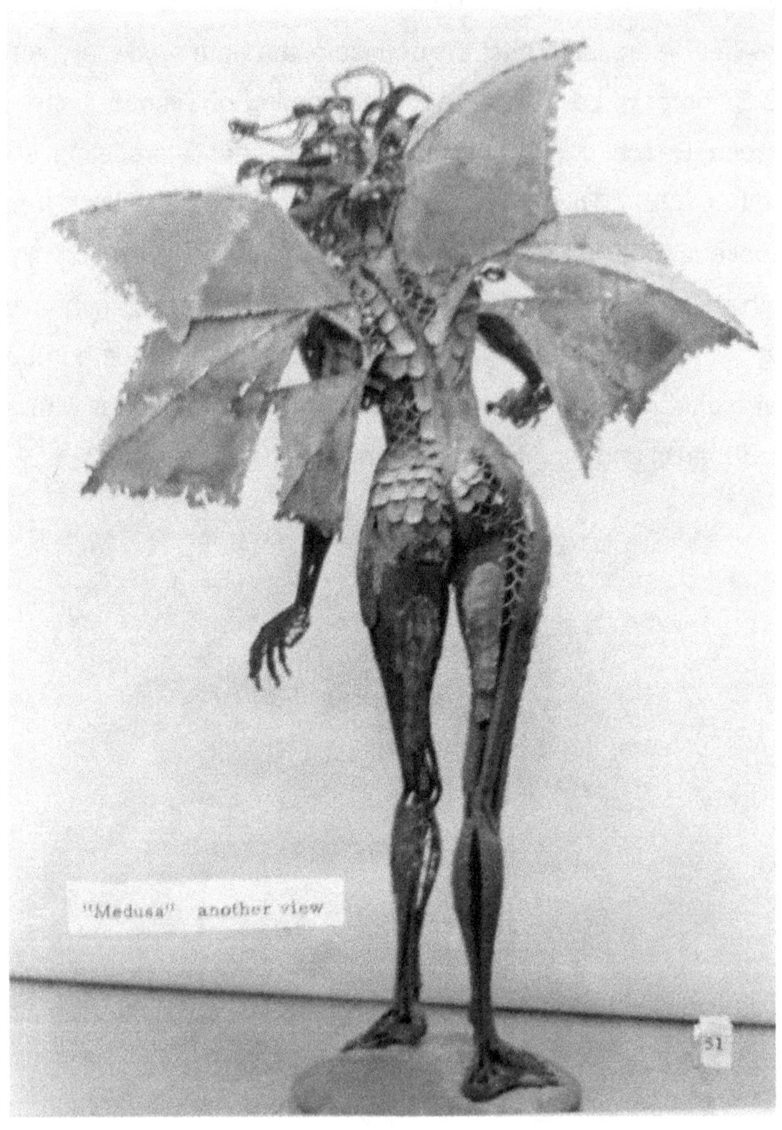

Figure 27: Back view of "Medusa," 8' welded metals, by Dion Wright, 1964. Photo by Neal Wolfe

Chapter V

A Drum Scene

In the summer of 1960, I returned to Laguna Beach for my second season at the Festival of Arts quite beat-up from the mad events of the prior year. I was getting a sense of the profound depths in this Art Game I signed up for. There was an increasing sense of a gap between the excruciating importance of what I was perceiving that Art was all about, and the soporific disconnect of the presumed professionals who surrounded me at the Festival. One might have supposed that to them, it was no more than home decor with egos attached.

Getting removed from the environs of ex-patriot Mexico, the Wichita Vortex, the Beat Generation and the Batman Gallery, to get implanted into sunny Laguna Beach in the summertime, could have opened a window of relative tranquility, but a committed seeker can find weirdness anywhere, as it turned out.

Certainly, there was nothing too weird about the artists and their Art at the Festival in Laguna Beach, although their opinion of me may have been somewhat different. My wardrobe had become odd, and my lingo was now full of affected hipster phraseology. My major piece that year was the sculpture of *Bob Branaman*, which captured the man well enough to disturb passers-by in Laguna Beach, who were primed for sunset seascapes, but were not ready for striding Dr. Death. One woman went into hysterics about it, shrieking that it was the essence of evil and the Devil's handiwork. That's some review. Maybe it was true. In any case, I was rescued from this hysteric by another ex-sailorman, Bennet Bradbury, who painted seascapes like Al DuPont did, but with substance.

Bennet's works were wild and furious evocations of seas in moody turmoil, just like he himself was. He was a medium-sized, tan, slender, leather-featured man who had a lot of body hair and a long crew cut. When he was exorcised, which was often, all this hair stood on end, and his lips drew back into a snarl. His blue eyes opened wide, and he resembled a baboon about to attack.

When the gibbering woman started screeching about the *Branaman* sculpture, Bennet Bradbury lit up with righteous indignation and came rushing out of his booth to defend Art. He swarmed the woman like a mockingbird badgering a raven and drove her clean off the grounds. Nowadays, such a thing could not happen.

So I was attracting some notice, and not only among the "squares." My little teenybopper was back again, hanging around in a posture of twinkling availability, but I had taken Al DuPont's counsel to heart about jailbait, so I was pleasant to the scrumptious nymphet but kept her at arm's length. Bobbi-baby was a different story.

The first time Bobbi-baby, a redheaded, jump-and-jive Betty Boop type, came chattering into my orbit, I could see that she was bursting with hormones and loaded to the gills on what turned out to be a habitual combination of speed and pot. I enjoyed her in that particular moment as a rip-roaring passing phenomenon but didn't regard her as more than a fleeting pleasantry to look at. I took a different view when she came back the next day, cooing

"Ooooo, baby," this and that, which was her characteristic mode of speech.

She was a compact number, with all of her wriggling volumes in the proper proportion. She looked just great but somewhat young, and I was prepared to hold her at arm's length also, like the aforementioned nymphet, until she revealed that she was a widow.

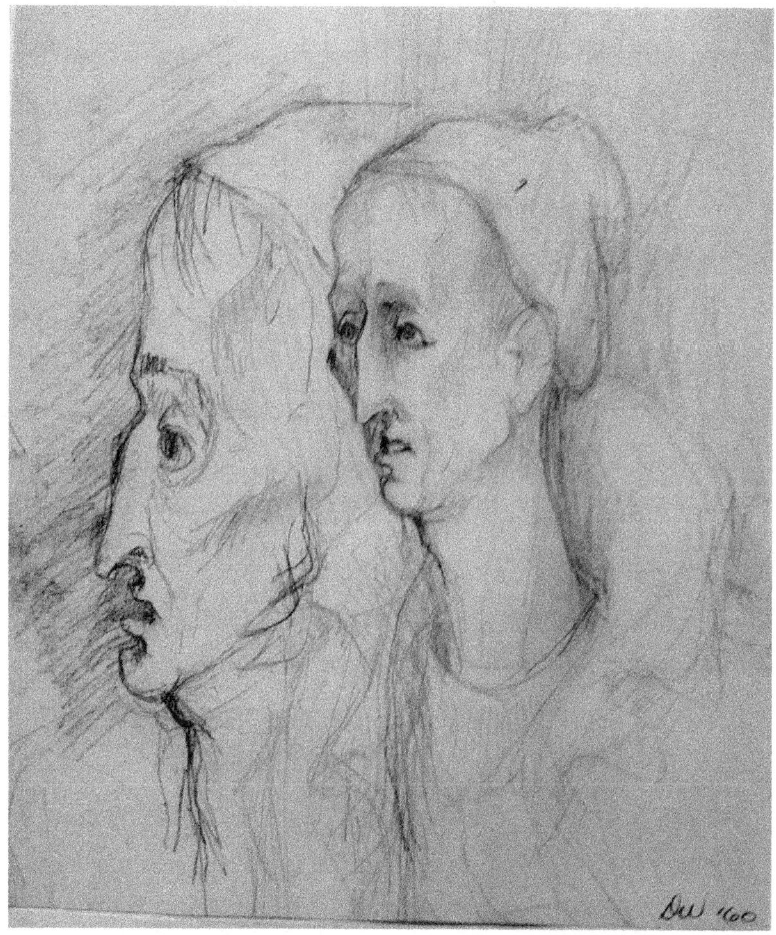

Figure 28: Sketches of Branaman by Wright

"There's no game fairer than a widow," I thought. Her deceased husband, one Edleigh Clarke, had been a cool jazz drummer who met a fiery end on the highway in a car crash. Bobbi-baby hardly seemed to be the grieving widow type and was eager to hang out with me more intimately than just chewing the fat at an Art fair. We arranged to meet that evening at ten when the show closed. She took me home with her.

Home was on a motor yacht in Newport Harbor. We got there via dinghy, and climbed aboard into comfortable cabin quarters, provided to Bobbi-baby by the current paramour of her mother. It was all as convenient as if it were staged, and quite a change of pace from my recent San Francisco reality, where everything had been difficult, and not least in the romance department.

Now I was well-and-truly back in the Land of the Lotus-eaters. "Don't get too comfortable!" she said, unbuttoning my shirt. She had a terrific superstructure, which she held proudly, all the while vibrating like an electrocuted hamster, cooing and giggling in lunatic fashion. A little reflection should have informed me that this personality could wear thin fast, but for the moment, raging hormones ruled over cool judgment. As it has been so truly said, a man has enough blood in his body to run his brain or to run his genitals, but not both at once. We smoked a big old bomber and fell into a passionate rut that lasted for months.

The weeks at the Festival of Arts crawled by drowsy day by drowsy day, each one followed by a wild night of sex. I fell asleep in the afternoons while sitting there in my booth waiting for somebody intelligent to turn up, as happened from time to time. Finally, the summer ended, and Bobbi-baby suggested that we go visit her jazz musician friends in Santa Barbara. She filled a handful of ill-begotten prescriptions for her favorite speed-based weight control pill, Obetrol, and we scored a couple of lids from

Suwanee the piano player, and away we went to a place called Mountain Drive, high in the hills above Montecito.

Exiting Highway 101 reached these Bohemian precincts after driving through the mansion district near the beach and ascending into a series of climbing switchbacks, until an enclave of individualistic handmade houses, each of a different but solid character took over. They all had plenty of room around them. Bobby and Floppy Hyde, who originally owned the whole mountain, had established this elevated neighborhood. They lived in the most Bohemian and capacious adobe on the hill with half a dozen Mexican orphans they adopted in their later years. Bobby Hyde wrote a book about it called *Six at Sixty*.

There were other writers around the neighborhood and all sorts of artists. Bobby sold his lots only to artists, not only that, but only to good artists. He rented out a bunch of places as well, to artists who were probationers, as it were, hoping to achieve endorsement under Bobby Hyde's high standards. Bobbi-baby's friends were renters who had a one-story adobe farther up the hill, perched where it overlooked the city of Santa Barbara, the sea, and the Channel Islands. It was nearly as spectacular as Big Sur. We wheeled into the drive and parked.

A large black man wearing an afro, the first I had ever seen outside of *The National Geographic*, was standing in the yard. His eyes were deeper and more spacious than the horizon. He was well groomed and casual, with clear skin, erect posture, and the sleek look of a seal. I had never met a mystic before but I was primed for one from all the esoteric reading I'd been doing while on the Beat scene in San Francisco. This man had a strong presence, which I perceived as being like the unruffled surface of a reflecting lake. The mental air around him washed over me like a nourishing zephyr.

Bobbi-baby's friend and mentor of musical hipness, Arloa Vineyard, came out of the house. The two women embraced in a cloud of jazz idiom. I was appreciating this great meeting, but when I turned to see how my first mystic was reacting to it, the guy had disappeared. Arloa had a less flattering perception of the man. "Ahhhh, that's just Stanford," remarked Arloa, "He appears and disappears like that all the time." She was not impressed by Stanford's mental spaciousness as I was. I never doubted my own perceptions and wondered how she could dismiss such a person with such blasé nonchalance. I soon figured out that this was the essence of Arloa's cynical and all-too-realistic personality.

Arloa was a looker, about ten years older than Bobbi-baby. She was also a harder-edged item, conventional but hot, a wisecracking cynical girl who always had a cigarette hanging out of one side of her mouth. Bobbi-baby burbled on, but Arloa never said anything she hadn't thought about first. She had a nice trim figure, emphasized with cocked hips and smoldering glances. She was sexy and sisterly both. The sisterliness was for everybody, but her romantic inclinations were only for her old man, Doug Vineyard.

There were other people living there, the first I noticed being Danny, a towhead boy of eight or so. He was Arloa's son, an internalized little boy who seemed to live in a state of self-created insulation from the world surrounding him. Inside the house, I met Conrad Riley, a man who had been following Arloa around since they had been in high school together in Belmont Shores.

Conrad was a bony and lantern-jawed specimen with lank and none-too-clean straight locks, which tended to fall across his eyes. His mouth hung forever agape, and until one heard some of the hip things which he sometimes said, one might think he was the village idiot. His non-compass-mentus appearance, Bobbi-baby whispered, was due to electric-shock therapy treatments Conrad had received at Lexington Hospital in Kentucky, where convicted junkies used to be sent to "take the cure."

"He's lucky they didn't lobotomize him," said Arloa out of the side of her mouth to keep her cigarette from falling out. After a while, her husband, Doug, came home from his job as the skipper of a Stearn's Wharf water-taxi that serviced the offshore oil platforms. Doug Vineyard looked like Superman, a reduced version, and was about as laconic as it gets west of the State of Maine. He was USMC 2nd Marines and a graduate of the Korean War, I later learned. He was friendly enough, shaking hands, but silently, and giving away nothing by his facial expressions. It was his habit to stand at the edge of his yard, where the land fell away, staring out to sea with his arms folded over his chest, tight t-shirt sleeves rolled up over his muscular biceps, and a sphinxlike patience pervading his entire dignified being. It seemed that he was guarding his castle like a stone lion in front of the library, but the truth was that he was just waiting for his smack connection.

All of these people were spliced together through the same jazz world once inhabited by the deceased jazz drummer, Edleigh Clarke, one-time husband of the Widow Bobbi-baby. They all, in turn, were connected like remote satellites to the legendary junky piano player, Joe Albany. Joe Albany had some chops, but not enough to justify the way these acolytes worshiped him.

His reputation rested mainly on having been Charlie "Bird" Parker's L.A. pianist in the '40s before Bird took the heroin cure by *"Relaxin' at Camarillo,"* a song he wrote there in the California State Hospital. The cure didn't work: it didn't work for Bird, didn't work for Joe Albany, and didn't work for Doug Vineyard, but it seemed to have worked for Conrad Riley...but at what a cost. Conrad was also a jazz pianist, but his brain was so scrambled that he could no longer play more than two bars without losing the thread.

Conrad lived in a wardrobe closet with an upright piano. There was no room in there for both a bunk and a piano bench, so Conrad sat on the circular top of a piano stool suspended by ropes that hung from the ceiling, and was put up onto the piano at night, so Conrad might go to bed.

He hung there for hours on end playing Bud Powell improvisations, but all chopped-up and abbreviated. It was odd to hear a sudden chain of hip notes ringing out, then truncated by silence. One could look in since there was no door, and see Conrad sitting like a puppet with its strings cut, staring vacantly into the corner, out of which reverie he would soon awaken to bang out another Powell phrase. He made his living as a dishwasher downtown.

The connection whom Doug Vineyard awaited so phlegmatically was George the piano-tuner, who looked like a fat Viennese innkeeper, with sagging belly and walrus mustache. George carried a wrinkled paper bag around with him, which contained various pills of many colors, which he ate like jellybeans. "Hell," he said, "These aren't habit-forming, and I should know. I've been taking them since 1941." He always tuned-up Conrad's piano when he came to deliver some smack to Doug.

I saw all of this because Bobbi-baby and I had rented a cabin just up the dirt road at the very top of the highest ridge that was accessible by car. On days when the fog rolled in, stopping just below the level of this house, we could look out across the surface of the fog bank to see the Channel Island summits stuck up in fine detail from the muzzy gray cotton. We carried on like a pair of rabbits.

At the bottom end of the Mountain Drive community, down in the holler under the live oak trees lived the Wooly Aphis. That wasn't his real name, poor man, which was Jon Lazell. Arloa had dubbed him that absurd name, perhaps because of the fuzzy blonde body hair that covered him and his buggish facial features, goofy and crooked-toothed. He also had another pair of those eternal eyeballs that I had noticed on Stanford. He was an outlandish-looking skinnymarink who habitually wore sandals and khaki shorts, period.

Jon and his wife Ruthie and two little boys lived there in splendid decay on family money, while Jon spent all of his time constructing huge, excellent conga drums, except on Mondays. On Mondays, the whole family went to Los Angeles to a P.G. Ouspensky group and studied the esoteric philosophy of Georges Gurdjieff. On the serious side of music, Jon Lazell worshiped Harry Partch, a percussionist/composer who wrote music which began from a classical mode, but soon spun off into eccentricity of the most unique and individual sort.

Jon Lazell longed to be a cosmic drummer, but although he had rhythm, he didn't have chops. He was one of those individuals who can see what Art and creativity are about, but can never break through into the heart of spontaneity. Therefore, he kept making bigger and bigger drums, which he called "tumbas". He kept them for himself to play, which he did in an interminable series of overlapping thirds. That was the basement of the music.

The guy who did have chops was the black mystic with the afro, Stanford Hayes. He had a drum that looked like it had been around since the last Ice Age. Its surface warm with decades of use, it had so much spirit in it that it seemed to be his silent partner. Stanford kept a rich cloth tied around the drum, sash-like, which only came off when he played. There was a suggestion of naked sexuality about the drum when it was denuded.

Weekly drumming sessions on the mountain began on Friday evening and didn't stop until Sunday. Stanford ruled the roost so long as he chose to blow. Badass conga drummers showed up from all over to play with him. Nobody came close to his cosmic virtuosity except a guy named Mitch, who arrived now and then with his own entourage who treated him like the boss bull.

Mitch was into an esoteric system called "Subud," and he usually talked in a garbled way, "talking in tongues" without the Christian fundamentalism. Nobody except Stanford Hayes had a clue as to what Mitch was talking about, but Stanford seemed to understand completely whatever Mitch's babbling meant, and the two of them went on between drum sessions with a discourse that left everybody else out. Stanford did not respond to Mitch with the same gibberish, but said monosyllabic stuff like, "Cool," or, "Mellow." Who was this Stanford Hayes, anyway? He was so esoteric, and while he appeared to be as open as the view from the mountaintop, he remained enigmatic.

Arloa, who wasn't a person to be impressed by such folderol, said, "Ahhhh, Stanford. He's just a spade from New York who likes white pussy. He'd like some of mine, but forget about it." I knew that there was far more to Stanford than that. I found Stanford rummaging around inside of my head telepathically, which was a hitherto unheard of thing. At first, I thought I was hallucinating, but when I locked eyeballs with Stanford, I learned better. "Mellow," said Stanford, when I looked at him in some alarm the first time this happened, "Are you hip to it? You're 'saved'. Are you hip to it?"

It all became even more profound when I reestablished my peyote connection with Moore's Orchids in Texas. The already hypersensitive and acute mental atmosphere that was pervading that supercharged extra-conscious community accelerated into overdrive by our warty little vegetable ally. "This is mellow, very mellow indeed," said Stanford, eating peyote buttons like cookies. While the rest of us barfed our guts out, Stanford hummed and strolled around the yard with unruffled equanimity. He seemed to be glad to have others joining him on the expanded plain of consciousness where he already habitually existed. And the drums played on.

It would be no exaggeration to say that it was one romantic scene, carried to cosmic levels that lasted little more than a few months.

In early October, there was a conjunction of events that changed everything. All the leaders of the world were coming to New York City to meet at the U.N., and simultaneously my grandmother was on her deathbed in New Rochelle. She summoned her relatives to come see her one last time. My mother asked me to go with her, so we arrived in Manhattan at the same time that Fidel Castro came to stay at a hotel in Harlem (to the fury of the State Department), and Nikita Khrushchev banged his shoe on the podium at the U.N.

I should have taken Bobbi-baby with me, but the idea of traveling in tandem with this particular girlfriend and my mother was ridiculous. Not with this girlfriend. Not with that mother. I had a lurking feeling in my subconscious that leaving Bobbi-baby on her own was not wise, but I pushed the little voice away and threw myself into the New York Art and jazz scene for three weeks, with visits to my dying grandma in between.

My Uncle George was a trumpet player with a good lip, but his musical career had been squelched in the '30s by this same ill grandmother, his mother. He still played when he could, although by then he was a master machinist. "I'm going to Birdland to see Dizzy Gillespie!" I told Uncle George. "Aaaaaaa, Diz is old hat!" said George. "He's worth seeing, of course, so long as you're here, but you really ought to check out Horace Silver."

That was the greatest advice, especially since the Horace Silver Quintet was alternating sets with Diz's group, allowing me to satisfy two agenda items at once. After a few days, the booking changed to Art Blakey and the Jazz Messengers alternating with Chico Hamilton. My life was full of drums, wherever I went. Diz's drummer at the time was Philly Joe Jones, the most virile and skillful drummer ever, including Blakey. I went to Birdland every night I could and was as dazzled as any other rube by the sophisticated hipness of the Manhattan music scene.

All the celebs hanging out in Birdland were fun to see. On one night I saw Phil Harris, Peggy Lee, Candido and Babs Gonzales, the inventor of the word "bebop". Diz got Babs up to sing "The Preacher," him barely able to stand up, hanging from the mike stand like overcooked noodles, but "lahba dahba doobahing" his heart out. I wanted to hear Art Blakey and Horace Silver in the same group, and later I found them recorded together with Miles Davis.

All day long, day after day, marinating in the Met, the Modern, and the Guggenheim, I soaked up Art. One day on the subway I saw the stop, "Columbus Circle," and got off there to see what that place was all about. It was really a traffic circle, and across the diameter of it from where I emerged from underground, I saw a five-story white building, which turned out to be the Huntington Hartford Museum, which I'd never heard of.

It was a striking building by Edward Durrell Stone, which I later learned was held in low esteem by the Bauhaus minimalists. Their low esteem was an early piece of de facto evidence to me that in the Art World the emperor might be naked. Be that as it may, I went in to discover that the entire five-story museum was given over to a retrospective of the surrealist, Salvador Dali. A visitor was carried by elevator to the top floor, where Dali's earliest work was, and then proceeded downward and chronologically through the collection toward the present, with Dali's work becoming more weird, draftsmanly, and monumental as the present day got closer. By the time I staggered out onto Columbus Circle, my senses were bludgeoned by overload. And that was just *one day*.

On other days I went to other museums and stopped several times at the Museum of Modern Art, where Pablo Picasso's "Guernica" was installed. This was Picasso's passionate and enraged, black and white protest of the Luftwaffe bombing of a defenseless town in Northern Spain, as an experimental exercise to test early air power. The huge painting was housed in a room by itself. It had to be by itself. No other work could be near it without seeming to be trivial.

I decided that "The Guernica" was the greatest painting of the age. I went to visit it repeatedly and spent hours soaking it in. It was the premier expression of abstraction wedded to content, I thought, warmly remembering my professor, Howard Warshaw, and wishing that man and his intellect were with me to shed more light. I decided that this "Guernica" was the gold standard; this raging outburst of the Spaniard, Picasso; and the creative moment against which I would forever measure everything and everybody who pretended to Art and artistry, including myself. This has never changed.

On my last day in New York, I saw Marshall Tito of Yugoslavia zooming up 5th Avenue in a limo. "That's Tito!" I cried to a sour-looking cop on a horse. "Yeahhhh. I wish they'd all go home, already," replied the cop.

When I made my way back to the top of my mountain in the Santa Barbara Land of Oz, I found my pad trashed, my record albums sailed into the brush like Frisbees, and my girl gone. Jon Lazell the Wooly Aphis told me that the party had started the day I left and never stopped until it was learned that I was on my way home.

There followed a long period of heartache. I was injured, exploited, and lonely. I chased after Bobbi-baby to San Francisco, where I tracked her down at Kirby Doyle's pad on Sutter Street, of all places, where she was being seduced by Jack Kerouac, of all people.

What chance did I have against such a big gun as that? Tears. Recriminations. Derailment. Ah, the hell it, I finally decided. I rebooted my brain and went back to Mountain Drive to see Arloa and Doug and Conrad...and Stanford Hayes. They looked askance and sideways at me to assess my cool, and life went on.

I couldn't say I was heart-broken since my heart was not all that involved, but I was humiliated and pissed-off. My pelvic region was the area most afflicted. Horny enough, I was. There was a lot of balm from the expanded nature of my consciousness, which was a sort of by-pass of matters of the heart, as far as I could see then, not yet having realized that Love is the motive power of the Universe and that Love did reside in the heart.

I welded a large figure of Charlie Mingus, hunched sexually over his bass, whom I had seen the past year at the Jazz Workshop in San Francisco with accident-prone, literary-minded Dan Hutson, another bass player. Plugging away making stuff was always my ground of sanity, and my life preserver.

On Halloween, Arloa and Conrad and I thought it would be a fine occasion to eat peyote, and we invited Stanford Hayes to join us, fully aware that the mystic conga-drummer would own the most serious consciousness in the group, if not in all of Southern California. "This is mellow, very mellow indeed," said Stanford Hayes, emitting a warm flood of deep satisfaction that wrapped everybody up as in a cozy, purple, psychic comforter. We ate our peyote and got sick, except for Stanford, who remained unfazed, and away we went into the night and the city, with Stanford at the wheel. He drove like a Zen archer shoots arrows.

Wherever we went, citizens who saw us did double takes, as if they suddenly were taking All Souls' Eve seriously for the first time. We went up near the Santa Barbara Mission to a monastery and parked outside. "If we think LOVE hard enough," said Stanford, "the Brothers will come out, bringing us some wine." We loved for all we were worth. No monks came forth, but the arched sky seemed as royally purple as the richest wine in the universe. That was the Mountain Drive swan song. I soon left for further disastrous adventures.

Later, I heard through the grapevine that Stanford Hayes had taken the name "Krishnadevananda" and was up around Big Sur. That was no surprise. We never met again, and I sometimes feel impoverished by it. I could have become Stanford's disciple, and related to him as the guru, but I drew back from the prospect. The guru should seem holy, and for all his amazing powers, holiness was not the quality I felt in Stanford. Among the admonitions I had absorbed in my occult readings was the one to beware of false prophets, and to avoid yogis who display their powers overtly. So I was wary, with or without sound reason.

I packed my rucksacks again and returned to San Francisco, to see if that was where I'd left my wholeness. San Francisco was as it had been, and nothing turned up. Bob Branaman and Susan were living in the Mission District, all strung out, and the whole scene was so down-and-out that I wondered why I'd returned. I scored a matchbox of weed from Bob and headed back south to San Clemente, where I could crash at my parents' house, and try to find some bearings. That matchbox of pot led to my betrayal by my best friend from childhood, and my jailhouse blues.

Chapter VI

Aldous Huxley & Timothy Leary

In 1955 Aldous Huxley and his friend Dr. Humphrey Osmond, a Canadian psychiatrist, invented the name "psychedelic" to describe mind-expanding chemicals such as mescaline, the active agent in the otherwise vile peyote cactus. Osmond had come to Hollywood in 1953 to give mescaline to Aldous Huxley, who was not only an eager guinea pig but was the most articulate one in history. Huxley's two 1953 books about mescaline, *The Doors of Perception* and *Heaven and Hell* were written with a slight separation in time, but immediately became joined in fact and the public mind, sold vigorously and still do sell well.

Aldous Huxley had been using his prodigious intellect to try to get at the essence of existence and had always been ultimately frustrated. The arc of Huxley's evolution as a writer and thinker had been from early celebrity as a humorous satirist of social mores, dealing with substantive ideas, through several novels, until his interest began to turn to emblematic historical ironies.

As he pursued his mental growth, he started to evolve beyond some of his readers. By 1943, insulated in the Mojave Desert from World War II, Aldous wrote three very different books, all on the theme of the possibility of man to grow and change.

The first of these was *The Art of Seeing*, a clinical narration of his own struggle to regain some of his sight, almost destroyed at the age of twelve by a sudden attack of keratitis pigmentosa.

The second book was *Time Must Have a Stop*, another excursion into the novel form, investigating the nature of consciousness beyond physical death.

The third book, *The Perennial Philosophy*, was a summing up, through the fantastic erudition and stupendous intellect of Aldous Huxley, of all the wisdom of all the great mystics of all the world's religions, or as individuals, with the intent of unifying beatific vision in a compendium of spiritual analogy. He accomplished this in the deep isolation and vast distances and silences of the Mojave Desert, in environment much like the places where his saints had meditated. All this dense work was accomplished by a sickly man with minimal vision in less than a year. The books speak for themselves.

Huxley's cadres of devotees, however, were struck asunder by the idea that their clever and witty entertainer was going "mystic" on them. They bitched and kvetched like debutantes at a rained-out soiree. Aldous Huxley paid them no mind, and serenely continued to plow the seas of creative writing with more tonnage than any others, with a robustly evolving certainty about where he was going (which turned out to be ever deeper into psychology and parapsychology), when, he struck up his life-long friendship with Dr. Osmond, which was inaugurated by the opening of the doors of perception.

Taking psychedelics and then writing about it favorably drove many literary people to fury. They denied that he, or anyone, could receive true enlightenment through a chemical. Meanwhile, Aldous became more and more serene, as testified by his wife Maria, who said that the formerly difficult genius had become a sweet saint.

During this same period, Timothy Leary, thirty years younger than Aldous, had been pursuing his own stellar career. His brilliance was a given, if his social behavior left something to be desired, as might be inferred from the fact that he was cashiered from the Academy at West Point for "conduct unbecoming"...something about co-eds on a train. Poor Tim endured shunning, for a semester, receiving the silent treatment from one and all. He rode over his vicissitudes, perhaps with some of his later aplomb. After climbing the academic ladder at other institutions, Leary became a behavioral psychologist (!), and wrote such a good textbook about it that it is still in use.

For all his brains, Aldous refused to accept the gradual waning to cancer of his dear wife, Maria, who was literally everything to this quirky, sickly, unpredictable sage. He made light of her ills until reality crashed in on him and devastated his world. His meditations on transcendence kept him aloft and productive. Timothy Leary also lost a wife and the mother of his two children when she committed suicide.

At the time of Maria Huxley's drawn out and agonized death, Aldous had moved philosophically from Hinduism toward Mahayana Buddhism, and had become saturated in the Tibetan Book of the Dead. As Maria slowly perished, the heartbroken Aldous, tears streaming down his face, read softly into her ear from the Bardo Thodol to facilitate her transition. Aldous later quoted Shelly:

"Why linger, why turn back, why shrink, my Heart?

Thy hopes are gone before: from all things here

They have departed; thou shouldst now depart!"

Timothy Leary, Richard Alpert, and Ralph Metzner later elevated the Tibetan Book of the Dead into a sort of textbook for the LSD experience. They called their book, *The Psychedelic Experience*, and dedicated it to...Aldous Huxley.

By 1955, vast amounts of LSD were available in America, thanks to Captain Al Hubbard and the CIA. Aldous had his first LSD experience and was able to remember at long last his mother's death when he was a child, and to access his long-buried feelings, and to grieve for her. He experienced LSD several times in 1955 and '56 before coming to the conclusion that when it comes to psychedelics, less is more, reflecting that once a year was plenty to provide an intelligent person with fodder for contemplation and self-improvement.

When the LSD psychiatrists began to flourish, providing LSD sessions to whomsoever had a hundred bucks, Huxley was incensed at the irresponsibility and materialism of it. Later he came down four-square against the growth of the so-called "drug culture"...but by then it was too late. It was also too ironic, as Aldous Huxley's own two revelatory books, *The Doors of Perception* and *Heaven and Hell*, had kicked-off general interest in the subject. As he back-pedaled and became more and more conservative, Aldous Huxley found himself in the uncomfortable, not to say "absurd", position of being at the center of the international media cyclone which was, as usual, more hysterical than thoughtful, and more hip-shot opinionated than informed.

Aldous Huxley gradually became close to Laura Archera, a family friend, therapist, and concert violinist who had been Maria's intimate friend. In the course of a mescaline session monitored by Laura in 1956, Huxley became saturated in the Vedanta dictum that there is no difference between the subject and the object; and to the music of Bach's 4th Brandenburg Concerto, the idea for his final book, *Island*, was born.

This was to become the visionary template upon which the Merry Cricket, John Griggs, wanted to found his Utopian community, and which vision was corrupted by the venal needs of Dr. Timothy Leary. As for Aldous and Laura; they were married in the Drive-In Wedding Chapel in Yuma, Arizona, and lived happily ever after, which truly didn't last all that long.

Aldous Huxley had one of the most beautiful and mellifluous of speaking voices. One time in the restaurant of the Algonquin Hotel in Manhattan, home of the famous Round Table, Aldous was dining with some friends when he was seized by the topic of conversation, and took off, ex tempore, composing and delivering an essay on the spot. Talk at the other tables fell off to silence as Aldous developed his thesis. When he was done, the entire room erupted in applause. By 1960, Aldous Huxley had received the diagnosis of cancer of the tongue. Surgery would end his career as a lecturer, and he refused the knife.

Meanwhile, Aldous was struggling with the *Island* utopian novel project, which he couldn't get to "behave". He was also booked for a lecture series at several universities, and in October of 1960, he found himself lecturing to fifteen hundred people at MIT on the subject of *What a Piece of Work is Man*. Over from Harvard in the audience was a new professor from the Psychology Department, Dr. Timothy Leary. Leary and Huxley, and Osmond all met the next day.

It is startling to learn that when Humphrey Osmond and Aldous Huxley compared notes after first conversing with Dr.

Timothy Leary, they both thought that he was remarkably square! This is quite an insight, for when I met Dr. Leary myself some five or so years later, I, too, regarded him as a bit fusty, which academic cobwebbiness he was rapidly dissolving until he became the now and happening creature we all love to remember.

As I think of it, I suppose that psychedelic seasoning brought out a natural, perhaps Irish, talent in Tim to channel personalities. I saw him be Jean Lafitte, a dumb tourist, Dr. Feelgood, Thomas Jefferson, good-time Charlie, etc., all played to perfection. Will the real Timothy Leary please stand up?

Come to think of it, Aldous Huxley insistently described human beings as "amphibians" inhabiting differing media and environments, not necessarily mutually congenial. Too bad, he didn't live long enough to appreciate Tim's bravura manifestation of his idea. Also too bad, that Tim was so impetuous and headlong that he failed to apprehend the deep gravitas of Aldous Huxley, much less reflect it.

Serendipity was in play. Aldous Huxley's lecture and meeting with Timothy Leary happened just as Leary, Richard Alpert (Baba Ram Dass), and Ralph Metzner were beginning their psychedelic investigations with psilocybin "magic" mushrooms. Aldous was folded right in to this commencement, along with Alan Watts, Allen Ginsberg and the whole suite of what would emerge as the leaders of the Psychedelic Movement.

The topography of what was said between Timothy Leary and Aldous Huxley remains sketchy, especially since some of the dialogue was reported later, from memory, by Leary, and sounds not much like Huxley. We can know that Aldous counselled Tim to be restrained and conservative in his approach, because, as he warned, the Academic Establishment would view poorly encroachment upon its territory of being the official agents of enlightenment, as happened. "Don't cock a snook at Authority," urged Aldous, to the foremost snook cocker of the 20th Century.

Aldous returned to his Hollywood home, which promptly burned to the ground, consuming his priceless library and generations of manuscripts, becoming the first instance, if one were moved to see it that way, of “Shiva” in conjunction with Timothy Leary. Aldous saved only the manuscript of *Island*, and Laura saved only her priceless Guarneri violin. Everything else went up in flames except the firewood stacked in the driveway.

Aldous Huxley continued as ever to persevere in the face of dire vicissitudes and completed *Island*. His cancer returned and slowly killed him. He died on November 22, 1963, the day JFK was shot. He died on a double dose of LSD.

Timothy Leary pursued his demons, or they pursued him, as follows as a portion of the tempus fugitive saga.

Chapter VII

Jail

When I hit San Clemente after my compromised exit from San Francisco with my matchbox of pot from Bob Branaman, I went immediately to find my old pal, Bobby Miller, whom I'd known since the 7th grade. He was a clam who kept his mouth shut, except at home and with me. We were both outsiders. I had many friends despite my alien state, while Bobby's only friend was me. He had brilliant parents, brilliant siblings, and was brilliant himself, but socially inept and too introverted to talk about it.

We had both been the odd characters in school. We were non-conformist and outside the pale of the vapid American conformity and social savoir-faire of the '50s. We were both tardy maturers, biologically, jointly neotonistic to a fault, and mostly untroubled by that state-of-being until we were getting into the upper class standard at high school when we found ourselves socially more and more strained and excluded. We responded to the pressures of that condition differently.

The basis of our friendship was a fascination with wild nature. We didn't talk too much, but were on the same wavelength with each other. With others, I was somewhat challenged and stilted as to being able to communicate, but Bobby couldn't do it at all. If he spoke but little to me, he didn't speak at all to anybody else, and this caused him plenty of trouble, especially in school. Meanwhile, we went all over the land and sea, penetrating deeply into the interesting ecosystems (as yet an unknown word) that made up our world, discovering, hand over fist, and exploiting our discoveries for money. We gathered plants and animals and sold them.

Bobby was a non-conformist. He absolutely refused to wear shoes, and suffered for it within such social institutions where the compulsion to conform was important. He wouldn't, and didn't. It wasn't rebellion with him so much as a conviction that the constraints of behavior that Society dictated were silly. Still, he was looking for an identity to inhabit as a pre-teen, and went through several theatrical incarnations wherein he assumed the persona of some slice of the social fabric and carried it forth until he ran out of gas.

He tried-on being a Marine for a while when we sold newspapers on the Basilone Road exit from Tent Camp Three. This was where the Marines left Camp Joseph H. Pendleton every afternoon. Bobby was given a cap with the anchor and world emblem on it by a happy-go-lucky Marine, which he wore proudly.

He became a sort of mascot for the Marines, who day by day outfitted him with various elements of uniform and accessory until the MP's came and made him go back to ordinary boy clothes; either that or get lost. It depressed him. The fact probably was that some officer couldn't abide seeing him barefoot in uniform.

We both were engaged with the sea, the tides, and the creatures that lived there, but with Bobby, it was an amphibious life. We both did stuff like swim around the pilings at the end of the pier and collect lost tackle off the mussels and the horse neck barnacles, but Bobby would go farther, often swimming out to the edges of the kelp beds with spear gun in hand, or to the offshore reefs, even in the fog, and all by himself. He was intrepid, and quite at home on the edge of existence. The published tide tables were our almanac, and every winter our lives centered on the minus tides that occurred every two weeks, more or less.

A minus tide meant that vast expanses of normally hidden intertidal acreage would be revealed in that Southern California landscape where the drop-off of the beach was so gradual. This meant that we could scour the flats for a few hours, finding many organisms that were normally under water, beyond our easy reach. We collected all sorts of invertebrates: starfish, clams, urchins, octopi, crabs, worms, etc., etc., etc., which we then immersed in preservative fluids, packed in cans, and shipped to Kansas for a payday from Quivira, a biological supply house. We had money, and we didn't have to have a job. This modus operandi went on for six years or so until I went away to college and Bobby went off the deep end.

It was never a topic of conversation between us, as we pursued the fruits of Biology, the real nature of our own personal Biology that had us, still on the wrong side of puberty years after our peers had made that transition. Not talking about it didn't mean it wasn't a tormenting thing within us, however. In my case, I just waited and suffered until I finally caught up naturally.

Bobby, however, forced the issue. He took quack treatments from some doctor having to do with testosterone enhancement, and Boy Howdy, it worked, all too well. When I returned one year from college, I found Bobby had morphed into a beetle-browed, husky character so extreme in appearance that he was known down at the drive-in as "Magilla Gorilla". He can't have liked that, but he was compensating with a powerful muscle car and the pursuit of fair damsels. This was the guy I was seeking on my return from San Francisco early in the Kennedy administration. I asked around and learned that he was living on the end of the abandoned Capistrano Beach pier.

It was well after dark when I got to the old pier, on foot, as I had no car. Bobby's black muscle car sat parked at the foot of the abandoned pier. I wriggled through the chain link and barbed wire, which were ineffectively intended to keep trespassers from going out on the pier and breaking their necks. I ventured out, gingerly feeling my way from plank to plank, testing ahead for solid footing, and across the gaps where there were no planks at all, until I approached the dilapidated building on the end of the pier, which had once been a cafe and tackle store.

Below, the sea surged in its perennial rhythms, swells gently rocking the pilings and making the pier creak and sway slightly with each passing wave in the sucking sound of its passing. I found Bobby inside, cooking a can of Dinty Moore beef stew on a Coleman stove. A wadded-up and none-too-clean sleeping bag was pushed against the wall. The only other furnishings were a Coleman lantern, a couple of rickety chairs, and a few hundred books.

We took up where we had left off, sort of. Bobby had new preoccupations and wanted me to go with him to the Breakers drive-in at San Clemente, where the guys showed off their cars to each other, and tried to seduce girls within. Off we went, roaring down the coast road in a fine display of automotive might and power. I fired up the skinny joint I'd brought from the tiny Branaman stash, and we smoked that lousy pot, which failed to get us very high, but nonetheless filled the interior of the car with odor.

When we pulled into the drive-in and were chomping our burgers, a nervous young man suddenly got into the back seat. He sniffed the air and started vibing me out by talking about pot. Did we have any, could we get any? He was Larry Mansur, a fisherman well-known to us both. His behavior was quite out of the normal, and his questions seemed aggressive and inappropriate. This was altogether too weird for me, so I jumped out of Bobby's car and made off across town on foot. I was already habitually in a quasi-paranoid state, with my perceptions sharpened, so I avoided further human contact and sat on the bluff overlooking the sea for a time until my emotional body simmered down. Then, I went back to my parents' house.

They were already asleep by then, so I sat down and watched a TV program about the beginnings of the Kennedy era. As I watched, there was a soft tap at the door. When I answered, there was Larry Mansur, asking me if I wanted to see some good weed he had. It's still a mystery to me why my hitherto acute sensibilities then deserted me, but I left the house and went out to the street where a car was parked.

Suddenly a big fat man in a suit, wearing glasses, jumped out of the shrubbery and hurled me to the asphalt. He was twice my weight and was flattening me against the driveway. As he snapped on the cuffs, I saw his trouser leg ride up his calf, exposing white and hairless pudge. Larry Mansur fidgeted uncomfortably as the fat man, Detective John Guyer (which happens to mean "vulture" in German), braced me against the car and started in threatening and bullying me.

My little stash was well-hidden and there was no warrant. I was green and innocent, to tell the truth, so when Guyer told me how he was going to go into my parents' house and turn it inside out in a search for contraband, I was intimidated so thoroughly that I showed him where it was, tucked under a stone next to the garage. Off to jail on the spot and onto the next phase of my education.

It turns out that after I left Bobby's car, Guyer had joined Mansur, and they bullied him into admitting that the pot they smelled was mine. Betrayal.

If I had then been persuaded to betray Branaman, who knows how much better my fate might have been? Whether I should have given him up or not, I didn't. It was a stronger value not to snitch than to face incarceration. At the moment of getting busted, I wasn't taking it as seriously as I should have.

The amount of pot was so insignificant. The nature of pot itself was so unthreatening. The idea of pot being a "stepping stone" to harder drugs seemed absurd and still does. So, I took the fall.

The whole experience of sitting in cells and getting mixed in with a lot of distasteful characters has been exploited in media ad nauseum, so I'll be brief about it. I was bound over to the Orange County Jail (the old one on Sycamore Street in Santa Ana), the next morning by Judge "Gavvy" Cravath, who had been a professional baseball player in the '20s. Now, he was a liver-spotted old curmudgeon with the attitude of a snapping turtle. I was the first arrest for pot possession in the history of San Clemente, and everybody seemed bent on making an example of me. So I landed in Sycamore Street, pending bail.

The entire Gothic plant on Sycamore Street was under the dominion of one Sergeant Brusso. This guy matched his name and was an example of life imitating Art. He was an overweight and thuggish man who had thick rolls of fat around his neck. I had almost no contact with this monster, thank God, who reminded me of Gletkin in Arthur Koestler's *Darkness at Noon*. I was shunted into the holding tank, jam-packed to three times its capacity. The overflow "fish" awaiting disposition, slept "on the beach", which is to say, the concrete floor.

While dozing fitfully that night, a chinless Mexican in the mold of Alfonso Bedoya nudged me awake with his toe and asked what I was in there for. Out of the depths of my grogginess, the slang Mexican word for pot I'd learned in San Miguel de Allende came spontaneously out of my mouth: "Llesga." My interlocutor looked non-plussed and went off to the land of his peers at the end of the tank, where the head Mexican absorbed the information with a thoughtful expression. I went back to my shallow slumbers, and when I awoke in the morning, my coat and my shoes were gone.

Then I got bailed out by my mother.

We hit the pavement before she noticed I was in my socks. Being the take-charge executive type whom she was, she immediately charged back into the Sycamore Street Jail, over my strenuous objections, leaving me on the sidewalk, knowing full-well that no good was going to come of this. After some elapsed time she reappeared, triumphantly carrying my coat and shoes.

A period of slow months passed, during which I welded up my sculpture of the bass player, Charlie Mingus, and prepared for my third season showing at The Festival of Arts, which I was going to miss, being otherwise detained.

My well-shaved and ponderous lawyer was named Norm Rudolph. He had a fascinating single eyebrow that ran above his eyes, a short crew cut, and an overly loud sport coats. He was a nice enough guy, but criminal defense was not his specialty. He knew enough to schedule my appearance before the kindly Judge Hamilton rather than the hanging Judge Gardiner, and with the docket set, we awaited trial. I was going to plead guilty, in the expectation that such a trivial first offense would be dealt with mildly.

My day in court arrived, but Norm Rudolph didn't. He was tardy. I discovered, with nobody to intervene for me, that my case had been given to Judge Gardiner after all, who was less than delighted when I revealed that my attorney had yet to arrive. Instead of being first up, I was moved to the back of the line, where I watched the stern-visaged Judge Gardiner hand down harsh sentence after harsh sentence all morning.

Norm Rudoplh eventually came puffing and blowing into court, full of apologies that mollified nobody. His speech to Judge Gardiner was fractured and fumbling. The judge looked at him from under the most threatening brows this side of a Zen roshi and advised him coldly that his behavior left much to be desired. Then, he turned to me and socked me with six months in the County Jail and three years of formal probation. I was hauled off in cuffs, and never saw Norm Rudolph again. (Several years later, Norm Rudolph became an investor in a company manufacturing one-man helicopters. He was killed falling from quite a height, riding one…too much weight, too little lift). So, I landed in Tank 8 on Sycamore Street, the block dedicated to drug and sex offenders.

That was one tense place. The Mexican gang was on the east end of the tank. The black guys were on the west end. In between were the flotsam and jetsam of white underbelly. This tank was also overcrowded and “sleeping on the beach” was the prospect.

A soon as I was dumped into this cage, the head Mexican, Angel "Joe" Lopez, came up to me. He was rather courtly on the whole, but still very sinister. He informed me that he had been the guy caught with my shoes and coat, had done time in the hole (solitary) on that account, and that I owed him. He was a dandy sort, with a pencil mustache and hair that naturally looked Marcelled, so there were layers of overtones when he said he wasn't going to claim my ass, but was going to claim my food. He left me to contemplate this situation. As I sat there, I heard a rich baritone voice singing *I Apologise*. A black man who looked roughly like a large cinder block covered with scar tissue was the source of this singing.

"Hey man," I said, "You sound just like Billy Eckstine." That weak remark saved me. The man broke into a gleaming, shining grin and steered me into his cell to meet his mate, Clarence Chance. We talked jazz non-stop, until my benefactor, Rocky by name, who had sized-up the situation out in the tank, said I could sleep on the floor under their bunks and assured me that nobody would bother me as their client. I should think not. Rocky looked like the only thing that kept him from walking through the wall was his good nature. Clarence was the image of an NFL superstar, although he was really just a dumb cluck with ten kids and not enough sense not to commit armed robbery while sporting a bright red Afro. Dumb or not, Clarence was sincere and decent to the point of high dignity, but it would take a real fool to start something with him.

So I was a saved by the black guys, and spent my days in Tank 8 talking music and drawing pictures for Rocky and Clarence, mostly of sexy women. We had a good old time, much like high school, until for want of space we all graduated from Sycamore Street to the Theo Lacey Security

Theo Lacey was in no way actually a farm, as there were neither crops nor livestock there. It was a series of dormitories set up like spokes on a wheel, at the hub of which were the jailers, who could see everything in all the dorms through the glass walls facing the control booth. Out behind there was a shop building, and to this, I was assigned. Since I was an artist, they didn't know what else to do with me. Because I was a dangerous dope fiend, they couldn't send me off-campus in one of the parks or roads crews.

In that shop, was the closest thing to a farm item, namely the shit-kicker who ran the place, Jim Newcombe. He was a Hank Williams look-and-act alike who had the humor of a shovel and the brains of a wheelbarrow. At the other end of civilian management was Earl Williams, the recreation director, who was as smart as Newcombe was dumb. These two birds didn't get along at all, since Newcombe was a white hick from the South, and Williams was a black college graduate. In between these civil functionaries were a number of Sherrif's personnel who were more subject to satire than respect, from Sergeant Skinhead at the desk through Deputy T-Bone and up to Lieutenant Burrell M. Batelle

I had various jobs at the farm, including making a large model of the facility to be shown at the Orange County Fair. I was given a day out of jail to go to the fair to install this excellent piece of work, under the custody of Captain James Broadbelt, a county narc who was still bent on extracting the name of Branaman from me, at which aim he failed.

He was a canny and civilized sort, a cultured man in the wrong role. I spent a lot of energy trying to persuade Lt. Batelle to let me muralize the attractive blank wall in the cafeteria, but he demurred. I could have done a good job of execution, but who knows what the content might have been? I might have been the Orange County Jail's answer to Diego Rivera at the Rockefeller Center.

The major work I did do, with my fellow cynic, the inmate folk singer, Russ Thomas, was to build a jogging track around the entire perimeter of the grounds. This was a good addition to the accoutrements, and gave Russ and me a chance to develop a long and intricate dialog that was thoroughly aware and beyond the capacity to be bugged. Close relationships form in jail, but afterward, they melt into nothingness.

Before I knew it, my sentence was up, and I was released into the surveillance of a probation officer, and constrained to go to work at an architectural hardware manufacturing company in Laguna Canyon known to its wage slaves as "The Doorknob Factory". That place employed me for a couple of years, and is worthy of a book along the lines of *Tortilla Flats/Cannery Row*, which I may eventually get to write, should I live so long.

As for my friend Bobby Miller, he became the postman for the southern portion of South Laguna, where he lived out his life. I went to see him twenty-some years later, ambushing him out behind the Post Office, assuring him that I forgave him and bore him no ill will. He looked as if he might explode. After that, we had occasional contacts up until his early death from diabetic complications in his early fifties. He was not found until the odor of him informed discovery. An amazing irony revealed itself after the demise of this close-lipped and interior man. He had assembled the largest known collection of the world's bivalves, i.e. clams, which are now the property of the Dana Point Marine Institute, located down where we used to go to collect.

Chapter VIII

Psychedelic Psychologists

Donald Duck introduced me to the idea of psychologists.

Kids who became fans of Donald Duck in comic books learned that several people drew and told the stories, and that one of these persons was so superior to all the rest that he was known as simply "the good artist." He was the American cartoonist Carl Barks. Walt Disney invented Donald Duck, but Carl Barks turned the character into a literary phenomenon. It became habit to take a quick glance into each comic as it hit the stands to see if Carl Barks had drawn it or not, and if not, to put it aside, un-bought. Apparently, many fans did this, because eventually, almost all the Duck stories were by Barks. We did not know him by name in those days, just by style. It was not Walt Disney's practice to credit any individual for anything pictorial, other than himself. A man marvelously named Ub Iwerks, invented Mickey Mouse, but he only got the credit for it through the grapevine.

Huey, Louie and Dewey, Uncle Scrooge, Gladstone Gander, Gyro Gearloose, the Beagle Boys and the evil Magica de Spell (Daisy's alter ego) were invented by Carl Barks. Carl had a sense of story that was always topical and interesting, imagined in epic terms, once his characters had entire comic books as the format to play out an adventure.

Take *Lost in the Andes*, for instance, when Donald and the boys go off on the trail of square eggs, or when they're selling steam calliopes to Alaskan Indians who use totem poles as the pipes, or when they're catching the Loch Ness Monster by tricking him into eating hot chilies.

Barks also drew the opening eight-page stories that began all the *Walt Disney Comics and Stories* monthlies during the late '40s and the '50s. The stories had mostly local situations occurring in and around Duckburg. One of these stories featured a child psychologist.

Now, in the standard Duck story presentation, the three nephews are more grown-up than Donald is, who is often portrayed as selfish and unrealistic, and given to fits of emotionalism, while Huey, Louie and Dewey are responsible "Junior Woodchucks", Barks' version of the Boy Scouts. When it suited his story, however, Barks would make Donald become the harassed parent while the boys acted out juvenile behavior. In the story in question, the nephews are unruly, and misbehaving so badly that Donald takes them to a child psychologist. The psychologist, a bearded entity (none of Barks' characters is ever drawn as quite human), who looks a lot like Sigmund Freud, presses his fingertips together and advises Donald that he should not repress the little boys, but should allow them the freedom and license to develop without inhibition. The last frame of this story ends with one of Barks' signature panels, of characters in silhouette against the night sky. The nephews are running for their lives, pursued by the psychologist brandishing a switch, while Donald brings up the rear, shouting ironic questions at the maddened doctor.

The message was clearly that the psychologist was talking a lot of pretentious gobbledygook, which had humorously dissolved in the face of reality. This apprehension fitted in very well with the attitude of my parents.

My mother, agreed with by my father, regarded psychology as bunk, and psychologists as pretentious charlatans. Nobody will be shocked to learn that both of my parents were extreme neurotics, desperate to present themselves as normal. In those days, everybody thought that there was such a thing as normal. Any system like Psychology, which probed beneath the surfaces of image to try to understand the roots of behavior (as I understand it now) was regarded as a deadly threat to the tenuous and fragile balance that my parents expected and assumed they had, but never really owned.

Leaving aside the nature of their particular psychological problems, which were actually quite prosaic (for all the energy put into obscuring them), the seminal fact for the purposes of this story, is that I entered intellectual life, groping for experience with a deeply skeptical attitude toward the entire field of Psychology. Then I began to meet actual psychologists.

The first one of these was a slender and dark professor named McClintock who lectured the required units to a class hall filled with several hundred snoozing undergraduates. Professor McClintock could scarcely have rendered himself less interesting had he been embalmed. His voice buzzed inaudibly like the "veena" drone instrument under an Indian sitar performance, methodically and exhaustively intoning the words with no sense of communicating anything of any interest whatsoever. So far, so good, no threat here, had I been even thinking in those terms. I was otherwise preoccupied, thinking mostly about nearby females, which no doubt had far more interesting psychological ramifications than anything the soporific Professor McClintock was liable to say.

I moved off campus into a Bohemian enclave, though nobody in it yet realized that's what it was. I painted a knock-off of the central figure of Paul Gauguin's, *Who Are We? Where Do We Come From? Where are We Going?* on the front door of our board and bat beach bungalow, and in retrospect can only be glad I identified with Gauguin rather than Van Gogh! That scene of sexual probing and artistically tentative revelation went on for a couple of years, leavened, in the last months, by the Beat Generation and its books.

Jack Kerouac's *On the Road* and Allen Ginsberg's *Howl*, were broadsiding us, the nascent counter-culture of the University's latest crop of almost-graduates, on the eve of our matriculation into the real world. We were enthusiastically ready to go "on the road", not having the wits to discriminate between X and Y socially, creatively, responsibly, and dare I say it...psychologically.

As soon as we had enough gas money after graduation, my pal George and I took off in his black '40 Ford coupe. We roared up US 1 through Big Sur. The CHP stopped us at the Big Sur Inn for a broken taillight glass (even after putting one of Ma Deetchen's red rose petals over the bare bulb with a rubber band). Next, we stopped at Nepenthe to ogle at Henry Miller conversing with his friends, and at last entered San Francisco in a rapturous state of enthusiasm. It only took the couple of days we had there to inoculate me permanently with the wonder of San Francisco, and I was from New York!

However, no psychologists yet, none in Laguna Beach or in San Miguel de Allende either, at least I hadn't crossed paths with any. It was over a year later when I returned to San Francisco in a more permanent way that I met a real one...but...

Just now, in real-time, a colleague wrote to ask how I had managed to avoid being sucked into unlikely belief systems such as Astrology. The answer seems to fit into this essay/memoir just right, so here it is, before plodding along down the chronological path of constraint:

Regarding successful sidestepping of the trap of being bamboozled by nonsense, I tried to "judge each tree by the fruit it bears", and had some extreme lessons by example early on.

I took the time to learn the esoteric systems exhaustively for a few years in the early '60s and came down on the side of the yogic disciplines as the most likely way to get off the wheel of reincarnation. The fruit borne on that tree was not only genuine, in a psychic sense, it also required a lot of hard work to get anywhere with it. It was not just a self-deluding "Leap of Faith", that easy way out so comfortable for so many. As for the *I Ching*, I have a lot of regard for it as offering chances for personal insight, which beats prognostication every time.

There was no Science, as such, the way we now understand it, right up until the last few hundred years, but there certainly was the hierarchy of the Church, which did not care for any ideas that might go against the grain of dogma. Alchemists and such were a real threat to the Establishment, where found, and anyone appearing to be operating outside the accepted rituals was routinely burned. For that reason, the knowledge that existed was buried in symbolism, laminated onto pagan calendar rites, and became the Kabbalah (and other systems). This somewhat preserved the notions of primitive Science in a way that allowed it (benighted as it all was) to survive the Dark Ages, and become the launch pad for Chemistry, Astronomy, and the rest.

Within a very loose chronology, here is my view of how the phenomenon of Art, and eventually of Psychology, were derived from Neolithic cave society. We could go back a lot further than that, assessing roots, but it seemed to me that the point at which symbols are made is a reasonable starting point to cast a little light on our contemporary predicament.

The basic division I see, leaving out indecipherable (so far) gender issues, is the early division of the tribe into the political wing (chiefs and warriors) and the religious wing (priests and medicine men). When these basic social communities started symbolizing their ideas, they gave rise to a third wing: the artists. An uneasy tension has existed ever since. The priests and the warriors (which originally overlapped) couldn't approve nor understand why these kooks had to behave so outside the box, even in Solutrean times. They were uneasy, but put up with a lot of personality rancidness and behavioral hooey, if they wanted to get their symbols made.

The dynastic levels of success at bending artists to bureaucratic molds has waxed and waned throughout History and is getting out of control again. Especially now that phony-baloney poseurs are claiming to the mantle of creativity without in any way deserving it, and since the Babbits who run the so-called Art World have driven quality into the ditch for the sake of artificially manipulated value (not to mention specious definition).

Nobody knows anything anymore, except the real artists, who are secure in what they do. It will be fascinating to see how this all works out, should we live long enough.

The artists have been here right along, watching the sundry splits and permutations, socially, among the Politicals and the Spirituals. The huge current tribe of 'businessmen' are descendants of the scribes who kept the accounts for Pharaoh, gone off to set up on their own while mouthing the right phrases to get along with Church and State (i.e. plenty of flag and cross waving). Therefore, they derive as hybrids from both the warrior-chief and priest-medicine man sides of the equation. After all, both sides needed accountants!

Psychologists are a late-blooming phenomenon within the aforementioned loose definitions, but their roots are definitely in the priest-medicine man (or, "witch doctor") tradition. In fact, psychologist/psychiatrists are sometimes called "witch doctors" which may be more accurate than it is flattering, but less insulting than "head-shrinkers". Both terms are evidence of ongoing suspicion in the general public's mind about people who wish to cure, and sometimes seem to need curing more than their patients, and who assert that they are practicing a Science, while Psychology is such an overwhelmingly subjective effort, compared to, say, Physics.

It seems to me that the Psychs are really doing something halfway between Art and Science, but without the constraints of manual dexterity, nor the imperative of talented vision. That is why so many practitioners of the psychological doctrines, up to and including Dr. Timothy Leary, told me that psychologist/psychiatrists are in a mutualistic symbiosis with artists. That's from *their* point of view. Some artists, while acknowledging the symbiotic nature of the relationship, regard it as a parasitic one. In this equation at least, the artists do not regard themselves as the parasites. The Psychs love the artists and are fascinated by them, while, because of the wild-card nature of artistic inclination, a sound analysis of them, singly or in multiples, is always doomed to frustration.

And now, on to specific thumb-nail sketches:

So, let's see, to give chronology another whack at this compendium, where was I?

Back from Mexico, I passed through a second season at the Festival of Arts in 1960, then journeyed into the heart of the 2nd generation Beat scene in San Francisco. My friends from UCSB, Mike and Jane Lewis, brother and sister, had a flat on Oak Street, third floor, just off Fillmore, where many artists came and went. Mike worked as a writer for *Newsweek*, and because of the nature of his job, he was not scorned by the clubbish illuminati, who all hoped (though they didn't say so), that he'd get them into print in the magazine.

Oak Street was but one 'pad' of a constellation of them, where agitated arty people circulated restlessly, looking for what hadn't yet been found. They knew it was there, because Kerouac, Burroughs, and Ginsberg told them so, or so they thought. One of these centers is a place that still exists, although its location has been changed. It was the flat of Glenn Todd from Texas. Doyen of a Beat archive, he was the host for the luminaries who stopped at his place when they passed through San Francisco.

Just a few years ago, when Glenn's building at 1403 Gough Street was due for demolition (so "Progress" might occur) such an uproar arose from the arts community that Glenn was found another, similar Victorian mansion nearby, where he could transfer his archives, and continue his literary centrality. As they were moving a sofa away from a wall, Glenn found Neal Cassady's driver's license on the floor, where it had fallen decades earlier. That was the kind of place it was, and where I met my first psychologist, who was actually a psychiatrist.

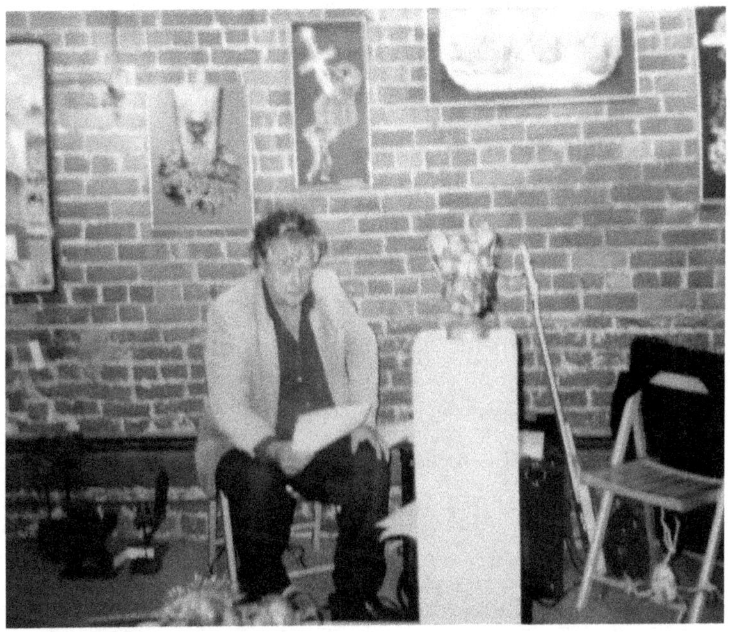

Figure 29: Sterling Bunnell reading his poem in the Canessa Gallery, San Francisco, at Dion Wright's 1990 opening. All the rhyming words were Aztec; muatl, Quetzalcoatl, axolotl, etc., etc. It was on this occasion that he looked upon the next generation and reflected, "Some of them never leave the larval state." Photo by Dion Wright

All psychiatrists are psychologists, but not vice versa. Psychiatrists are psychologists who have earned an M.D. and completed analysis themselves. This guy, Sterling Bunnell, seemed too young to have done all that. He was a carelessly dressed, cherubic man with a hank of black hair falling across his forehead, and an intent, preoccupied look on his round face. He reminded me of a youthful Clarence Darrow. He was trying to turn off a radio on top of the refrigerator that was not turned on. "Don't bother him," whispered Glenn, "He's on scopolamine." I didn't bother him, and later he played a large role in my life.

Then I had to go back to Laguna to get busted, and had all of those fine jailhouse adventures which are told in another chapter. When I got out of jail, my meanderings curtailed for a couple of years, as the probation department thought I should have a regular job, which turned out to be at that doorknob factory in Laguna Canyon. During that time, I observed several local psychiatrists in their natural habitat. The most impressive one of these people, and the one who set the stage for so much of what followed, was the LSD therapist, Dr. Frank Dunne. I watched him with all my attention, but kept my distance.

But to continue in order: While I was working at the doorknob factory and hanging out with the swashbuckling Perry Duncan on Van Dyke Drive, there was a psychiatrist living across the street from him named Mark Jocelyn. Mark Jocelyn was a bearded Dane of imposing brow, whose deep-set eyes were coolly neutral, and whose features were always swathed in the smoke from his pipe. He could sometimes be seen downtown in Dilley's bookstore shouting and arguing at the top of his voice, in Danish, with his landsman, the Laguna Greeter, Eiler Larsen.

Who knew what they were yelling about? Eiler always vocalized by shouting anyway, but Mark Jocelyn was a very quiet man the rest of the time. He was then in the throes of trying to extricate himself from his domestic arrangements, to pursue a new tomorrow with Nan Wing, a fey poetess. Nan, the sister of painter Andy, was madly in love with Mark. This illustrated for me that a psychiatrist can have the same sorts of imbroglios as anyone else, and not necessarily be able to think their way out of them.

At this time, I was part of the stable of artists at the Albatross Gallery in Balboa, owned and run by another psychiatrist, Ray Herold. I got in there through my friend Phyllis Bailey, an immaculate draftswoman of multiple faces and multiple hands that were worthy of Raphael, but non-sequitur. She was Ray's patient. He opened the gallery so that she would have a venue. Everybody made a few bucks. I liked Ray very much, and found him a reasonable human. The thing I remember best about him is that he installed a roof on his house that rolled open, like in a stadium, so he might gaze at the night sky when he felt like it. The problem was that in Southern California, overcast and light-pollution leave little to be seen.

Back in San Francisco, Beth Branaman was part of a group that rotated around another psychiatrist, Mike Agron. LSD was just breaking onto the scene, and Mike Agron was using LSD in his consultations with sundry geniuses from the arts community. In those early days around 1960, the chemical was legal and had no negative associations laminated onto it yet. Quite the contrary, it was widely rumored to be the gateway to higher consciousness. It was then the province of psychiatry, but was beginning to get loose into society as a whole. Beth Branaman made it her mission to come down to Laguna from San Francisco to turn me on to this LSD. It was in liquid form with one dose on each Pez candy she had in her purse. We went down to the rocky beach below Dana

Point, where there was no harbor yet, and where the deserted shoreline at the base of the cliffs was still pristine.

I sat on a huge metamorphic boulder and soon understood how it got that way, while Beth kept quiet. It was a sacrament, without the priest (Agron) but with the earth mother (Beth). It would be up to John Griggs, five years later, to set the chemical into its spiritual reality, even as the nature of the LSD itself became more and more compromised. I was a pagan, and accepted my expanded consciousness as a natural thing.

Viet Nam was still below the horizon, but coming on fast.

Shortly after my "Baptism by Beth," Dr. Frank Dunne appeared in Laguna at a sumptuous cliff-side suite overlooking the Pacific. He was turning artists on to LSD for $100 a pop. As in any "Art Colony" there was a spectrum of excellence and hip savoir faire among the artists infesting the place, and the most elegant ones were lining up to get the treatment from Dr. Dunne. Something about him made an alarm go off down around my medulla oblongata, so I just watched his act from a distance.

Some years ago, when I first tried to write about Dr. Dunne, I started with a quote. It still seems apropos:

"This monarch often laid down with a heart filled with love, and the next morning rose with as much indifference."

- Madame de Pompadour on Louis XV

Dr. Frank Dunne was a large and ruddy, red-haired man who smiled and whistled as he wheeled his shiny red Cadillac convertible through the hilly neighborhoods of Laguna Beach. A pronounced widow's peak pointed to the space between his ferociously saturnine eyebrows. He had wide shoulders and slim hips, and dressed immaculately to enhance them. He was a charismatic force of nature at the top of his game, and surrounded by admirers. Part of his duty was to go from blossom to blossom on a service loop, when he was not keeping hours in his well-appointed suite of offices across from the Victor Hugo Inn.

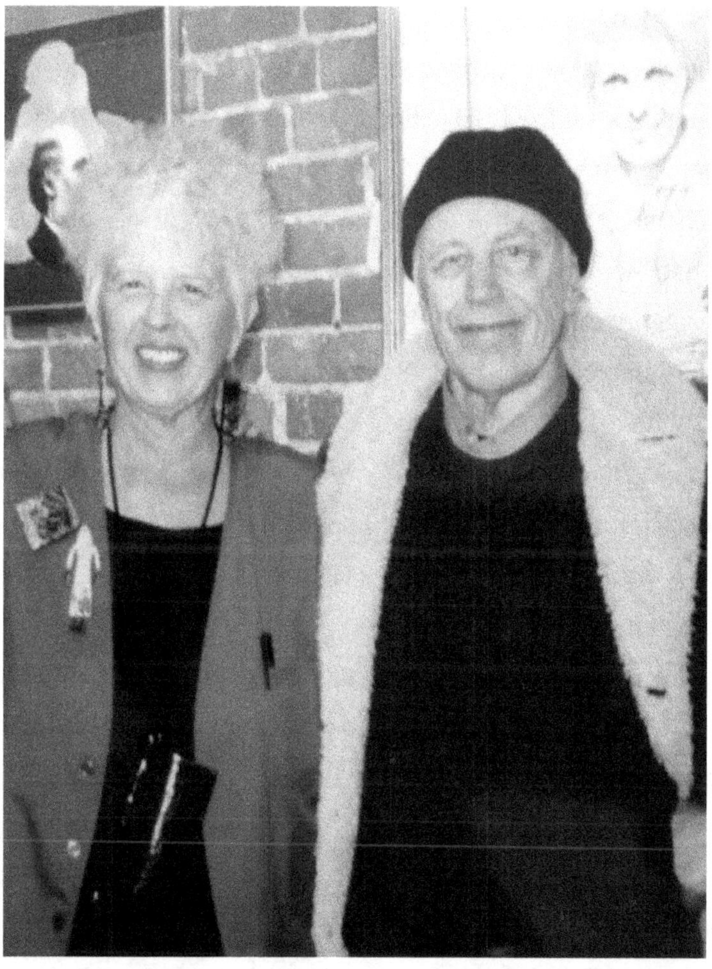

Figure 30: Beth Pewther, nee Branaman and Mike Agron at Dion's 1990 Canessa Gallery show in San Francisco. Charles Darwin and Amelia Earhardt in background. Photo by Dion Wright.

This red-haired giant was Laguna Beach's first LSD practitioner. He liked artists better than anybody else, and any pretty lady artist was his favorite "patient" du jour, but he was an equal-opportunity savant, and had issued a public invitation to the Mayor and the City Council to come on down and get enlightened.

If Dr. Dunne wasn't a Leo, he sure looked and acted like one.

He also gave habit-forming vitamin injections of a power-recipe of his own concoction. There was a press to get an appointment for the LSD initiation, narratives of which, I had from numerous artist friends.

The super-sensitive graphic artist Gayl Stenlund told me that she had her session with Dr. Dunne in trade for a picture. He ushered her into an office which was floored with mattresses, and left her there listening to Mantovani as she came on. After a while, Dr. Dunne returned and sat down next to her. He began to caress the back of her neck "ominously," as she put it. "Would you like to have me make love to you?" asked the satyr. "No thank you," replied Gayl. "Good!" cried Dr. Dunne, "I've had three patients already today, and I'm exhausted."

The funniest raconteur, and arguably the best artist in Laguna of his era, was the suffering neurotic hypochondriac, Leonard Kaplan. Lennie was laid up with a bad back for years and years, so, due to that immobilization, Dr. Dunne made a house call.

"He came to give me a shot of muscle-relaxer for my back spasms," recalled Lennie, "but he got the syringes mixed up, and gave me LSD instead. I had a rebirth! I rose from my bed, but couldn't breathe! Dr. Dunne came over and beat the shit out of my back, and shouted, "You're reborn!" I believed it. I sent Harry the Horse out to find me some blue clothes. Then I went over to

Judy Bernard's nursery and spent the day on the little boys' side. After that, my back REALLY got bad.

He continued, "Lieutenant James Broadbelt of the Orange County Sheriff's department had an attractive wife who was modeling for me at that time. He was a big narc. He came by one day and told me that he knew that I was part of Dr. Dunne's 'love cult'. "I know that you're on something, Kaplan," he told me. "What are you on, anyway?"

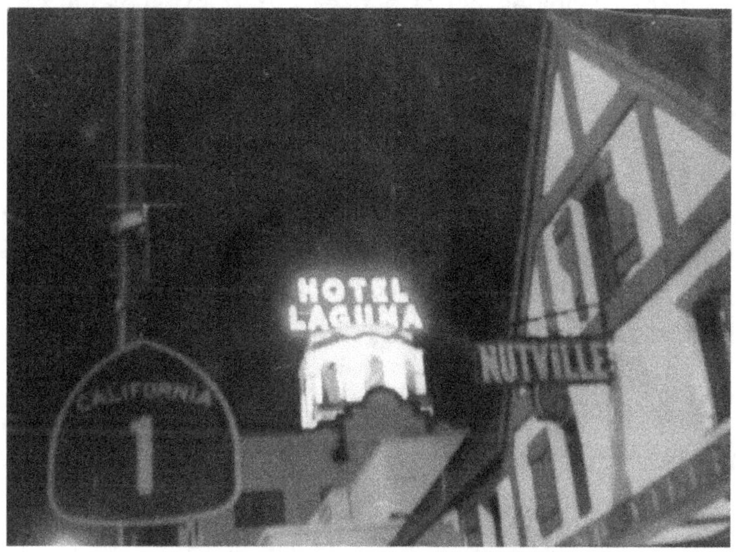

Figure 31: "Nutville." Photo by Mike Chaney

"Anybody could see that I was on my back, but he kept at me until I dragged myself to the refrigerator and took out a substance that I ground finely and handed to him. 'THIS is what I'm on,' I said, 'Don't take any, or you'll never kick the habit.' He put it in a little plastic bag and took it off to the police lab in Santa Ana to get it analyzed. It was Turkish halvah."

"After Broadbelt left I saw that I had unconsciously drawn his picture on the same page, and facing, a sketch of Dr. Dunne."

Dr. Dunne was not only protected by being a physician; LSD was also still legal, so on the surface of it, he was acting legally, if not altogether ethically. As William James had remarked around the turn of the century, with regard to pharmaceutically-induced religious experiences, "Having a religious experience does not necessarily lead to living a religious life."

Dr. Dunne was skating on thin ice as to what was permissible social behavior. He was also exploring new territory psychically, and making a guinea pig of himself in the investigation of bio-chemicals. The psychiatric community watched him with growing fascinated anxiety. The cops were trying to figure out a way to bust him, while the doctors were afraid that Dr. Dunne would humiliate them professionally. Dr. Dunne was the pilot of his own destiny, and his foot was against the floor on the accelerator pedal.

He began to see bugs.

"They did in the dinosaurs!" cried Dr. Dunne, of the red dinoflagellate plankton bloom that turned the sea rufous in some summer seasons. He saw the bugs as universal imps; the source of all ills. At this time, Dr. Dunne's self-medication consisted of a recipe of scotch whiskey, heroin and LSD.

He began picking bugs off people on the street as he was conversing with them.

"He picked them off some people more than others," said Tom Hurst. "He was always pickin' 'em off of this guy, Keith. I asked him, "How come you're always pickin' bugs off of Keith?" He said, "Well...he deserves it."

Lennie Kaplan said, "I can show you a little scar where he picked a bug off of me. He took a quarter inch of skin along with it. I TOLD him! "You're a psychiatrist! Don't you know the classic sign of disturbance is seeing bugs?" He paid no attention. He was too far gone."

Then Dr. Dunne got hooked on his muscle-relaxing agent, Pavocaine. He took it frequently. While passing the time of day with an acquaintance on the boulevard he would sometimes reach into his pocket for his syringe, and shoot himself in the hip, right through his slacks.

The psychiatric association finally acted, and committed Dr, Dunne to Norwalk Hospital for observation. His female patients continued to go see him there. Presumably, he simmered down to relative normalcy in the absence of his cocktails, and was released. He returned to his practice in Laguna, and was soon acting more bizarre than ever. At last, he engineered his own fall by being caught, supposedly in drag, trying to smuggle heroin across the border at Tijuana. He went to prison, and was never around again until years later, when Lennie Kaplan claimed to have seen him selling used furniture out of a van.

The journalist Craig Lockwood, upon reading the foregoing, added another dimensional perception. Craig's parents were among Dr. Dunne's closest "patients," so Craig saw quite a bit of him at the time. Craig is and was a militarily-oriented young man with a deep experience in that world, as well as a sharp perception. In retrospect, Craig reflected that Dr. Dunne was a very typical example of a certain military type, the Sergeant Major, but with a strong intellectual component. Craig pegs him as an intelligence officer of some stripe, maybe Naval, but more likely CIA.

This fits well on so many levels that I'm amazed at myself for not having seen it before. After all, it was the CIA who first had their hands on LSD in American society, and who were so irresponsible about uncontrolled dosing of each other, convicted prisoners, soldiers, and residents of madhouses.

The apprehension of some of those Langley double-domes like James Jesus Angleton was that this LSD, if brought under control, might prove to be a truth serum that could be used on Communist agents, etc. The CIA was shot-gunning psychedelics into some parts of society long before Ken Kesey, Tim Leary, et alia, ever had their hands in it. It also makes sense that Dunne was an agent of some kind, from a perspective of intelligence gathering.

Many of Dunne's "patients" were not only artists, but had been card-carrying Communists back in the '30s. Playing with fire, as unstructured and random distribution of psychedelics must be seen as, was a function of the immemorial human hubris, in a modern mode, as symptomatic within the CIA. They were arguably so arrogant about their own expertise that they goofed irresponsibly with the cosmic unknown, and not only got burned in their own particulars, such as Dr. Dunne going off the deep end; they also were the trigger for the chemicals' explosive and uncontrollable effects in society, and the scene-setters for Dr. Leary and company.

Whenever I reach this nexus of the story, I especially lament the passing of Aldous Huxley on the very day that JFK was murdered. Just on the cusp of general disaster, with his parting, whispered injunctions to Tim Leary about exercising caution and responsibility evaporated. Those whispered words whipped away on the wind, unheeded, as the brilliant Irish brat tore off down the pike in pursuit of kicks.

As for Carl Barks, he died just recently, having lived to almost a hundred at Hemet; hale, hearty and socially reticent to the end. During the '80's, in retirement, Barks began to paint large oil canvases of the Duck Clan, marvelously executed in the manner of Jan Van Eyck. When he tried to show them, Disney came on with lawyers enjoining him to cease and desist. Eventually an accommodation was reached, whereby Disney printed the paintings, licensed the images, and marketed them. You can buy one.

To round-out my life-survey of the psychological community, it remained for me to get a load, on personal terms, of the most colorful psychologist of all, and the one who modestly dubbed himself "The High Priest", Dr. Timothy Leary.

Chapter IX

Neal and Lorraine

In 1962, I was on probation for pot-possession, and living in a studio apartment on Summit Drive in Laguna Beach, California. The apartment was half of a duplex mirror-imaged over the garages below, with a long covered porch running the length of the building, and a terrific view of the Pacific Ocean with its spectacular sunsets over Catalina Island. I was working as a polisher and grinder at the local doorknob factory in Laguna Canyon, a job that avoided stultification by containing a wonderfully zany cast of characters who were a daily delight. It was a nice life for a convicted felon, the worst part of it being my probation officer, a man named Howard Fen.

Howard Fen hated my guts, and made no effort to hide it. He had been in an automobile accident some time earlier, a consequence of which was the snipping off the end of his nose. His pale, watery-blue eyes seemed to brim with hurt resentment. He was a large, curly-blond, red-faced mesomorph, dressed in wrinkled polyester. The raspberry in the center of his puss did nothing to enhance his looks. It did nothing to enhance my relationship with Howard Fen, either, because the other driver in the wreck that had truncated his schnozzola had been a loaded pothead.

Howard Fen made an equation in his mind between that guy and me, which left him in a permanently-soured state-of-mind. I could plainly see that he yearned to violate me, and return me to jail. I was being a straight arrow, giving him no cause to destroy me. My immediate problem was to resist collapsing in mirth whenever he unexpectedly appeared, because while he was funny looking enough to begin with, he drove the world's smallest red Fiat, a sort of prop worthy of a circus act. Watching this large and lumpy clown-cop extricating his bulk from the world's tiniest car, I intuitively knew it would be a mistake to guffaw at the man who held all the cards against me.

This was also a most sexually active period. The girls' coming and going, noted by Howard Fen, must have made him angrier yet. My landlady's daughter was also an artist, and she sometimes lived in the next-door apartment. She was a pretty girl upon whom I launched a vigorous campaign of seduction, which failed. She looked at me as if I were "a bug," in Terry Molloy's phrase, which response sent me packing. I made friends with her younger brother, Steve, and that friendship continues to this day. Eventually, I settled into a lustful affair with a precocious senior from the high school and skated the statutory edge with aplomb, while Fen, I imagined, gnashed his teeth in envy.

That studio apartment the place where, late one night, I was in bed with my girl, when there was a knock on the door. When I opened it, there were Perry Duncan and Sheila Casey, naked and drunk. Perry was the big old soldier-of-fortune bon vivant who had befriended me because he liked my Art. He lived up the hill on Van Dyke Drive in a glass-fronted, redwood house he had built himself, and where the parties were more-or-less non-stop. Among other things, Perry was a relentless pursuer of comely females, and Sheila Casey, his neighbor, was certainly in that category.

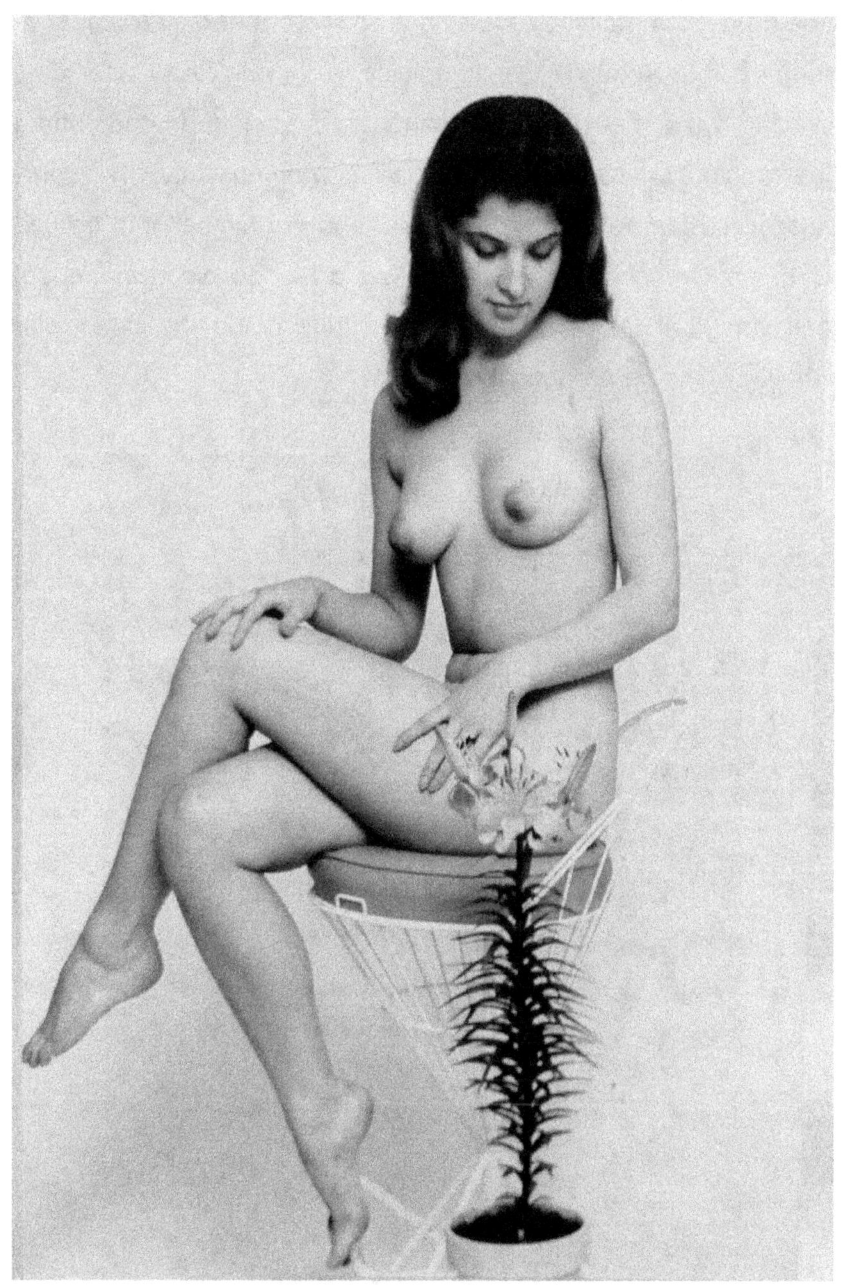

Figure 32: The Girl Friend. Photo by Chuck Everts

Sheila's husband was a USMC jet-jock at El Toro, with whom she traveled a rocky road. Being a bon-vivant herself (compared to her bilious spouse), Sheila quickly fell in with Perry's cupidity, and the two of them were the scandal of the neighborhood, rutting like minks whenever the poor pilot was on duty. The pilot suspected the truth of the situation, and got himself into trouble with the Corps when he ran power-dives on his own house, believing that Perry Duncan was within, doing the deed with Sheila, which he probably was.

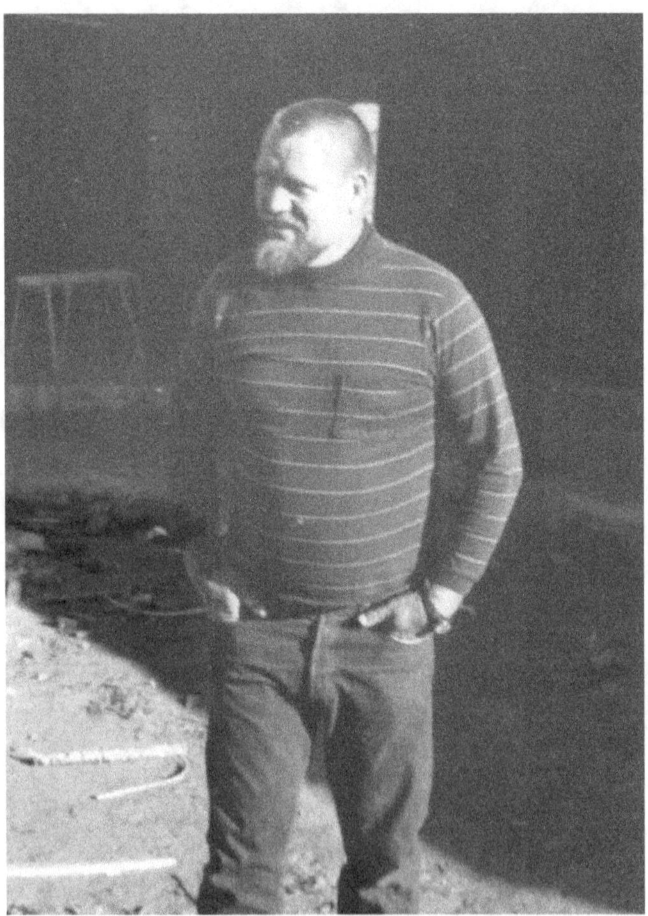

Figure 33: Perry Duncan

So, there Perry and Sheila were, that late night on my balcony, in the buff, giggling like hyenas, and bearing bottles of cold champagne. Now we will discreetly draw the curtain on that fetching scene, and allow the reader to exercise the imagination.

I worked on my sculpture in the street-level garage there on Summit Drive, with the doors open so I could see the world, and the world could see me. I had many visitors stopping by, and made numerous friends. My next-door neighbor was George Beringer, a matinee-idol from the days of silent films who was now an old codger.

I saw a photograph of George dressed in his tuxedo and erect as a Prussian colonel, and could scarcely equate the image with the bent and toothless, bewhiskered old wreck who came over every day to jaw with me. He was lonely. George had been working on his house for years, and the work he did consisted of mixing up a wheelbarrow full of concrete, and pouring it into a form, adding to the mighty buttresses that surrounded his modest bungalow.

"Keeps me in shape!" said George. He was an old man, though, and eventually died. After George had passed, his home came into the possession of a gay man of the town, whose paramour was the Episcopal priest, an apparently wonderful man, in his interfaces with the town, but who suffered a dark side in his domestic arrangements. This fact was proven when a lover's spat turned into a conflagration that incinerated the old Beringer cottage. For years afterward, the melancholy sight remained of George Beringer's mighty concrete works brooding on the hill, like a relic of war.

Time passed, and many events unfolded, all punctuated by ongoing visits and conversation with my Pasadena pal, Steve (the brother of the aloof princess next door on Summit Drive). We saw eye-to eye on life, especially on matters of Art, and on the pell-mell progression of the so-called "Psychedelic Revolution." Steve came to Laguna, and got a job working for the Parks Department at just the time that Mystic Arts World was slowly coming into being.

The luck of the draw was that Steve found himself working side by side with none other than "The Farmer," John "Happy" Griggs, who was just then ram-rodding Mystic Arts World, and making ends meet by working for the City of Laguna Beach. The municipality, in a deeply ironic move, had hired much of the Brotherhood of Eternal Love to be on the maintenance crews in the parks. It's a wonder that dogs and their walkers did not collapse left and right from the pot fumes in the air. Inattentive Brothers one day flooded the bocce-ball courts, to the indignance of the old men. John made a terrific impression on Steve, as he did with everyone. The Summer of Love was right around the corner.

As it happened, I had an opportunity, unconnected with the social burgeoning in the Haight/Ashbury, to have a one-man Art show at the Canessa Gallery on Montgomery Street, to last for the whole summer. Of course, I jumped at it. John Griggs helped transport and set up the show, with his customary energized overdrive. One of the architects who was part of the firm sponsoring the gallery gave me a second-story flat on Shrader Street in the Haight-Ashbury to use, which overlooked Haight Street and the end of the Golden Gate Park Panhandle. It was a ringside seat. That flat became a humming hub of activity. Steve came by for an extended visit, and brought with him a friend from Scarsdale, Neal Wolfe, a photographer.

Neal Wolfe was a big man, mellow and contained, with deep-set blue eyes, a high sandy pompadour of thick straight hair, and a deep voice worthy of a newscaster. He was an intelligent and unflappable person who had a sharp appreciation for the absurdities and ironies he saw everywhere, and a posture of amused tolerance for all of it. Neal's most recent position had been as the staff photographer in New York City for the prestigious *Paris Review*.

It was unclear how he had found his way to hippie-central. Perhaps he was on assignment. His sense of humor was pointed and dry, and went right over the heads of many of those flower children, although he consistently cracked up the most intelligent persons on the set. I remember Ralph Metzner falling off the couch laughing at one of Neal's witty remarks.

Neal decided he wanted to make a project out of photographing all my numerous welded sculptures, and this effort went on for many days. In the end, I had a catalog cross-section of my oeuvre to that date, and I still have most of the pictures. Neither the photos nor the sculptures hold up as well as we regarded them at the time. Neal assessed the job as a creative endeavor of his own devising. He gave me a dual set of the pics, and charged me nothing for it, a great generosity. More time passed.

Mystic Arts World finally opened, and became the next cultural phase after the collapse of the Haight/Ashbury. Neal Wolfe was one of the enthusiastic visitors to Mystic Arts in the first flush of its optimistic beginning. He arrived with his girlfriend, Lorraine, a shy and pleasant Scandinavian-looking blonde, pretty and sweet natured. They were obviously crazy about each other. Neal took more pictures, and they left, not seen again for several years.

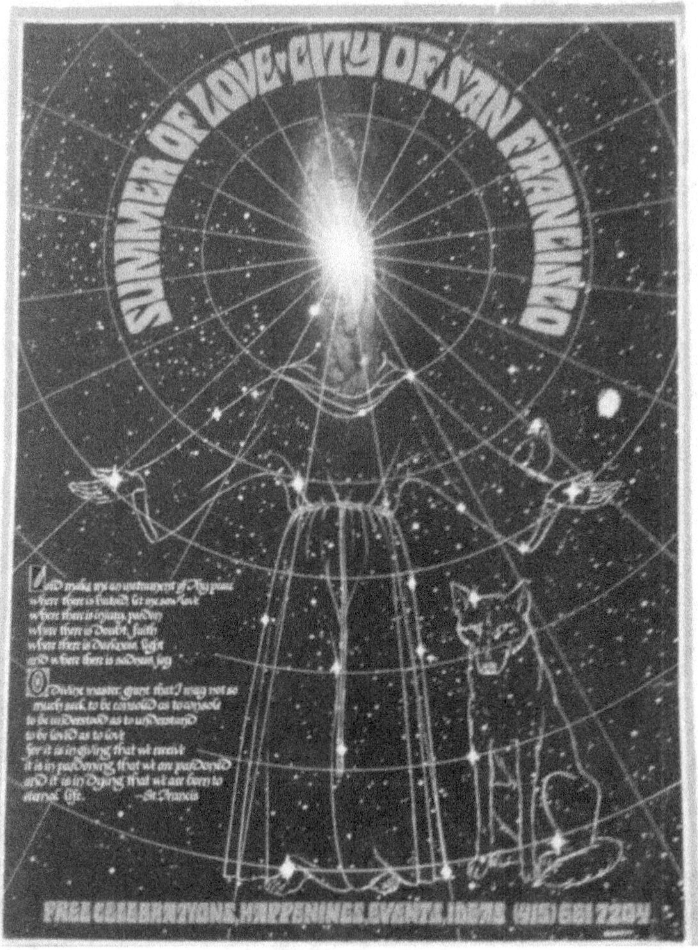

Figure 34: The poster of early 1967 inviting flower children to come to the City of San Francisco.

The next time I saw Neal and Lorraine, they were in company with Neal's mother and her boyfriend. She was an attractive woman who was fighting the downhill slope, and had this guy with her who looked fifteen years younger, as cool and breezy as a real estate salesman. They were civilized people visiting the natives. Neal's mom bought a piece of sculpture, and took it away with her to Scarsdale. Then I lost track of Neal and Lorraine until some years later when I had a letter from them.

They were living in Hailey, Idaho, near Hemingway's old stomping grounds at Ketchum. Why didn't I come visit? Life was chaotic just then. I was breaking up with my wife, and trying to put something reasonable together. I filed the invite for future reference, and went to work as the staff artist at the Arizona Sonora Desert Museum for a couple of years, during which my wife left the country. I had to give up my dream job, to go rescue my kids in San Diego, where my wife had precipitously abandoned them. At loose ends, I went on the road, and found my way eventually to Hailey.

Neal and Lorraine were living the life of the prosperous avant-garde, raising two boys, and inhabiting a cozy cabin at the foot of a long and mighty slope that featured a bald-crested mountain, patches of turning aspen trees splashing down the grades. We hiked into those woods and discovered football-sized white fungi, which Neal happily explained, were “deliciously edible”. We fried them like abalone steaks. Neal was now a computer whiz making his living in cyberspace, networking into the present from his remote idyll. Lorraine was the Earth Mother. We spent a congenial week together, and I left for Colorado. More time passed.

I had been making large sculptures for the Chart House Restaurant Corporation for a number of years, when one day I went into corporate HQ in Solana Beach on some mission or another, and was looking over the various brochures and other

PR items in there, and noticed the dis-unified quality of it. I told my friend John Creed, the CEO of the outfit, that he needed to get all of these images made by the same aesthetic eye; that the shotgun approach to imagery was not a success. "OK," says John, "You do it." He had never seen a single example of a picture I had taken, but he gave me money and a meal ticket for the Chart Houses and sent me off around the country.

In brief, the tour was a great success. I returned at last with many images, the best of which went into the catalog for potential investors, as the Chart House went public and issued stock. "Dion," said John Creed, "We're going to hire you to make a sculpture for every new Chart House we open!" This sounded great since they were opening two or three of them a year. They never opened another. The stock failed, and the corporation was dismantled.

Be that as it was, during our circuit of America, we stopped in Portland, Oregon, where Neal and Lorraine Wolfe had moved. They had a farm, raised thoroughbred horses, and Neal was still making his way as a computer wizard. Their spread was gracious and grand and looked like something out of Country Gentleman. The sons, Kyler and Solon, were almost grown. We had a fine nostalgic visit and soon went off, back on the road.

A decade or so later we heard through the grapevine that Lorraine had contracted breast cancer, and fought the brave fight. She went into remission, and things seemed OK. It must have been true love with Neal and Lorraine, because when the cancer returned, total, mortal and inoperable, they got into their car, and Neal drove them into the path of a speeding freight train.

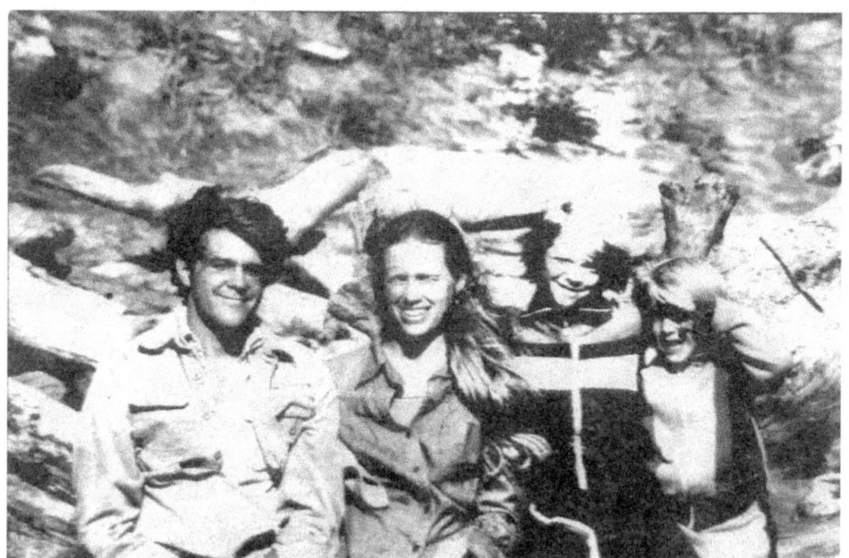

Figure 35: Neal and Lorraine Wolfe in Idaho with their sons, ca. 1972.

Chapter X

Communities

If you weren't there, you may be unaware of the subtext of hysteria in America through most of the 20th Century that blazed around the word "communism". It was weird to note that the experimental and/or idealistic sociological experiments of the 1960s were being called "communes". That name was begging troublesome connotations, at the very least, if not outright attack by right-wing zealots.

Still, by 1967, "communes" were a now-and-happening buzzword. As a phenomenon, they had been around since those first ape-men left Africa to seek a better scene with more elbowroom. Idealistic social experiments have always been part of the American scene as attempts to build something better, but in the 1960s many of the new communes were trying to get away from something worse. The idealists were taking to heart the terse slogan of Dr. Timothy Leary: "Turn On, Tune In, Drop Out".

Folks who really tried to do that soon learned that it was impossible. Everybody knew how to turn on and tune in, but nobody could come up with a successful means of dropping out...although dropping dead was sometimes an option.

The first communal situation an infant encounters is the nuclear family, in whatever unique form that may be for each individual. As little children, everyone perceives whatever is happening around them as the 'normal' situation. That normalcy becomes more and more doubtful as the individual child matures, the smartest ones catching on the fastest, as usual. Growing up has to do with coming to terms with the particular parents and siblings one is dealt. In some cases, it happens organically and easily and in others, it never happens at all.

In the 1960s, people expanded by psychedelics demonstrated a tendency to re-invent community on a wider front than ever before. The general perception was that the best way to be sane was to abandon the failed societies seen around us. This included abandoning the compromised family units all the distraught individuals had emerged from, to try to cobble together something healthy with a few like-minded friends. The folly in this approach was in thinking that better forms and behaviors could be invented in the present, than those that had taken millennia to develop. Commune founders thought that their idealism would be proof against historical human flaws. Few of these brave new societies continue into the present.

As I think back over the series of communal situations I've witnessed, they all seem to be full of sex, as well as idealism. Even primary school, for those who have had no siblings of the opposite gender, were role-identity seminars.

Schools are the first social communities people have to cope with outside of home. At home, children are programmed at the basic level of walking, talking, and using the potty. Once these basic functions are in place, little children may be thrown in among their peers to sink or swim, and get confronted by that surrogate parent, the teacher.

Teachers are responsible for filling little heads with information, but the subtext charge of all schools is also to plasticize rampant juvenile egos into a malleability that will allow them to be formed into good citizens, i.e. cannon fodder, taxpayers, and busy bees in the bowels of commerce. Individualism gets a little lip service within primary academia, but conformity comes first. The Germans were the best at this, but all national societies do it. To *not do it* is to be absorbed by the neighbors who do.

I was a fortunate native, as far as it goes, encountering these tough early community imperatives in becoming an acceptable citizen. At nursery school, I resisted the alien experience of lying down on a canvas cot among many others for a "nap time" when none of the kids was in the least tired, the clock on the wall ticking off the seconds as if stuck in mucilage.

This introduction to social compulsion made me a non-conforming rebel by the age of five. I went to half a dozen grammar schools, learning as best I could to adapt to the latest change of scene, before being blessed by an idyllic four years at high school in the rural and beautiful environment of San Juan Capistrano, and then another four years at the equally congenial Santa Barbara campus of the University of California.

These eight years of learning coincided exactly with the Eisenhower administration, a smug, prosperous and soporific period during which even teenagers weren't very rebellious. My course in life was conditioned during these years by my neoteny, or slow maturation. It was anxiety making to be physically several years behind one's peers in the process of growing up, especially as I had been so precocious as a wee tot. I lost out on most of the social norms of those years between ten and twenty because of my lingering juvenile appearance. I caught up eventually and made up for my losses big time. That was on the physical level.

Mentally I was always ahead of most of my contemporaries, but emotionally I sometimes wonder if I've caught up even yet.

The university environment, as community in the grand sense, meant freedom from parents. It took a couple of years decompressing, to get our bearings. Several of us who were already long-enchanted by a romantic idea of Art had blossomed enough to try to invent our own community. We moved off campus. Since we were artist-types, the atmosphere we created was Bohemian, from an old perspective, and Beat, from a new one. We were oblivious to such intellectual categories, however, being all wrapped-up in trying to know what Art is so that we could make good versions of it. We were also chasing each other around in a state of permanent priapic arousal and frequent inebriation, which was restricted to weekends.

Our neighborhood was Isla Vista when it was still a few beach cottages and mostly open fields. As a community milieu, it served as a launch pad into further scenes, all of which were far more serious than the play-acting of misunderstood existential youngster parts we were inhabiting, and that in a few cases soon become desperately real.

The community on the San Clemente Pier, where I had summer work, provided a counterpoint to the undergraduate hi-jinx of college bohemianism. That was a very Steinbeckian scene, the sport fishing business on the pier, chock-full of colorful characters, hardly a one of whom would have fit in at UCSB.

I was at some pains to "'hide my light under a bushel" there, as I had grown up around similar people and knew in front about how much tolerance they had for overt intellectualism, not that many of them weren't bright. This interesting milieu is described elsewhere.

When I went to graduate school at the Instituto at San Miguel de Allende in Guanajuato, Mexico, the community I learned about was one of ex-patriots. In those days the number of gringo retirees was small, but there were plenty of others. Artists, students, remittance men, WWII vets, ingénues, sinister schemers, divorcees, writers, poseurs, soldiers-of-fortune, gigolos, sycophants, raconteurs from wall to wall, almost everybody drunk most every night, if not both night and day.

Nobody was getting high on anything but booze, so far as I could see at first. That constant drinking fueled the boozy society I fell into. It's hard to know where to begin, with such a suite of wild characters, who surely deserve their own book, many of which have no doubt already been written.

My particular center of social interaction was La Cucaracha, a rich and dark saloon around the corner from my high-ceiling pension room in a 17th Century building off the square. La Cucaracha means "the cockroach," the title of Pancho Villa's marching song, and was in an even older building than my rooming house. It was run by a couple of brothers named Chucho and Freddie, who poured the booze as fast as they could, and watched the antics of their clients with a combined tolerance and anxiety.

The rows of beautiful bottles gleamed richly in the subdued light. The rooms were heavy-beamed and tall: dark, warm, and full of huge leather furniture, in which lounged the regulars; Louie Brock, Hal Harwood, Archie Macdonald, Dennis "the Mayor" Wigand, Minor Avon Neal, Gabriella Duvalier, and "Petunia," among others, all of whom were unbelievably good joke-tellers. I've never laughed so long and so hard in my life, and I've always hoped I'd stumble into another such funny situation...but I never have.

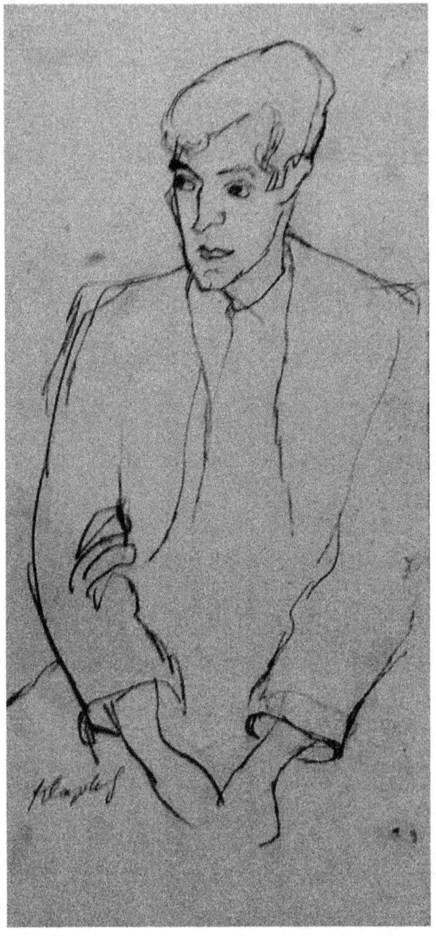

Figure 36: The author, as seen by Mel Klapholz at San Miguel de Allende in 1960. Mel quoted Dion as remarking, "This town must be a nightmare for atheists."

Gabriella "Gabby" Duvalier was the daughter of the Haitian dictator, Papa Doc, and she was a raging bi-sexual nymphomaniac with a style that was nothing if not colorful. She was a regal presence, taller than most men in that scene, except for when Karlheinz Wertmann came into La Cucaracha. Karlheinz was not a joke-teller, by any means, and his appearance was like a cloud passing in front of the sun. He was a refugee Nazi who operated as a jeweler in the ancient colonial town. He was an enormously tall man, spare and rangy, with hooded eyes that sucked all the warmth out of the room. Luckily, he never stayed long. One time he arrived already quite drunk, bursting through the door, snapping off a Third Reich salute, and clicking his shiny black boot heels together smartly as he shocked everybody with a booming "Heil Hitler!"

The WWII vets hated Karlheinz Wertmann, but he had them all intimidated. He came to a bad end when it was discovered that he was smuggling cocaine in hollow jewelry. The Federales raided him one night, beat him to a pulp, and hauled him away, never to be seen again.

Gabby Duvalier died suddenly soon thereafter, under whispered circumstances, and a gloom settled on La Cucaracha that failed to lift. As a sad footnote, some years later Neal Cassady, icon of the Beat Generation, came to San Miguel de Allende, and died there; found on the railroad tracks where the fast Swiss train ran between Ciudad Juarez and Mexico City. Ken Kesey wondered what Neal was doing there, and decided that he must have been counting the railroad ties, that compulsive man.

The Art school at the Instituto Allende was an entirely different place from the dissipated La Cucaracha. My sculpture professor, Lothar J. Kestenbaum, was another German national who had survived the war and emigrated to Mexico. He was completely different from Karlheinz Wertmann, never alluding to the past. I always wished he would talk, because of my fascination with first person historical narration. Lothar, with his wooden leg from the hip down, clearly had something to tell, but he never did. The scuttlebutt about his leg came in two versions: 1. He had been run over by a trolley car in Berlin, and, 2. He'd had it shot off on the Eastern Front.

Neither of these rumors may have been the truth. Lothar was as Germanic as any Herr Professor could ever be, but leavened by a warm humanity. The man was skinny with deep-socketed eyes. He was shaggy and olivine, dark and haunted, but all of that made him a compelling teacher. His welding technique was honed to perfection and never hurried. He worked constantly. I learned from Lothar how accurate rendition and profound feeling can (and should) occupy an Art object. Lothar had no use for pure abstraction and saw it as a deviation from responsible artistic integrity. He taught the conservative principle that Art is intrinsically a communication exercise. That lesson has remained with me. No content: no communication; no communication: no Art.

With Lothar, I experienced a real and true master/disciple relationship of the sort, which never quite took shape with any of my college professors. That was an unexpected boon to experience in such a backwater academic community as the Instituto, for which I'm still grateful.

The San Miguel experience had become stale, and I was restless, not for the last time. I went to see my friends Mike and Jane "Chipmunk" Lewis in San Francisco, where they were immersed in the remains of the Beat Generation. A season of living among post-Beats on Oak Street in 1960 San Francisco, followed by incarceration in the Orange County Jail for six months, and my subsequent servitude at the doorknob factory in Laguna Canyon for a matter of years, are all related elsewhere.

As *communities*, the post Beats in San Francisco revealed that the nature of an Art movement may be generated politically as much as aesthetically. The jail experience was a refresher course in survival at the jungle level, and the doorknob factory was an immersion in an echo of feudal society as run by laissez faire homosexuals.

Then came Little Rome, an innovative community experience wherein both Art and sex were in full flower.

I met Robert "Bob" Young when we were freshmen at UCSB, just as he was busted in the dorms for having a case of beer under his rack. Bob was a couple of years older than I was. That was enough to make me see him as a sort of hero-figure; not because he flouted authority and not because he'd been an Eagle Scout, and not because he'd been a Marine. No. It was because he was tremendously successful with girls and obsessively devoted to painting. He was a physically fit beach-boy with blond hair falling across his forehead, and a twisted, constant, wide grin full of large teeth. He laughed loudly and often. His Marine Corps experience had ended badly. Bob spent the last six months of his hitch in the brig in Hawaii. Like me, he was also an Art major, and a fellow Sig Ep pledge, so we were thrown together a lot in those first years of our friendship, a friendship that continued to the day of Bob's death. Bob was already everything I hoped to become, both as an artist and as a bon vivant. I might have looked a little closer, with a less dazzled brain, I suppose.

Al Green was another ex-military guy at UCSB on the GI Bill. He'd been an Army top-kick in Germany during his enlistment and had developed such habits of command that he was put in charge of us as the Sig Ep pledge trainer. He was a tough, freckled little man with a crew cut and a tight-ass posture, who muscled his authority through a physique that looked like an assembly of cannonballs.

His heart wasn't in it, though, despite how well he played the part. His real inclination was toward Art, but he was conflicted about it and majored in Sociology. Still, he did make Art, and it was interesting. Al lived off-campus in a hovel down in Goleta and had created a mural there that he used as a prop for his romantic campaigns. He believed, with some reason, that the cachet of Bohemianism would help him to get laid.

This mural of his was made out of mustard, ketchup, peanut butter and Wonder Bread, which he had slapped up on the wall with amazing results. The thing smelled pretty iffy, and bits had a tendency to drop off in chunks onto the floor. Empty beer cans and ashtrays full of butts completed the aesthetic allure. Al was Beat before anybody heard about it. Like me, he was trying to figure out what was what, and who he was in it.

Bob Young never suffered a moment of introspection, unless one counts the decision process of what his next move would be on his current painting. He was content to follow Art, which floated on top of his devotion to three habits: beer, cigarettes and girls, not necessarily in that order. All were available to him, and he indulged them all until he couldn't anymore. As a senior in college, Bob had a girlfriend he called "Buddha Babe" who was the most stunning specimen of the sexy blond that existed on campus.

Buddha Babe riding her bicycle in her short shorts turned every male head she passed. Tongues hung out and panting occurred. Bob and Buddha Babe made love constantly, and even studied for mid-terms with their friends, while in bed, tearing off a piece whenever they felt so-moved, and without the least regard as to who else might be there. They were conservative, though, and never indulged in threesomes, although some horny fraternity brothers made hopeful overtures.

Al Green got laid much less than Bob did, and he complained bitterly about it. "I'm just a sad sack of sour owl shit!" he'd say. Still, he certainly was getting more than I was in those days.

After we were all out of UCSB, Bob Young went to Otis Art School in L.A., while Al Green became a probation officer for L.A. County. Both Bob and Al married girls named Joy, and neither of them received very much of that quality from their hideously misnamed spouses. They both had kids, they both got divorced, and they were both forever being chased for money.

Meanwhile, I had been to school in Mexico; gone to San Francisco to hang out with Mike and Jane Lewis and the Beat Generation; got involved with jazz people and the Mountain Drive conga scene; got busted; fallen madly in love with my precocious teenage girl friend; and suffered from the hostile intentions of my own probation officer, Howard Fen, he of the truncated nose.

Through all these passages I was welding sculpture with might and main, all the while getting better at it, and figuring out, more and more, what this Art thing was really all about.

After finishing up at Otis and getting divorced, Bob Young moved into his dad's summer vacation trailer at the El Morro Trailer Park just north of Emerald Bay in Laguna. Young had grown up there all through the summers with his brother Dick, living in the water as much as on land. One time the brothers speared a 350-pound Black Sea Bass at Scotchman's Cove and maneuvered it down the coast outside the surf line until they could leverage it onto the beach before the eyes of the astounded trailer park residents and their nubile daughters.

In his post-Otis, post-divorce period Bob was sleeping at El Morro, in the nearly deserted off-season trailer park, and bumping around Laguna in his bachelor mode, while I was living up on Summit Drive, and enjoying my foxy girlfriend. When that delectable girlfriend ran off with a guy wearing Italian threads, I saw her no more. I soldiered on, welding with a broken heart. Meanwhile, Bob Young found a rambling catacomb of a downstairs apartment at 703 Browncroft Street, near the high school, available for low-rent, and moved into it.

Soon Bob popped up one night on my Summit Drive balcony shouting, "Dion! Dion!" I opened the door to see what was happening, and he grabbed me by my shoulders and began to shake me violently, happily shouting, "Dick and Barb are here! Dick and Barb are here!"

I didn't know who this meant, but soon found out. Barb was a woman who liked to pull a train and Dick was a husband who liked to watch. The upshot of the evening was that I moved into Bob's new digs on Browncroft, with the Dick and Barb episode being the tone-setter for all that followed. In a short time, the place became known locally as "Little Rome."

John Severson was the surfing entrepreneur I had gone to high school with in San Juan Capistrano. He had earned a degree in Art and become the Art teacher at our alma mater. We shared a booth together at the 1960 Festival of Arts, after which he launched his career as a surf film producer and magazine publisher. When John left off teaching at "Capo," his position as Art teacher was taken by bright little Jan Volz, late of the mid-west, divorced with four kids. She was soon married to Norm Babcock, a Laguna cab driver who was head over heels for her perky self, despite her somewhat overbearing cheerfulness and tendency to direct.

Norm soon graduated from cab driving to being a cop and began to rise in the ranks. Jan quit teaching in Capo and became a force to be reckoned with in the Laguna Art community. Eventually, through their dual social roles, we at Little Rome came to their not-altogether-welcome attention. They were so determined to be part of the family, and we were so anxious about who they were. One good thing that happened was that Norm worked something behind the scenes that caused my probation officer, the ominous Howard Fen, to be replaced by a passive fellow for the last part-year of my durance.

Looking the gift horse between the lips, I wondered immediately if Norm's game was to insinuate himself into our merry scene, mole-like, which would be harder to do with an alarm-ringing bull like Howard Fen intermittently charging into the works. With Fen out of the picture, I suspected Norm thought we would be lulled into letting down our guard, and revealing the nefarious activities that he thought were going on in Little Rome. There really were none. We were licentious but legal. I finished my probation and got my sentence reduced to a misdemeanor. Then it was full-speed ahead with Bohemianism in spades.

Al Green was Al Green-with-envy of our new libertine empire. He yearned to move in there himself, but the reality of having to make his living in the L.A. County Probation Department kept him in the smog throughout the week. He rushed down to Little Rome for the weekends. Al spent summers in Laguna as a youth and was friends then with the swashbuckling Perry Duncan, who also took to hanging out in our party pad. Perry had his own circle of acolytes, so our scene was bursting at the seams, especially after young Ed Lutz moved in as the third roommate.

Janie "Chipmunk" Lewis, who was at loose ends once more, moved in also as "den mother," a real stretch of that nomenclature. She wasn't romantically involved with any of us householders but sampled the passing men as it suited her fancy. Al Green and Perry Duncan, as the elder statesmen, sat like fat pashas in the center of the swirl, plucking ripe numbers now and then as they whirled by.

Right upstairs in the apartment at ground level was the world's foremost decadent Bohemian, the brilliant and cynical painter, Italo Eugenio Camarini d'Andrea, known simply as "Italo." He was a stooped little man always dressed in black, including a beret, with deeply shadowed bloodhound eyes, and claw-like fingers dyed brown from the endless hand-rolled cigarettes he smoked. He also drank red wine from the moment he awoke until the moment he dropped into sleep again. He needed that wine to function, shaking and shuddering when he arose in the day, only steadying with a few glasses of Chianti.

His shakes amazingly vanished whenever he picked up a paintbrush, always under protest. He provided a post-graduate course in the realities of the Artist's Life, and daily opened pages to us, with the most side splitting delivery, that we had never read in college. He was a textbook archetype of the Romantic decadent, knew it, bemoaned it, and embraced it.

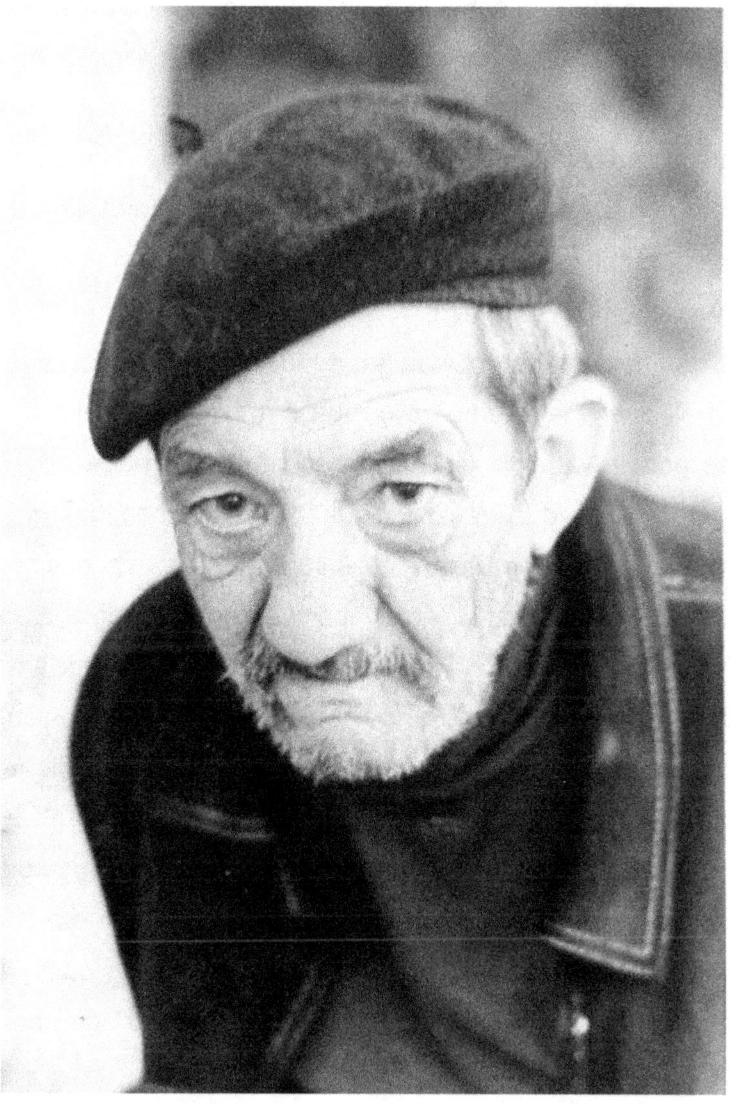

Figure 37: Italo Eugenio Camarini d'Andrea, the archetypical Bohemian, pictured midway on his long slide into oblivion. Talent won't solve anything much in the end. Photo by Dion Wright.

He could paint like an angel, but lived like a damned soul. He'd been forced into the lime-light by his adoptive dad, Martino Angelo, as a "boy wonder" in his early youth, and was stuck with it. He didn't really like being a painter, and only went to work at it when circumstances became desperate. He painted because that was better than getting a job. Italo was not only d'Andrea, he was also the painter of "Camarinis," "Sevingers," and other noms de plume aimed at fast production for different market slots. His long-suffering wife, Jean, never stopped heckling Italo with clever barbs of humor, which he returned with enthusiasm. "Italo woke up with a semi this morning," she would tell us.

Then he'd put her to work hand-making pasta noodles, which hung all over the apartment on the day of their creation. God, those people were funny. They also had a teen-age daughter, Idgi, who seemed to be less amused than we habitués of Little Rome downstairs were, by the senior d'Andrea's vaudeville act. Their pad was always full of the most intelligent, libertine, creative individuals of the town. Then the girls from Mississippi arrived. They arrived one night and never left. They were on an adventurous lark in the freewheeling environs of that exotic world, California.

There were three of them when they arrived, who indulged at once in a hormone-drenched game of sexual musical chairs, which soon displaced one of them, who moved in briefly with Perry Duncan, and some months later the second one, the one whom Bob had dubbed "Muffin."

This was a shortening of "ragamuffin," which their Marine jet-jock home-boy, Hardy Steiner, called her, but knowing Bob, we caught the double-entendre. Languid and relaxed, they drank enormously, and drawled their sibilant Mississippi dialect in the most charming and sexy way. They were classy chicks from upscale families, yearning to get some elbowroom to indulge the swampy and fervid fantasies they had imagined about California. They came to the right place. In the end, Muffin staggered back to Mississippi and left the field to "Miss Kitty," who oozed around Bob like good Delta molasses.

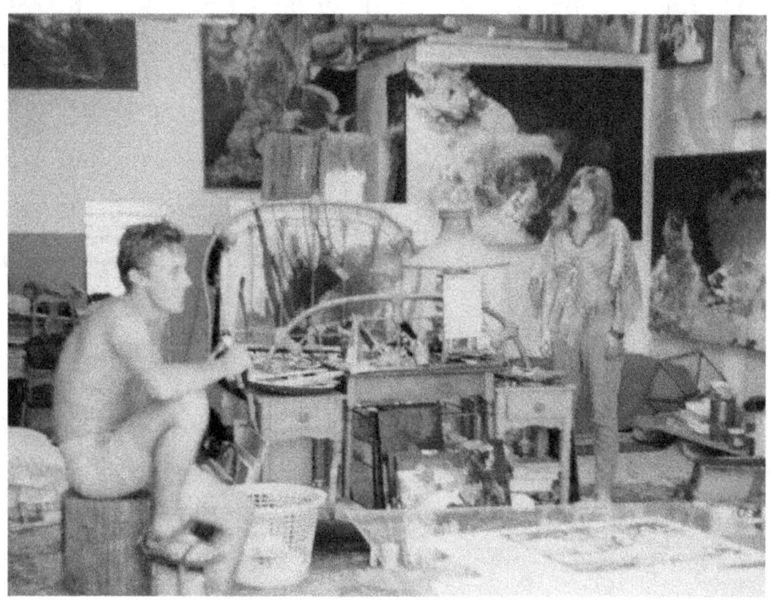

Figure 38: La Vie. Bob Young and "Miss" Kitty Cooke, in the artist's studio. Photo by Chuck Everts.

Little Rome was at last flooded out one day when heavy rains came. "Development" at the top of the ridge had left large areas of denuded ground cleared for building sites. Under an unusual downpour, all this dirt became mud, and the mud became liquefied, and it began to flow down the hillside arroyo, which happened to lead right through our backyard at Little Rome. Ed Lutz and I were up in Hollywood that day, trying to sell a bunch of Ed's paintings to an abrasive dealer on La Cienega Boulevard named Mirzelle. She low-balled Ed into a sacrifice-sale. We drove back down the freeway in an ambiguous state of disgruntled satisfaction, which immediately became catastrophic alarm when we saw all the emergency vehicles operating around our home. Norm Babcock came out and sadly shook his head. Bob Young told of how the wall of mud came rushing in, pouring into the patio, and then into the house.

He and Chipmunk and Miss Kitty barely got out of there in time, clambering up the cinderblock walls to safety, while the patio became a whirlpool, with Gordon Dodge, the sinister mole, clinging to a sofa for dear life, as it went around and around in the current. By the time Ed and I got there, the interior rooms were four feet deep in mud. It was a long and sad effort to salvage what we could and leave

Meanwhile, Ed had acquired Rosie, and I had acquired Charlene, and we all went off on separate tracks after the flood to seek our destinies. "Medusa" met "Batman" and all our marriages went on the rocks. Ed and I failed to get a ride on a flying saucer, for all our proactive intent, taking a lot of acid in the desert and trying to think one down.

By the end of 1965, Tom Blackwell and I had both been abandoned by our wives. Mine (the one who looked like Elizabeth Taylor) had run off to Mexico with the Wichita Vortex painter Bob Branaman, taking our infant daughter with her. Tom's wife Rosalie, the sexy spider girl, had also taken the best-friend route of abandonment, leaving in the dead of night in an XKE to NYC with the breezy psychedelic entrepreneur, Bill Baldwin. Baldwin was a perpetually smiling glad-hander who had lots of money, while Tom was a sober-sided redheaded guy with a heavily serious demeanor and a lot of painterly talent, but no dough.

Tom and I were at loose ends, and hanging-out together in a fog of mutual gloom. Since under average conditions gloom was our normal mode, especially Tom's, in our joint-state of uncomprehending desertion, we must have sucked all the joy out of every place we went. We were like fellow-survivors in a lifeboat, which we were rowing from island to island, trying to get cheered

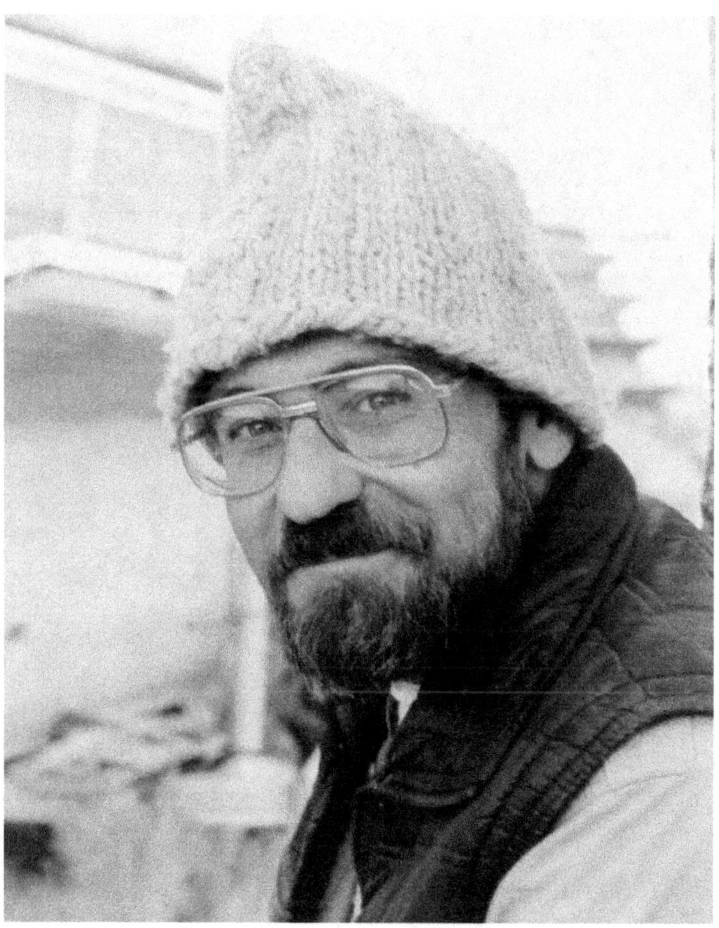

Figure 39: Ed Lutz in the 80s. Photo by Dion Wright

up by whatever native we found there. We had neither a home nor a car between us.

One of those whose beach we washed up upon was the hip Viking, Eldon Setterholm. Eldon, an exponent of physical culture and a free-loving pothead, was in his mid-forties at that time, and

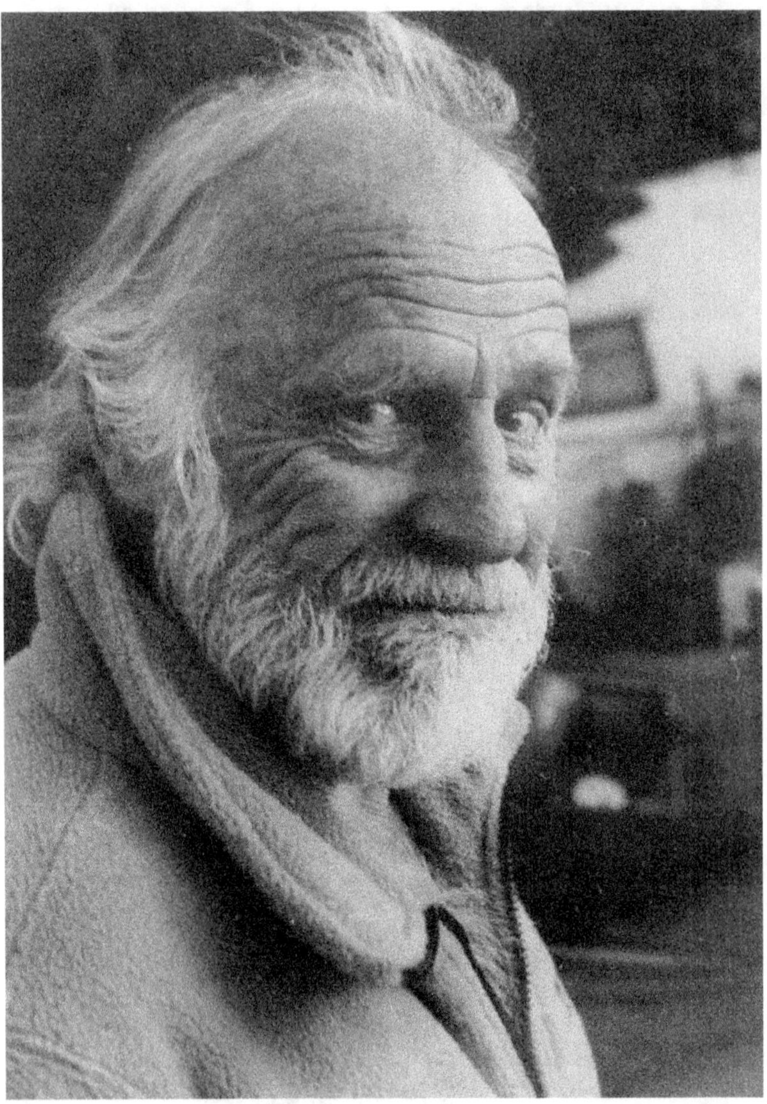

Figure 40: Eldon Setterholm, ca. 1985. "My brother became an admiral, but I had more fun." Photo by Dion Wright.

living in a wine cellar on Cleo Street close to St. Anne's beach. He went there daily to play volleyball, impress the unwary, and pluck such nubile plums as came his way. He was a heroic-looking specimen, so his options were many. Tom and I, in our desperate horniness, wanted to be just like Eldon. It was a foolish wish, which was beyond our assets to accomplish, but such are the delusions of wounded egos.

Eldon liked us a lot because we were real artists, a type of person he enjoyed and cultivated. He wanted to help us, being like a sort of deplorable scoutmaster, encouraging us to go out there and win our sleazy merit badges. Eldon had once been the local man-at-arms for the jazz comic, Lord Buckley, who had made a deep and dense impression on him, and all of whose routines Eldon knew by heart, and would perform at the slightest prompt. He did them pretty well, too, standing there in his mighty masculinity, chin tucked into his chest, shoulders thrown back and reciting verbatim from Lord Buckley's hilarious, but scurrilous, catalog. Eldon thought that Tom and I needed to buff-up.

Having been one of the beefcake exemplars of physical development on "Muscle Beach" at Malibu, where he hung out with Joel MacCrae, Stuart Whitman, the Arness Brothers, Gary Crosby and the rest of what he called "a regular clique of Hollywood guys," Eldon was well-prepared to be a coach. He had taught Leopold Stokowski how to swim. Eldon was passionately but unrealistically optimistic about our chances. We were motivated to get laid, but not to work our asses off trying to become muscular.

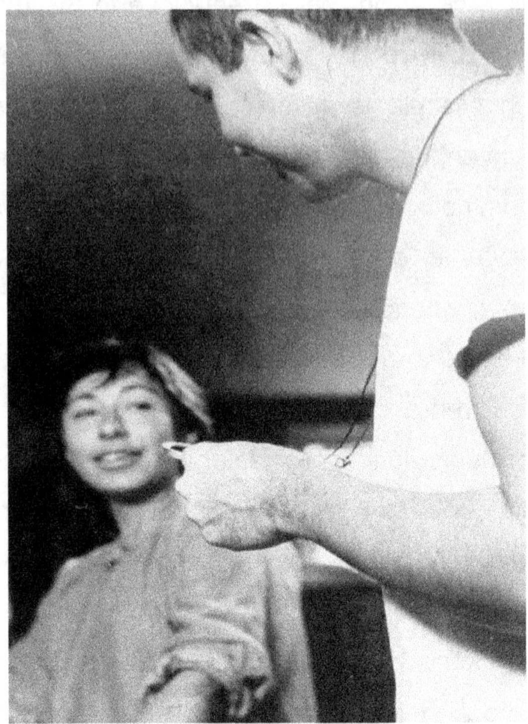

Figure 41: Jean d'Andrea wiseacering with Chuck Everts.

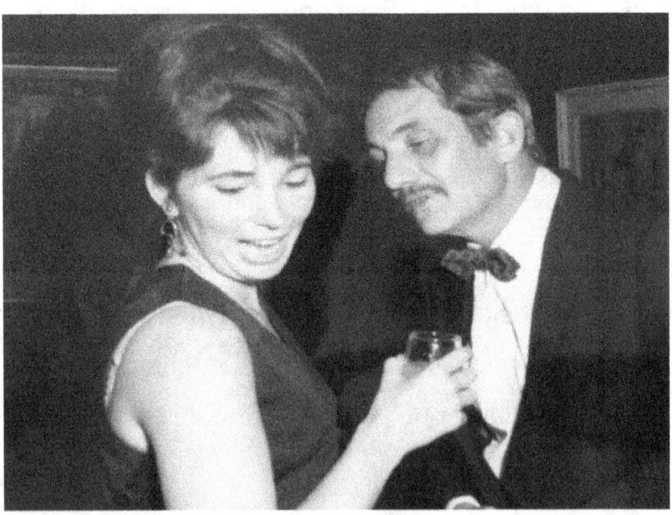

Figure 42: Tipsy-doodle. An opening at the Richard Challis Gallery. Italo d'Andrea leers at "Miss" Kitty Cooke. Photo by Chuck Everts.

One of Eldon's practices of mighty prowess was the way he could perform acrobatic miracles on a pair of rings he had hanging from ropes fixed in the upper reaches of a tall eucalyptus tree outside of his love-nest/wine cellar. He was a joy to behold, and he wanted us to achieve grace in space the same way. We tried, but stunk. Tom managed to get up there and start swinging, but lost his grip on the sweaty rings and fell flat on his back in the dirt with a frightening thud, knocking the wind out of himself. Nothing could induce either of us to get back on them after that.

We continued to hang around until we became a nuisance. Eldon was likely to show up at any hour with some round and firm and fully packed female he had glommed, and our lugubrious presence was hardly good for his romantic prospects. He was kind and friendly, but we could plainly see that we needed to find other beaches to wash up on, so we drifted away.

We weren't getting any work done, either, although we were both full of lofty intentions, plans, and inspirations. We were sort of leaning on each other like felled trees that would collapse to the ground if not holding each other up. We decided to go to Guadalajara to visit Jean and Italo d'Andrea, who had moved there shortly before the destruction of our libertine world at "Little Rome." Tom Blackwell had not been a resident in that seamy pit, but he was tangential to it and on close professional terms with Italo, who was one of only a couple of other artists who could paint on Tom's level. Although Tom produced like the sorcerer's apprentice, getting paintings out of Italo was like dental surgery. Tom and I had been through our marital collisions since then. We decided that Italo and Jean would just love to see us, and we headed south to the border.

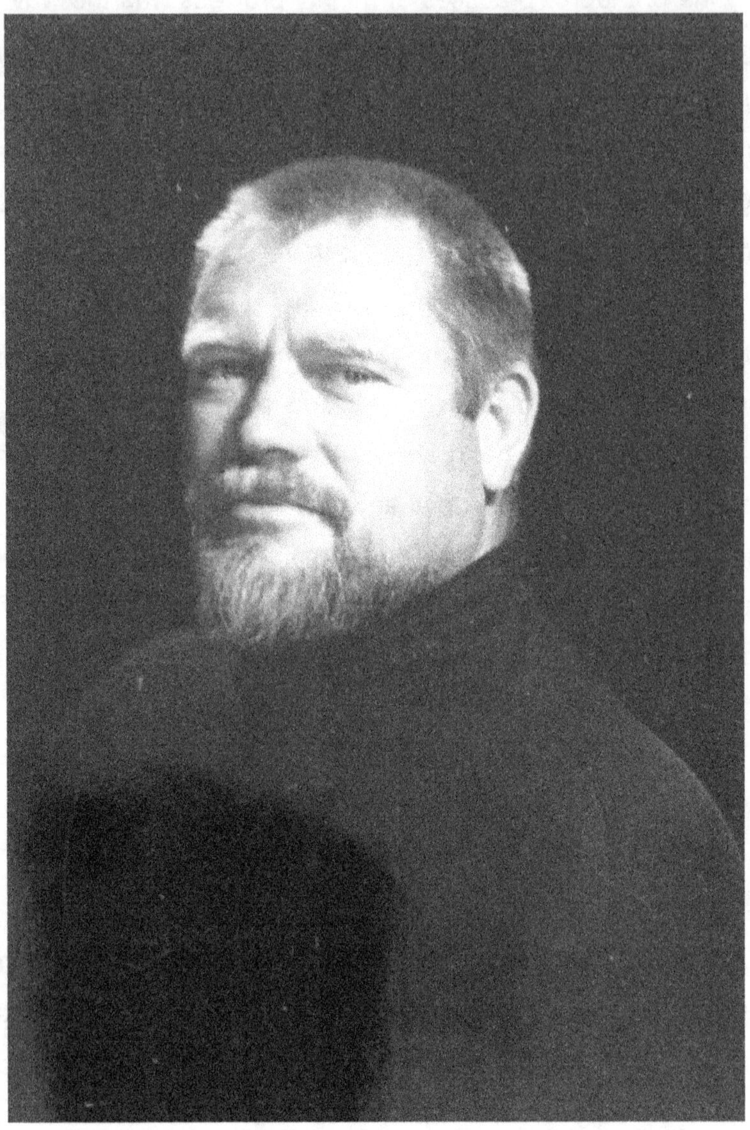

Figure 43: Perry Duncan at Little Rome. Photo by Chuck Everts.

Eventually, we staggered off the bus and into the friendly warmth of the City of Mazatlan, below the Tropic of Cancer, a city dear to me. I proceeded to give Tom Blackwell a look around, as he had never been there before. I showed him the beach near the Hotel Playa, where I met Eldon Setterholm eight years earlier, camping on the strand during Christmas vacation with college friends Mike Lewis and George Goyer.

Mike and George and I had been in the tide pools at low tide and had managed to extract a dozen big lobsters from under a flat rock, embedding many sea-urchin spines in our knees and feet. We were cooking these lobsters, and taking hits off of a big jug of Bacardi Rum, when the mighty Viking came striding down the beach, like right out of central casting. Noticing our grand surplus of rum and lobsters, Eldon, for that's who it was, ambled up and began to jaw entertainingly. He had the gift of gab, and a command of the jazz idiom that I was unfamiliar with, but took to enthusiastically. He invited us to bring our booze and bugs over to his ticky-tacky beach shack, built of old green driftwood planks. The shack was only half-roofed, the open part draped with fishnet. We were happy to be offered an opportunity to have a new friend and new experiences and were happier still when we saw that Eldon lived with Maria, a blond girl as stunningly feminine, as he was masculine.

We all set in to eat lobster and drink rum until the full moon rose and shone down into the candle-lit pad. Eldon asked us then if we were interested in smoking some of that "groovy green tobacco." Mike, who had gone to Hollywood High and had writers for parents, smiled broadly and started in to nodding his head, saying "yeahyeahyeahyeahyeah". George declined with pursed lips. I had no idea of what Eldon was talking about, but when he brought forth a big bag 'a stinky marijuana, I began to get the picture from various allusions I had read or heard in the past. I knew that this herb was considered a no-no in the States, but in my naiveté, I imagined that it was probably OK in Mexico, especially as Eldon was being so casual about it. I wised-up later and learned that Eldon had no need to worry since he was a sort of enforcer for Don Enrique Osuna, the local crime boss.

So Eldon rolled up some big fat bombers and they started making the rounds. Pretty soon I was as stoned as I ever was at any later time, and discovered myself out of body and looking down on the scene with myself in it, accompanied by the sensation of being pressed all over against glass. That went away when my attention shifted suddenly to the gorgeous Maria, who was disrobing. She stepped over into the corner of the room where the moonlight shone down and raising her face began to recite Poe's *The Raven*. She knew the whole thing, and went on stanza after stanza, with the shadow of the fishnet ceiling playing across her eye-popping anatomy. Remember that this was back in the Eisenhower era, and I hadn't seen many real live breasts before, and it would be years before I saw any others as perfectly spectacular as these were. "That Maria," as Eldon referred to her in later years, was to die for, physically, something that, according to the later Eldon, would have been OK by her.

Now, eight years later, Tom Blackwell and I were in this well-regarded former territory without Eldon, whom we had left behind in Laguna Beach swinging from his rings, puffing big bombers, and servicing the renewable crop from his local chicky farm.

Tom and I took the next leg of our trip, from Mazatlan, Sinaloa to Tepic, Nayarit. It was daytime, and the haul up the mountains out of the coastal jungles was so spectacular that even Tom cheered-up a little. We pulled into the interesting city of Tepic at dusk and tossed a coin to decide if we'd hang around for the bullfights the next day, a Sunday, or press on to Guadalajara, still

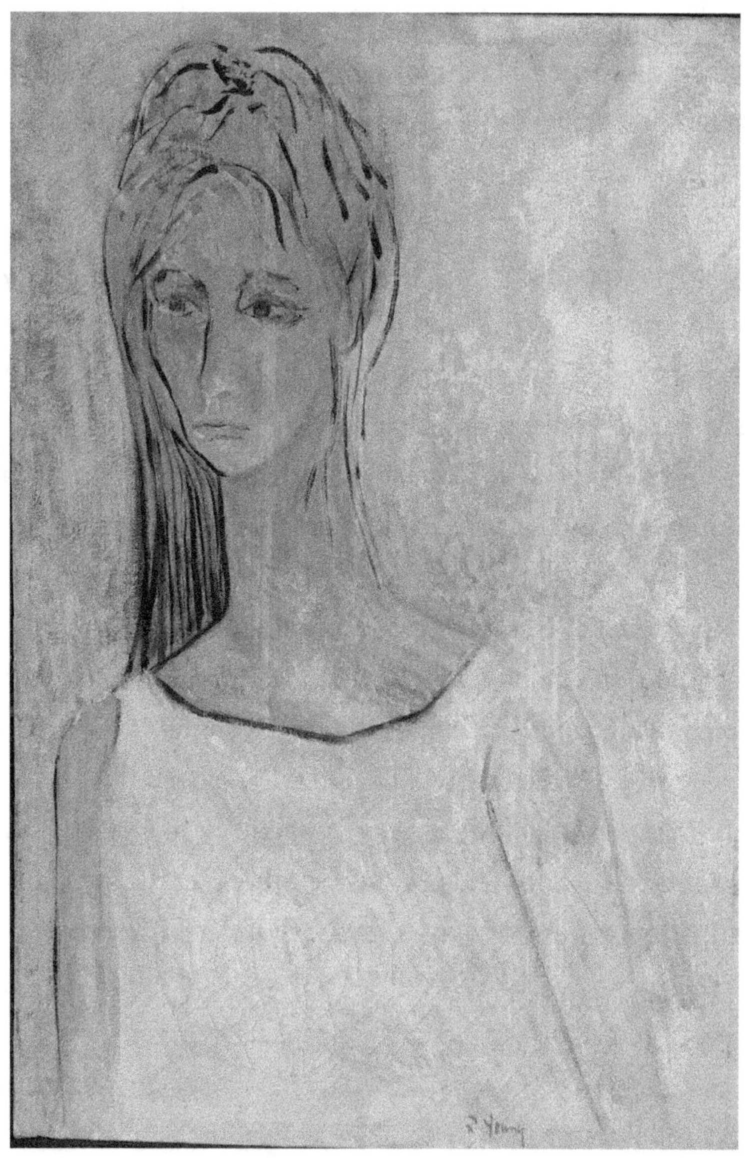

Figure 44: "Muffin" ("the ragamuffin from Mississippi"). Oil on canvas by Bob Young at Little Rome, ca. 1962.

a long bus ride southeast. We opted for the corrida, which was a marginal affair in that provincial capital, but of a piece with the raw nature of our entire trip. Eventually, we arrived in Guadalajara and made our way to the d'Andrea's place.

Italo and Jean's home was a rambling adobe one-story affair with the accustomed d'Andrea Bohemian atmosphere. Italo and Jean were unchanged, she pert and bustling, a cigarette hanging out of her mouth as she issued zingers, and Italo all in black, his accustomed beret still on his head, his sad bloodhound eyes looking up at one with their combined sharpness and reproachfulness, and his claw-like fingers as brown with tobacco stains as ever. They seemed glad to see us.

The house was on a residential street close by the Zocalo. There was the standard high wall all around the premises with broken glass set in the top, and accordion razor-wire on top of that that, both of which were backed up by the presence in the front yard of a vicious, ravening German shepherd bitch named George. "How come you named that bitch George?" I asked Italo. He cackled and said that he hoped the trans-gender label would piss off the dog and make her even meaner. In George's run there grew an odd spindly tree with tiny leaves and covered with strange and alien blooms made all the stranger by being crawling with large multi-colored beetles. I was charmed, Tom was repelled, and Italo liked the color juxtapositions.

Paco and Rudolfo were a couple of the many characters who came and went at Jean and Italo's, just as had been the case at 703 Browncroft. I mention these two because they were polar opposites, Paco being a chesty and in-your-face, macho bus-driver, and Rudolfo an aesthete who was "as queer as a three-dollar bill", as the phrase used to go before the advent of political correctness. Rudolfo and Paco didn't like each other one little bit, and if it weren't for the neutral platform of Italo's world, Paco might have hurt Rudolfo. Both of them looked at Tom and me with "wild surmise," trying to figure out who we might be, there in the bosom of d'Andrea hospitality. Paco thought that Tom was gay, and sneered at him blatantly. Rudolfo thought that I was gay, and made overtures. Italo laughed his ass off at the whole situation. Jean went "tut tut," and shook her head while she cooked an endless sequence of tasty dishes. George snarled at everybody.

Jean and Italo had an old lady friend who had been a camp-follower in Pancho Villa's army. She looked exactly like a proud raptor. I wouldn't have dared to cross this skinny and erect virago with her piercing black eyes, her determined jaw, and her drill sergeant's posture. I would have bet that she had six knives and three pistols and a machete concealed in her dress. One day President Adolfo Lopez-Mateos' campaign bus went down the street nearby, and the old Villista lady emitted a scathing broadside of colloquial Spanish in a high shriek that left nothing to be inferred or mistaken, even if you didn't speak the language. Lopez Mateos must have heard the decibels, even if he missed the content.

Tom and I hung out there for several weeks and went on many excursions with Italo, who was a great guide into the underbelly of wherever he was. He showed us many amazing sights, and delivered many good drinks and much savory food, knowing, as he did, where the best of the best was, and getting it at local rates because of his absolute acceptance by the locals as one of their own, and his mastery of the idiomatic Spanish of the streets.

Everybody in Guadalajara seemed to know and love him. In retrospect, though, probably the best thing Tom and I did in Mexico was to marinate in Orozco murals.

That was the swan song for Italo and Jean, had we but known it. After that, Italo fell for a teenager back in the States, the d'Andreas broke up, Italo fathered another daughter by the girl, who immediately disappeared for good, and Jean died of lung cancer. Italo lingered for another fifteen years, living in squalor in Ensenada, and coming to Laguna once a month to pick up his Social Security check at Walt Elterman's Marine Room bar, where he crashed on the floor in the storeroom. He continued to paint like an angel, bringing a few pieces up to sell each month, off the stretcher bars and rolled up under his arm. He was a 19th Century artist rushing toward the 21st.

After our return to Laguna, Tom Blackwell and I drifted in different directions. I hitchhiked to Woodstock while Tom moved in with the police detective, Norm Babcock and his perky painter wife, Jan Peters Babcock. Norm slowly convinced Tom that he should help the cops nab Bill Baldwin. Tom and I crossed paths once more in Woodstock, told in detail in another chapter. At that point, we really did sever our relationship, or rather; Tom severed his relationships with all his former friends. Now they are all dead, except for the two of us, in our separate worlds.

I hitchhiked off across America on the trail of a passionate girl artist after whom I lusted, ending up in Woodstock, NY, just after she had left. Undaunted, I moved into the abandoned cabin in the Catskills, that belonged to my eccentric great aunt, the difficult and temperamental actress/control-freak/hermit, Edna Aug.

I gradually made my way into town and met Gerd Stern, who was one of the principals of the experimental Art community called "USCO," standing for Us Company.

Chapter XI

Jackie Brown's Blacks

Toward the end of my pop music chapter, I wrote: "While I was in Woodstock painting my large Mandala, I fell in with the late jazz-mama, Jackie Brown," and I said she deserved her own chapter. Here it is:

When she was still a teenage white orphan girl named Jacqueline Morgan, Jackie Brown had been seduced by a Negro groom in the stables at Churchill Downs, or so she told it. Whatever the exact truth of the seduction was, she liked it. Horses and black men ruled her life from then on. Art ran a close third to plugs and studs. That cryptic passion for Art brought her into my world, a boon of ambiguous merit. She was a slender rail of a girl who had a hatchet face, but the best pair of legs this side of Atlantic City. Her hair was long and straight and black, and she had a cynical look on her face that could get informed by lust in a heartbeat. She moved like a cat. She also had her hands on the controls of her sexuality, and could turn it on like an appliance whenever she felt like it.

By the time she got to Woodstock she was a widowed mom with a couple of daughters; one a teenager named Jennifer, and a ten-year-old named Maris. I met her in 1965 while I was working away on my big Mandala about Biology and Taxonomy, and doing it in a cramped, converted corncrib. Jackie Brown knew the real deal in Art when she saw it and immediately laminated herself onto me in a non-exclusive manner that worked very well for both of us, up to a point. Jackie was older than the other dames I'd been conjugal with, and it showed in many ways, particularly in her candor and pleasant expertise. She was pushing 35, and I was 28. It would be somewhat misleading to think of her as a cougar; more like an alley cat.

I don't know how Jackie Brown nee Morgan got from Churchill Downs to Topanga Canyon, but that's where I picked up her story. She was a part of the pre-flower child, Beat Art scene that was Topanga before it was developed. Her husband was John Brown, of all the possible names for the husband of a woman devoted to black people! Knowing Jackie Brown as well as I did, I expect there was a psychological component in her choosing John Brown because of that name. They lived the Bohemian life, hanging out with poets and painters, riding horses, making Art, having the two daughters, fighting and separating, getting back together again, and complicating everything with seriously fractured psychological mechanisms and licentious substance abuse.

John Brown was another junkie, God help us. During one of John and Jackie's recurrent splits, he went off in his camper to be alone and commune with nature. He lit his Coleman lantern, and it exploded, burning him mortally, but not killing him on the spot. Jackie Brown saw him on his deathbed in the hospital, where he told her, "Be of good cheer." Remembering that incident reduced Jackie to tears, and tears were far from that tough broad's ordinary state.

She'd hung on at Topanga for a while, but soon got the notion that it was time to make a change; get out of the tragic circumstance; find new horizons...all pointedly spurred along by

Jackie's fatigue at fending off the tiresome wooing of Anita O'Day, who, Jackie claimed, had the extreme hots for her.

Jackie's idea of a jazz paramour ran more toward John Coltrane than it did to Anita O'Day, so she packed up her stuff in a medium-sized truck, hitched up the horse trailer with her two horses in it, stuck the girls and Hoss the Weimeraner in the back, and drove off to Woodstock, a trip we can only imagine.

Jackie Brown was a city chick in one-half of her incarnation, who ought to have been hanging out in jazz venues as her environment, but she was equally committed to horses, which have never been good companions in nightclubs. She chose Woodstock, an Art place where she could keep her horses and because it was also within range of Manhattan and the hip jazz scene. Personalities of the jazz scene were coming in numbers to Woodstock, another hip scene on its own, rural, terms. Woodstock was the easy destination of choice for creative New Yorkers who wanted to unwind a little in a country place where Art was happening. That meant that Jackie Brown might bump into black musicians here and there, and so it happened. Whenever she found one, she tried to have sex with him. She was obsessed with the desire to get pregnant by a great black jazz musician, preferably a drummer. She had recurring fantasies about Elvin Jones.

The Woodstock Art community was by far the most seminal one of any "Art colony" I ever saw. The Big Apple was nearby, you know? All sorts of luminaries were about, and it did one well to avoid being dazzled by them. Since I was working as a printer's devil, and spent much of my time smeared with ink and listening to the clackety-clacking of a Multilith 5000 press, I had a certain grounding that insulated me from getting star-struck. Jackie Brown lived in the hope of being star-struck, but she was particular about which stars might strike her. Black musicians were the flavor of choice, all others need not apply. Except me.

Jackie Brown was as multi-faceted as a cut crystal, and her various faces, while all sincere, were by no means in synch with each other. When she was a mom, for instance, she was a complete and devoted one, but that was only one aspect of her out of several. Horses were another, which interfaced OK with motherliness, but then there was the nightclub scene, which was at odds with the rest. Complicating the mix was Jackie Brown's recurring and passionate horniness. As a real artist doing major work I measured up to Jackie Brown's standards (even though I suffered from being white), so she worked me into her busy schedule. Since I was as horny as she was, this worked out all right, except for difficulties of scheduling.

Jackie had so many irons in the fire, that she conducted her sex life on the fly. I was always either in the print shop slaving to make a living or in the corncrib, painting my ass off. When it was the latter, at any time of the night or day Jackie Brown might suddenly appear, shedding her clothes almost as soon as she came through the door, and throwing herself into a fervent, wham-bam sexual catharsis that was always welcome, but never any more meaningful than a sneeze.

Her idea of foreplay was slipping out of her panties. It did keep tension within manageable bounds. That was an extremely intense period of carnality for me, as there were often other females on the scene. When that happened, Jackie Brown was the soul of discretion, and quickly turned on her heel and split, with zero attendant game-playing.

When Jane "Chipmunk" Lewis arrived reading J. R. R. Tolkien in her Nash Metropolitan to crash in the corncrib with me, that complicated the making of liaisons even more. My relationship with Jane was strictly platonic, but the corncrib was still a tiny pad, and ill-suited to more than one occupant, especially more than one occupant conducting a busy sex life.

It's a wonder that I was able to forge on with my painting, amid such bounties, but I did. I also ended up in the hospital in Kingston in a bronchial/asthmatic crisis, brought on by a combination of exhaustion, and oil fumes within close quarters. My lady friends all came to see me in the hospital, Jackie Brown bringing along her particular friend, Eddie White, who was exceedingly black.

Alan White, who was even blacker, also came to see me almost every day. He, too, was a satellite of Jackie Brown. Black Eddie White was the size of a linebacker, but black Alan White could slide under a closed door. Eddie White beamed warmly, and so did Alan, but unlike Eddie, Alan was a hip genius, full of poetry, lyrics, mojo, and excruciatingly penetrating perceptiveness. He was also twice as old as Eddie White, and might have been any age over 50. He shook his head over Jackie Brown, as a concerned parent might do, seeing her endless complications as clearly as they were opaque to her. We stayed friends, at remote orbit, for life. Alan White lived in a sort of lurid temple of his own creation in mid-town Manhattan, where he shared his life with a Puerto-Rican teen-age firecracker. "I saw this luscious ripe plum, and I plucked it!" he said.

Eddie White may have been servicing Jackie Brown from time to time, but he was certainly servicing Irmi Rosenthal, the sophisticated German-national wife of Phil Rosenthal, a NYC psychiatrist of the expensive grade. Bob Dacey, the Hip Leprechaun of Birdcliffe, who lived across the road from Bob Dylan, got us a job painting the Rosenthals' house. The home was an enormous wooden structure of three stories, which, for reasons known only to themselves, the Rosenthals chose to paint a burnt umber color that was almost exactly the color of Eddie White, come to think of it. That job took a while, and for me was an interesting window into a hitherto unknown world.

There were a number of big dogs stalking about, and Eddie White was like the biggest of these. His position in the household was sort of on that level, I thought. In any case, I appreciated his kindly visits to me in the hospital, and I noticed that after he and Alan White had come by, I received better treatment from certain members of the hospital staff.

The friendliest of these was a mop-pusher named Charlie. Charlie did not need to modify his attitude, which was purely loving throughout. Charlie was a wiry biological 'sport' who seemed to be put together out of mismatched parts. He was a freckled kid with a huge gap between his front teeth, with odd blue eyes that looked away at the walls on either side. He had a speech impediment that made his tongue get tied around his teeth, resulting in a garbled sort of delivery, which was, nonetheless, perfectly clear to me.

Charlie liked to hang around in the wee hours, leaning on his mop handle and telling me all about his church. I was reading Martin Buber's *I and Thou* at that moment, and Charlie made a congenial counterpoint. The nurse kept chasing him away, but he always came back, perhaps in the hope of converting me, but most likely just because he was kind. I remember him as one of the best people I ever knew.

After getting out of the hospital, I fell in more deeply with the geniuses of the communal multi-media Art group, USCO, centered in their 19th Century church down in Garnerville, halfway to New York City. Bob Dacey, the Hip Leprechaun, was part of USCO. The honcho of it, Gerd Stern, had a cabin on Maverick Road there in Woodstock.

This, as well as being a plunge into another and newer sort of creative milieu, opened the floodgates to a whole new set of women. I continued to conduct a sort of opportunistic series of intersections with Jackie Brown, who kept asking me to give fatherly advice to her daughter, Jennifer, who, at fifteen or so, was spinning off into normal teenage girl excesses of her own. I was willing but inept. What did I know? It seemed to me that conservative wisdom left me with only the option of telling Jennifer not to act like her mother and me. Anyway, Jennifer turned out all right.

The Maverick Gallery was Gerd Stern's operation, outside of Woodstock town a little, a completely freewheeling and experimental stable of artists doing their thing in a big old barn surrounded by hardwood trees, with a sparkling creek burbling nearby. That was a relaxed forum as unpretentious as any place I had seen, but at the same time advancing a high-octane sort of Art.

We all know what a bunch of posing egoists an assembly of artists can be, but even preening was at a minimum in the

Maverick Gallery. I think that the prevailing down-to-earth congeniality was directly a reflection of Gerd himself, simultaneously the most brilliant and least affected artist one could ever hope to meet.

Jackie Brown was keeping her horses in a rented stable at Bearsville, a rural place a few miles southwest of Woodstock. She was renting stalls in a bucolic and ancient barn, from an old man named George Schultis. He claimed to be over 100, and he sure looked it. He was the original wizened gnome, made ghastly by a huge suppurating growth on the end of his nose, and a personal hygiene that had not included water for years. He stunk, and so did his rancid quarters, which smelliness seemed to make no impression whatsoever on Jackie Brown.

Getting out to Schultis' place to feed her horses was a twice-daily chore, which, in the winter, could be a dicey run through driving snow. Still, Jackie Brown did it, and I went along sometimes. In the depth of winter and into spring, Old George Schultis boiled maple syrup. His house was as hoary and sinking-into-the-ground as his barn was, sagging so low that I couldn't stand erect in it, and, God knows, I shrunk from sitting down on anything in that septic environment.

In the middle of the room, there was a sort of open hearth with a hood and chimney over it. On the hearth sat a giant tub of bubbling liquid. This was the maple sap that Old George Schultis drew from his trees. He stirred it, looking like a revolting alchemist, and reminisced while doing it. "Yes, Missus," said he, "I've seen a whole lot of folks go underground." Amen. He'd seen history go by since the end of the Civil War and couldn't remember any of it. Looking at him was like looking into the undifferentiated past of the New Amsterdam Dutch peasants who had been in these mountains since the 17th Century.

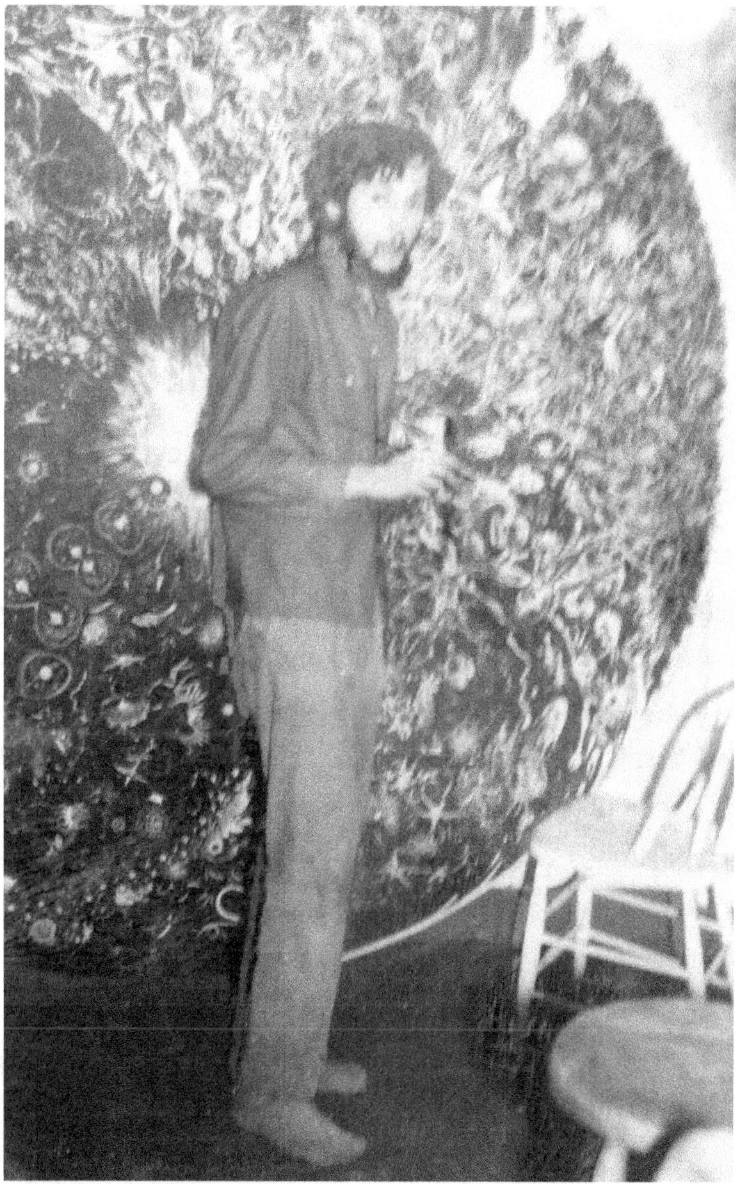

Figure 45: Dion Wright working on the Evolution Mandala in the corncrib at Woodstock, winter of '66. The near-death winter. Photo by Jackie Brown.

Lee Marvin was raised in a frame house along the Bearsville Road, and his parents still lived in it. He came to town occasionally to get drunk with his mates from high school. One day he and some friends were blotto and staggering on the streetcorner when we drove by on our way to feed the horses. Young Jennifer leaned out of the window, and with a stentorian bellow that almost shattered the windows of the neighborhood she yelled out, "HEY, LEE MARVIN!!!" The poor actor spun around and collided with the lamppost, almost falling on his ass, but for the support of his buddies. We sped on toward the Pit of Old George Schultis.

Janie Chipmunk was involved with a local poet, named Peter Allen; Jackie Brown was involved with a light-skinned black song-writer from Harlem, named Bobby Gleason (who was supposedly a friend of the bebop drummer Max Roach); and I was involved with a perfect Middle-Earthian elf/nymph (Oh, those boots!), who amazingly enough, lived right next door to Theodore Sturgeon, the sci-fi writer. Theodore looked quite unearthly himself...sort of like a fleecy golden lamb from God-only-knew-where. We were all in the throes of our fantasies come true, but passing and changing, passing and changing.

Bobby Gleason was a supercilious snob of a sort whom I would hardly have thought that Jackie Brown would tolerate. She tolerated him because she hoped hanging out with him would get her into the sack with Max Roach. Bobby had his nose so far up the air that "a cloudburst might drown him," as the old saying goes. He clearly hated my guts, which I supposed was some color thing, but no. "He doesn't like you because he knows you're a better baller than he is," advised Jackie Brown. How did he know this? "I told him," she said.

One day I returned to the corncrib from my servitude in the print shop to find the heavy oak door split and hanging loose on its hinges. Amazed, I stuck my face into my place and saw the sheepish faces of Janie Chipmunk and Peter Allen peering down from the loft. They were so apologetic. At least he fixed the damn door the next day. He was a handyman by trade, and competent to fix the damage he had wrought in his blind lust to assail Chipmunk. Peter Allen was a tall, knobby, and blond young man whose pre-eminent feature was a large and active Adam's apple, which you could differentiate from his nose because his nose stayed still.

This was all very well, so far as I was concerned, but a third body in that teeny place was not an option, so I bid them move into Peter Allen's place up on Birdcliffe, near to Bob Dacey, the Hip Leprechaun, and the never-seen Bob Dylan.

Soon Peter and Jane decided to get married and to sail around the world in a freighter. They were married in front of my almost-completed Mandala, with Jackie Brown and Eddie White and me as the witnesses. The ceremony was officiated by Milton Houst, the local justice of the peace. You could see what an odd scene it was for that poor functionary. Jackie Brown and I delivered the newlyweds to the dock in Manhattan and watched them steam off into the east. Bon voyage!

Due to her horsey predilections, Jackie Brown was momentarily taken up by a large dowager named Bertha Biers. Bertha invited Jackie Brown to a dinner prepared by her gastrophilic son, and Jackie was cautious of going alone. She would cruise right into the dingiest dive in New York without a qualm, but she was touchy and leery of any potential predatory women, which was what she imagined of the quite possibly innocent Bertha. Jackie begged me to go with her to this dinner, an occasion I would gladly have passed on, given my preference, but I went.

Bertha Biers lived in an immense mansion in the middle of spreading acres. She opened the door and we commenced a lavish meal with all the possible appointments, which wound down to a gracious farewell. We never went back. The odd thing was, Bertha Biers' chef son was never seen. He did the cooking and then hid upstairs.

My Mandala was completed and starting to move around, getting shown. I inherited Peter Allen's job of handyman at Birdcliffe, working for a Breughelesque foreman named Etherbert Van Kleeck. Change Bert's clothes and he could be one of the dancers at the *Rustic Wedding*, or the *Sleeping Peasants* taking a break from their mowing. I also inherited Peter Allen's cabin and was at once freed of both the print shop and the corncrib. Bert Van Kleeck was an easy boss, never demanding anything more than his daily bowl of "Campbell's Bean and Bacon Soup," which he always named in all its syllables.

Bert frequently offered me a bowl, which seemed to pain his dilapidated ectomorph wife deeply. Part of Peter Allen's shed life that I started inhabiting was a remarkable record collection. He had lots of spoken-word stuff, including e.e. cummings, reading his own poems, a quixotic counterpoint to the daily chores of fixing plumbing and shingles in the summer cabins. The cabins were rented to the favored intelligentsia of NYC, and bore cute bucolic names like "Wake Robin". All in all, the genie of serendipity seemed to be working overtime to enrich the tapestry of existence. My lubricious interlude with the mystic fox in tan boots shimmered and waned, and I fell in with my second wife, Margaret.

Jackie Brown never managed to get carnal with Max Roach, but she did succeed in getting pregnant by another jazz drummer of lesser renown. In the general diaspora of the next year, she left town to return to the west coast, Oregon, this time, where she delivered her baby within sight of Haystack Rock, and named him Malcolm, after Guess Who? A few years later, she died.

If you wonder what happened to the others, so do I. In fact, I wonder what happened to ME!

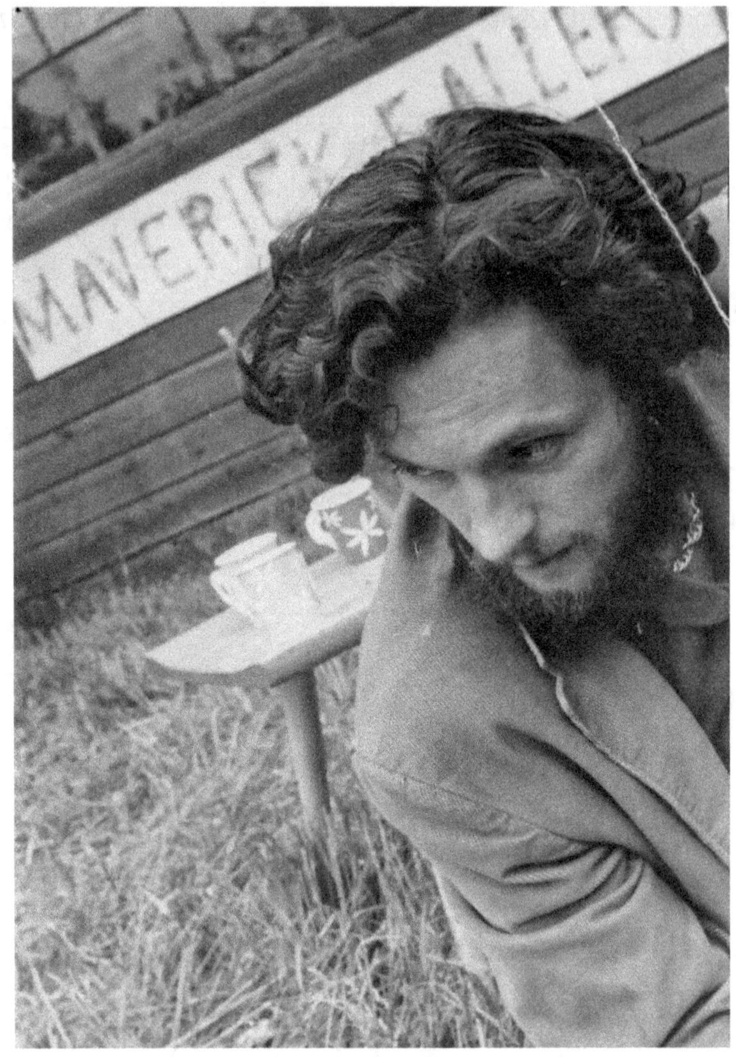

Figure 46: Dion Wright at the Maverick Gallery, 1965. Photo by Jackie Brown.

Chapter XII

USCO

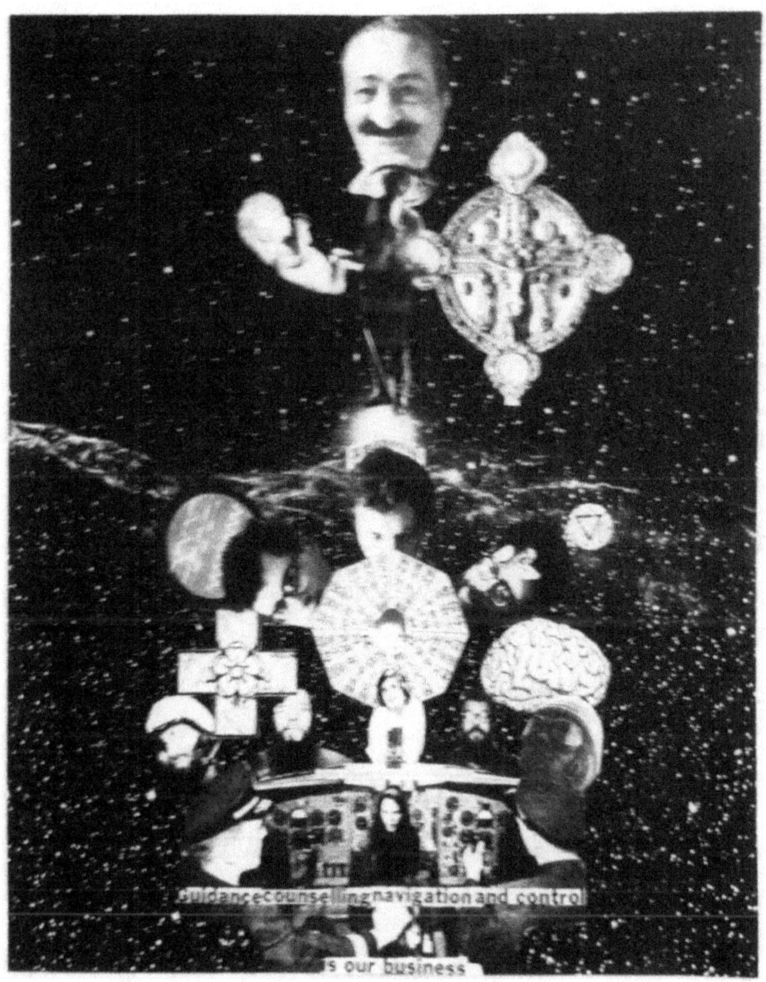

Figure 47: USCO Collage

USCO was lodged in a one hundred year old Methodist church in Garnerville, New York, while the LSD capitol of America was at the Castalia Foundation in Millbrook, New York, across the Hudson River. These communities were dual suns revolving around each other. Both were fueled by psychedelically accelerated consciousness, and staffed by the most elegant of minds. The Castalia Foundation was an academically oriented, culturally synthesizing, and intellectually speculating center that tried to steer and make sense out of the onrushing explosion of LSD awareness.

USCO was in the practical Art business of making physical objects, which mostly stumped and confused the general public, if that can be called "practical". These objects were artistic reflections of intellectual ideas and emotional revelations. Let's simplify that: USCO was both objective and subjective, while Castalia was more purely subjective. USCO seemed more an anarchic tribal scene, which was not what they exactly intended, while Castalia seemed to be more a hierarchical one, which was the exact intent. Such distinctions are made on shifty ground, and more for suggestive contrast than for definition.

The social systems were different between the two communities. At Millbrook, the place functioned in a very traditional way of a head man and his disciples. The brilliant, friendly and charming Dr. Timothy Leary was that head man, and he operated as both secular and sacred leader, styling himself, with plenty of sycophantic support from erstwhile followers, as the guru. He was also the chairman of the board. People deferred to him, and he did not hesitate to be the dean of the academy.

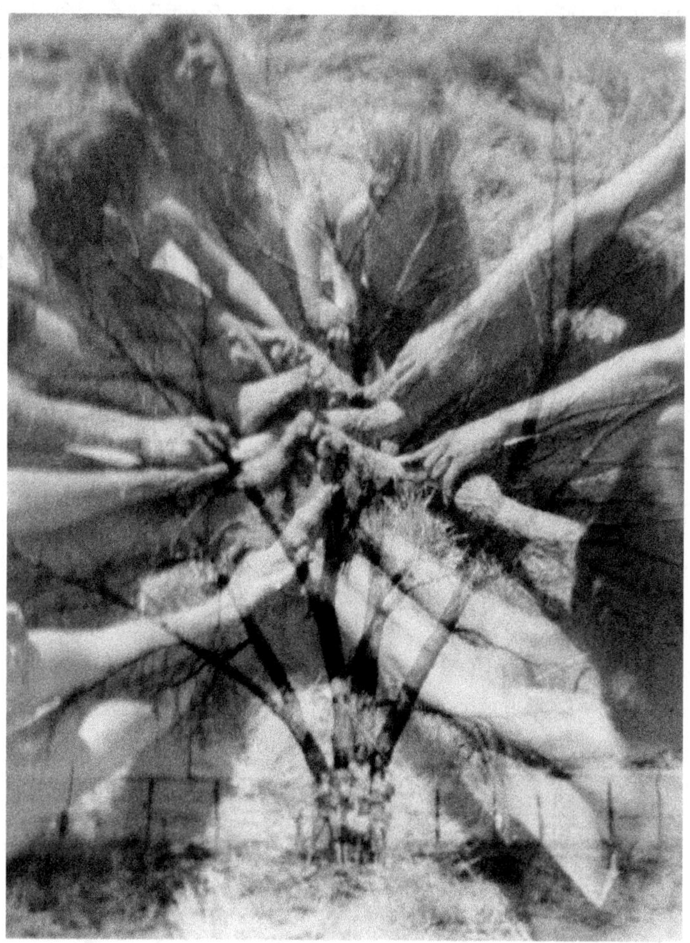

Figure 48: USCO "We Are All One." Photo by Stewart Brand or Steve Durkee.

At USCO, the social situation was qualitatively different. The aim at USCO was to have a mutual association without an executive head on it; a true brotherhood of equal opportunity from which visionary projects might emerge by general agreement and a sort of spontaneous creative combustion, with nobody getting too big for his britches.

That was the theory. In practice, the inertia of habit kept influencing the group to jiggle into a more traditional structure.

Most people wanted leadership, and some people tended to be leaders. Whereas Tim Leary was The Man, at Millbrook, within USCO there was an ever-shifting uneasiness of personality interaction. Three men who were powers within USCO illustrate the situation. Gerd Stern was the man most responsible for the apprehension of what USCO, the idealized creative community, might be. He was regarded as the chief, although he was always at pains to not *be* the chief. He was an alpha male of medium stature who surveyed the world through thick glasses, spoke in a nasal bass, and had the most elegant sense of humor, plus much hair, of any artist in History. He was the wordsmith who concocted the novel language convolutions that both described what was

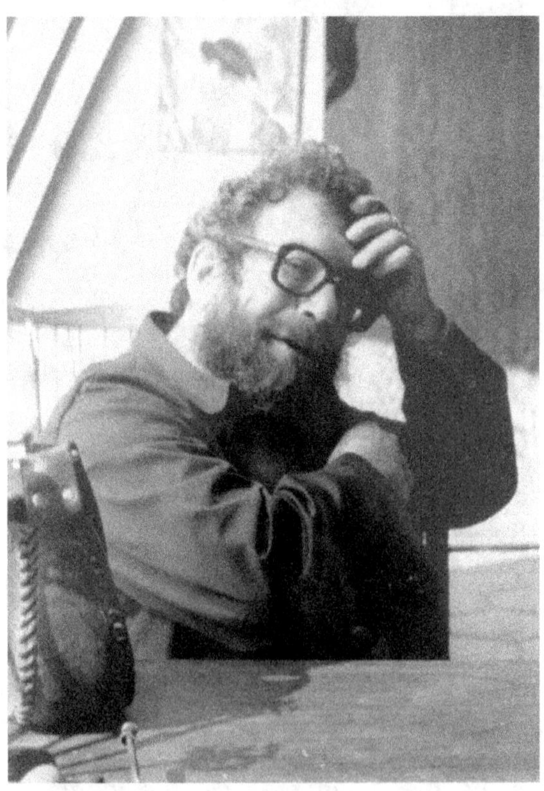

Figure 49: Gerd Stern at Castle Rock, 1984. Photo by Dion Wright

going on, and simultaneously obscured it, because of the utter novelty of the words, and the neo-recondite nature of the ideas they addressed and expressed. His accomplishments in this arena are all the more impressive when one realizes that Gerd's native tongue was not English, but German.

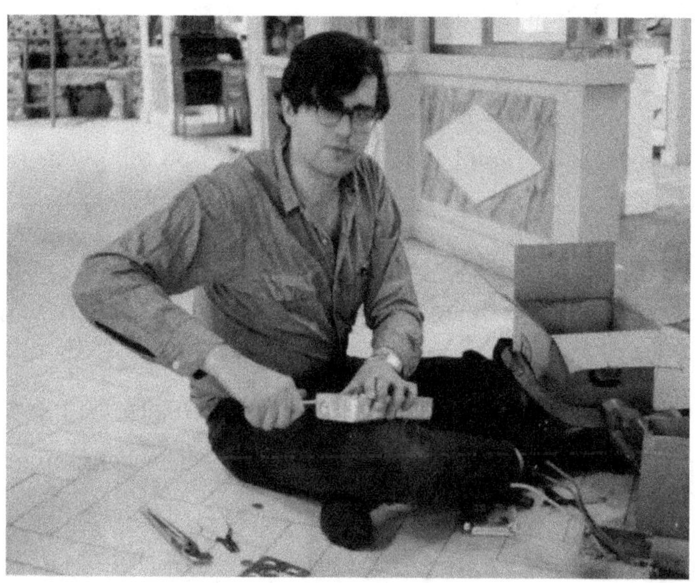

Figure 50: Michael Callahan ca, 1967. Bohematio layouts for USCO multi-media events. The electronic Dimension of Art. Photo possibly by Barbara Durkee.

Gerd worked closely with a young electronics genius he had discovered at The San Francisco Tape Music Center named Michael Callahan. Michael was a youngster, slender with dark hair that was forever falling across his glasses. Derived from the statements of the media-theorist Marshall MacLuhan, Gerd and Michael devised, developed and advanced circuitry that was electronic poetry. Hardly anybody was able to understand what they were up to, while nearly everybody was mind-boggled by the results.

Gerd's persona was counter-balanced by Steve Durkee, a fiery and physical artist who was another alpha male in the Church. Steve was raw-boned, ruddy, lanky, and seemed to be struggling at all times to contain a volcanic nature. He mostly succeeded at this, aided by a sense of humor that was equal to, and in synch with, Gerd's.

Steve's essential skill was as a painter, but he was also a widely eclectic and perceptive philosopher of religion. He was essentially a hierophant, one who knew he had a tiger by the tail with the psychedelics, but he seemed to be caught in a dichotomy. He was wanting to devote his huge faith to something in particular but was having trouble identifying that something. His origin was out of Roman Catholicism, which he had rejected, but the Catholic nature of hierarchy was bred into him, and he continued to yearn for its structure. Combined with the enormous strength of his charisma, he was always resisting his innate feeling that he, Steve, ought to be the Pope of USCO, to state it baldly. This conflict Steve tried to resolve by the introduction into USCO of a traditional Indian guru, whose pronouncements would be the scripture that the spiritual side of USCO would follow. This guru was Meher Baba, the man who claimed to be "the avatar (God on earth) of the age," and who had stopped talking many years earlier. He didn't stop writing, however, and had positions on everything.

Meher Baba had supposedly received his enlightenment about who he was one day as he was sauntering down the road past the elderly mahatma saint, Hazrat Babajan. The old lady took one look at Meher Baba, picked up a rock, and whacked him between the eyes with it. When he awoke, he was God. A huge painting of the saintly Baba, by Lynn Ott, a nearly blind devotee, hung over the head of the long dining table in the Church, the presence of which seemed to pour oil on the troubled waters of Steve's seething personality.

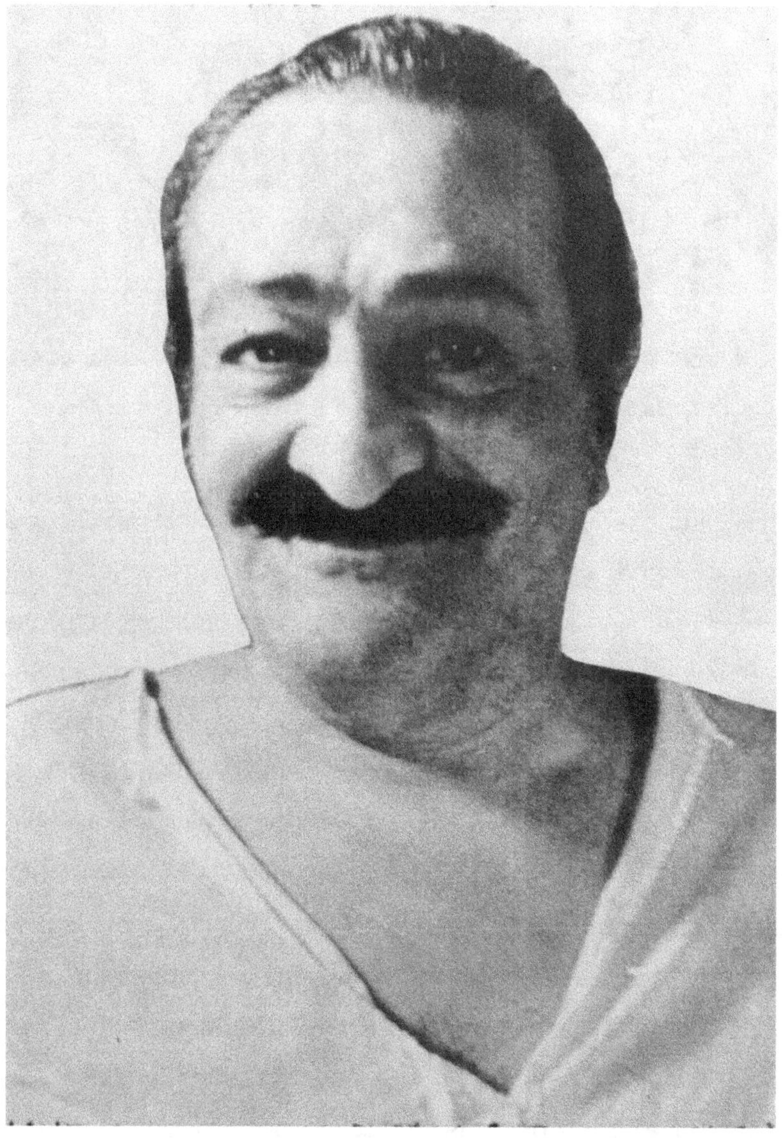

Figure 51: Meher Baba, Guru of USCO. "We are all one."

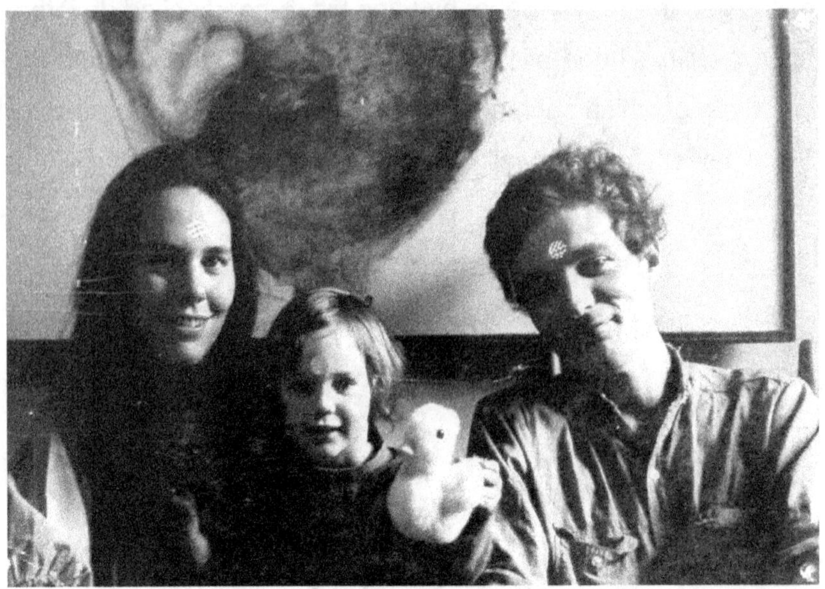

Figure 52: Barbara, Dakota and Steve Durkee at the church in Gamerville, NY, 1965. Photographer unknown.

The third example of a power-personality within USCO was Stewart Brand, a slender blond man with blue eyes, a Navajo wife named Lois, and a constant smile full of large teeth. He habitually wore a white mechanic's jump suit. He was just as bright as Gerd or Steve, and just as creative, but he held himself somewhat aloof. He knew that he had seminal influence within USCO, but he did not play in the power arena, except by existentially being who he was. As such, I suppose that Stewart was more the USCO ideal than either Gerd or Steve, who had concocted that ideal. He may have been able to be who he was by only appearing in the Church at intervals. Stewart was the USCO Man on the Road, peripatetically criss-crossing the country taking endless slide photos of all sorts of items, especially signs, which Gerd then assembled in Carousel trays to be folded into USCO presentations, and generically called, "The Verbal American Landscape".

This apprehension of Stewart and his position relative to the USCO group is not shared by everybody. Some survivors regard him as having been a sojourner, but in this writer's opinion, the laissez faire and inclusive nature of USCO was such that the distinction amounts to hair-splitting.

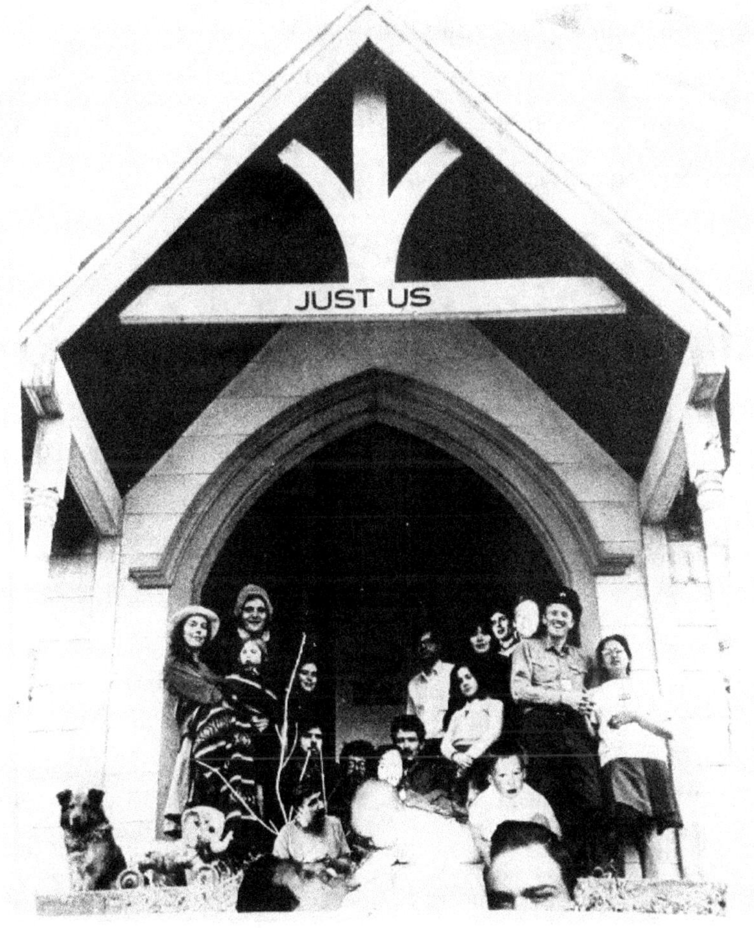

Figure 53: USCO collage of personnel. Stewart and Lois Brand at far right.

Stewart managed to be on hand for all the decisive events of USCO, which goes to show how psychedelically in tune he was with the ever-persuasive serendipity of the times. Stewart and Steve Durkee were involved in a sort of sub-set to USCO, a movement they called "America Needs Indians." That was all about Native American values of the land and its responsible use. Another one of Stewart Brand's cameos was the phrase, "Why haven't we seen a photograph of the whole earth yet?" which slogan was printed on a button he handed out by the thousands. Once we actually had seen such a photo, courtesy of NASA, that led Stewart to start The Whole Earth Catalog, which had the earth's photograph on the cover.

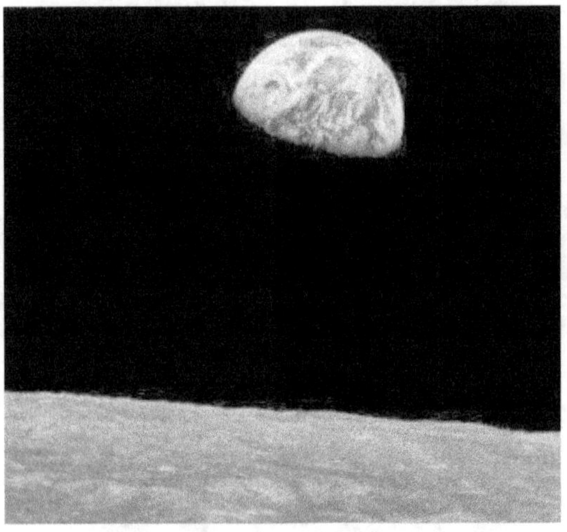

Figure 54: Whole Earth from moon. NASA photo.

Within the context of its creative chops, with Gerd and Michael, in particular, doing the programming, USCO produced the media-mix presentations that included Timothy Leary at the New Theater in NYC for the benefit of the Castalia Foundation entitled Psychedelic Theater.

Tim later expanded on this start in a lecture series called, "The Death of the Mind." This title made a philosophical point, but was, I thought, fantastically disingenuous since the entire effort was just about the most strenuous mental exercise I'd ever seen or heard of. It was as if Tim were saying, "When you have become a genius with all the answers, then you may embrace the void." Oh, really?

Bob Dacey was a Woodstock artist who was a part of USCO. I always think of him as "The Hip Leprechaun." He was a very Irish young man, as in the groove as he could be, and had both a slyly insinuating sense of ironic humor, and an unquenchable libido. There was to be a wedding at the Church in Garnerville, a psychedelic wedding between a warlock and a witch (so they thought), which was to be attended by the USCO people, and sacramentally accelerated by LSD from the Castalia Foundation.

Around this time, Dacey was picking up the sacrament at Millbrook, nearby across the Hudson River from Woodstock, and he took me with him. We left at the crack of dawn and pulled into the estate just as things were starting to stir. All the way over there, Dacey was singing "Just a summer romance"…" about his current sexpot girlfriend. It was a very entertaining rendition, to which Dacey was making up scurrilous lyrics. It was just the right atmosphere for a supposedly holy errand. We arrived in Millbrook and made our way into the countryside to the Castalia Foundation. I only spent that one day there, so my impressions are specimen, however, incised in memory.

The estate at Millbrook is in rolling country of open meadows and mixed woods. Brooks trickle gently through a congenial landscape. The gate to the place is a stone structure including roomy housing for the gatekeeper, who turned out to be the high E trumpet player, Maynard Ferguson. His wife, Flo, was best friends with Peggy Hitchcock, recent paramour of Dr. Timothy Leary, and sister of Billy Hitchcock, who provided the estate to the Castalia Foundation after the expulsion of IFIF from Harvard University.

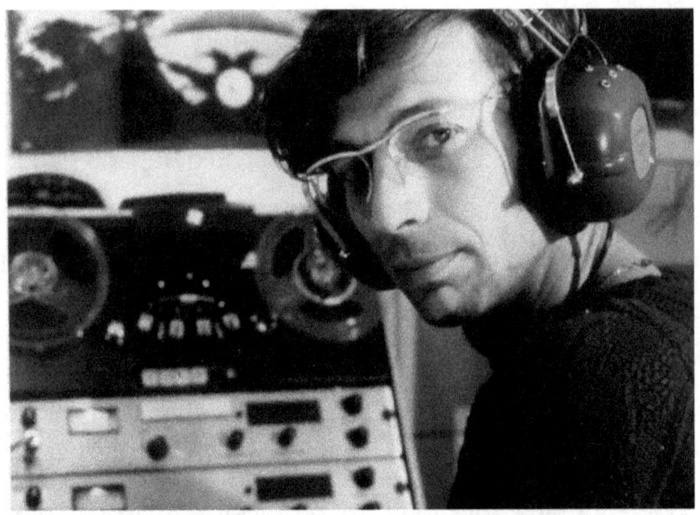

Figure 55: Bob Dacey editing Timothy Leary's LP, "You Can Be Anything You Want, This Time Around." Photo by Michael Callahan.

IFIF was the "International Foundation for Internal Freedom," which was the precursor to The Castalia Foundation. IFIF people got into trouble, including the expulsion from Harvard, and the deportation from Mexico, after the zany behavior of the IFIF-ites had enraged the administration at the university, and outraged the locals at Zihuatenejo, Mexico. Bud Hedrick later reported, "We had a nice relaxed scene going at Zihuatenejo before Leary came and fucked it up." At Harvard, Andrew Weil, who exposed and sensationalized the antics of the psychedelic professors within the pages of *The Harvard Crimson*. This accelerated his career as editor and fueled the successful eviction of Leary, Richard Alpert and their student colleague, Ralph Metzner.

The gatehouse at the Castalia Foundation set a medieval tone to come in on, immediately overwhelmed by the sight of the mansion itself as we approached. That structure was a Victorian/Georgian monster that looked back at you while looking at it. It had huge Buddha eyes of the sort seen in Bhutan and Nepal painted on the side of the building. We drove up the long circular drive and parked. We ascended the front staircase to the main door and entered.

There was nobody there, and the place was a textbook example of bad housekeeping, much to my disillusionment. I guess I was expecting something along the lines of a monastic-style, spare rectitude, rather than trash and chaos. At the foot of a wide staircase, Dacey left me as he went off in search of whoever it was that had the goods. I was standing there bemused when I heard a voice behind me say, "Share your light?"

I turned to have my first look at Dr. Timothy Leary, who was holding an L&M cigarette for me to light. The force of his personality was palpable. His narrow eyes were full of awareness, and his face registered an open friendliness. He was on his way into the kitchen to cook up a couple of pounds of bacon, which he was laughingly anticipating waving under the noses of resident Buddhist vegetarians. I was self-effacing, and withdrew to an observer's posture, to try to make sense out of what this supposedly ideal psychedelic community was. People started to stir, and it turned out there were a couple of dozen people in the mansion. More people drove in as the day progressed. They were a wildly mixed bag, united by a high degree of intelligence.

Whether any of them also had common sense was an open question.

The atmosphere was laid back and academic. Tim Leary surprised me by having a definitely fusty and fuddy-duddy aspect to his personality, which was quite professorial in feeling. It later turned out that this was the last gasp of that side of his persona. By the time he came to Laguna Beach, he had shaken off all the old cobwebs of his university life. At this particular moment, Timothy Leary seemed to be trying on the role of guru-holy man with indifferent success. He wasn't convincing as the spiritual leader, although that role was essentially the peg he was hanging his hat on to achieve recognition.

The chemical business of consciousness expansion stood its best chance of legitimacy as a practice protected by freedom of religion. We all know how well that worked out.

In mid-afternoon, Tim held "darshan." That's what he called it, anyway. The word "darshan" refers to the meeting of the master with his disciples, when blessings flow outward and downward to the faithful. This act of Tim's was theater without substance, as I saw but failed to feel it. He was dressed in a traditional garb of white robes, sitting in lotus posture on the lawn before the gathered populace, with incense burning and flowers, but the atmosphere was more like a boardroom than a spiritual retreat. Tim talked about this and that; business and procedural matters, as I recall, but I do not recall anything that felt holy about it. From then on, I regarded Tim's act as just that: an act. Dacey and I went back across the river to the USCO church, bearing what we were pleased to call "the sacrament."

Janie Chipmunk was living platonically in the corncrib with me and wanted to go to this exotic wedding. We were about to leave when Ed Lutz and Richard Remington III serendipitously drove up just in time to go with us. We forged ahead, and were welcomed, however, unexpected we all were. Serendipity was USCO's whole

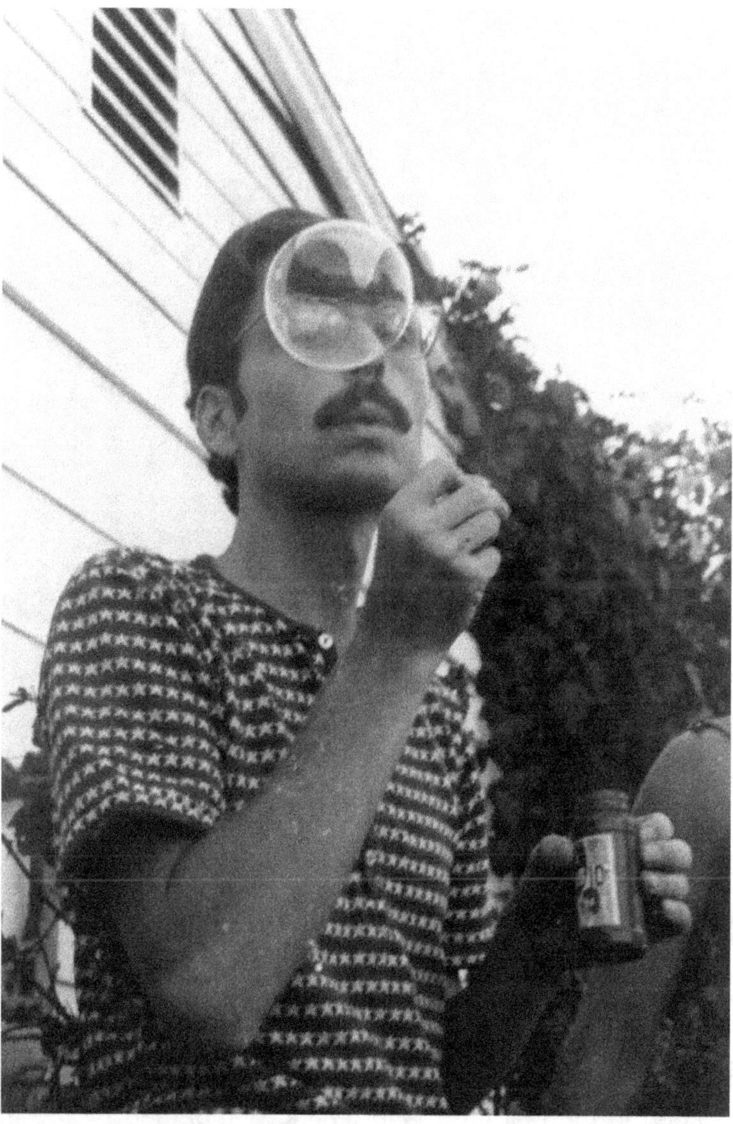

Figure 56: Ralph Metzner at children's birthday party on the Street of the Blue Lantern, Dana Point, CA. 1968, photo by Dion Wright.

point of having a church in the first place. It was, without doubt, one of the most holy and profound experiences of my life and it looked as if others felt the same.

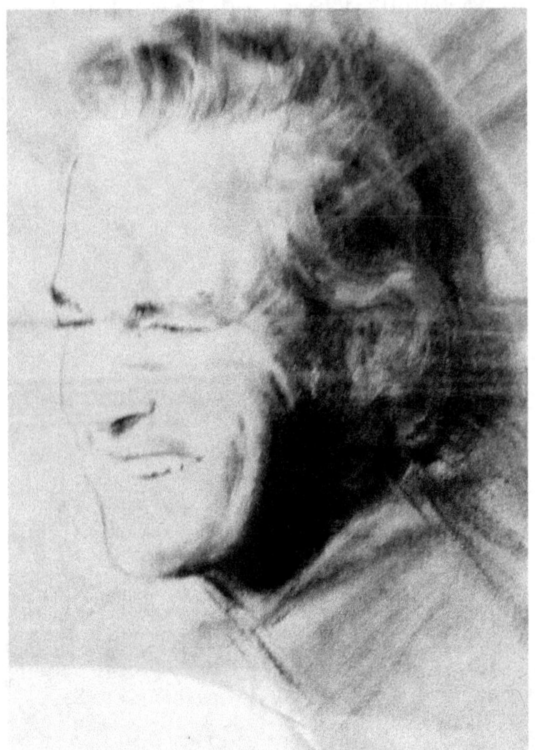

Figure 57: Timothy Leary as presented by the "San Francisco Oracle" during the Summer of Love, 1967. The image he cultivated.

A fire was made on a brazier in the center, and everybody sitting around it in a circle was given his or her dose of Millbrook acid from the fingertip of Gerd Stern, who had once been asked by the poet Michael McClure, "Where he got those weird fingernails?", to which, Gerd replied "The Museum of Natural History", (where he had once been an ichthyologist). Everybody was soon in the fast lane, and getting bombarded by the most spectacular psychic phenomena. Everybody surfed well; nobody freaked out, and eventually the dawn came. In the morning light, the guests drifted away on their separate karmic tracks.

I am told that this wedding was intended to occur within the format of the Native American Church's protocols for a peyote ceremony, but that Stewart Brand, in the way of an experiment, contrived to make the sacrament of this wedding be LSD instead. Nevertheless, these were objective matters, neither here nor there as per the subjective reality, which was big-time lift-off.

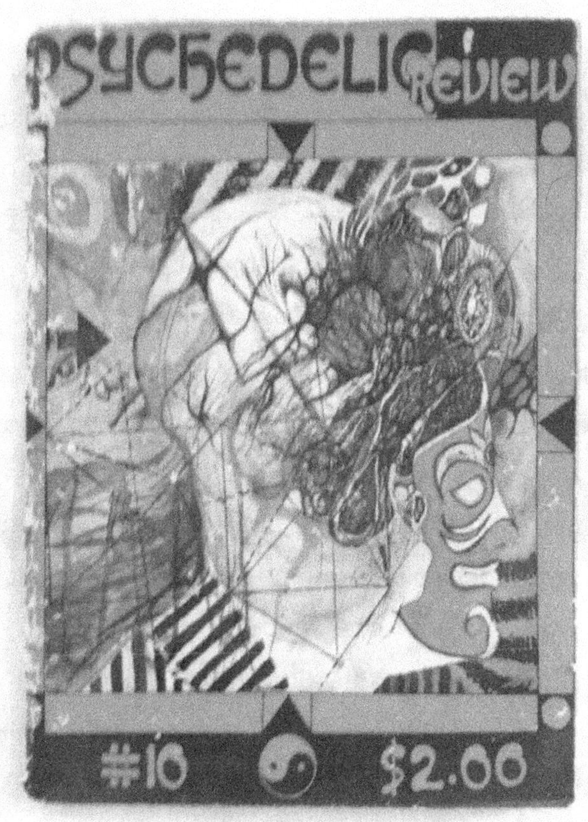

Figure 58: Cover Art by Ed Lutz.

The principals of USCO also dispersed, but it took them a bit longer. That dispersal occurred when the guru, Meher Baba, sent word that we should all stop taking LSD. That was the issue that splintered USCO. Steve Durkee didn't hesitate for an instant. The Father had spoken, and Steve obeyed. It was a display of character and commitment not matched by most of the rest of us, who, it seems, had indulged the primacy of Meher Baba without really taking him seriously. Everybody wanted to please Steve, but we all balked at the prospect of giving up our path to enlightenment. After all, this was the path that got us here in the first place.

The USCO Psychedelic Art exhibition at the NYC Riverside Museum, "USCO Down by the Riverside" was already in the works, and we all worked tirelessly to get it installed on time. It came punctually, but not without friction. One night Steve and Gerd disagreed about something, and the argument degenerated to "Fuck you, Stern!", and "Fuck you, Durkee!"

On this note the Psychedelic Art of spiritual enlightenment was about to be offered to the public. On the eve of the opening, Steve Durkee received the word, there at the Riverside Museum that his father had died. People moved away from him. He was standing there looking like the most lonely and isolated man in New York City. 'This is poor,' I thought to myself, and went over to Steve to offer sympathy. I tried to give him a hug, and it felt the same as if I hugged a tree. He was rigid, flexed, and unresponsive. I gave up and left. The next day the Psychedelic Art show opened with great fanfare. Much later, I learned that the relationship between Steve and his father had been strained.

Shortly thereafter, there was a diaspora with USCO persons leaving the Church for other venues. The Durkees went to New Mexico to start the LSD-free Lama Foundation. I took Margaret and started to return to Laguna, by way of San Francisco, where Stewart Brand was producing a sort of psychedelic media fair at San Francisco State College called “Whatever It Is.” The door to participation was open, and I was able to hang the Mandala at the student union during the run of the media festival.

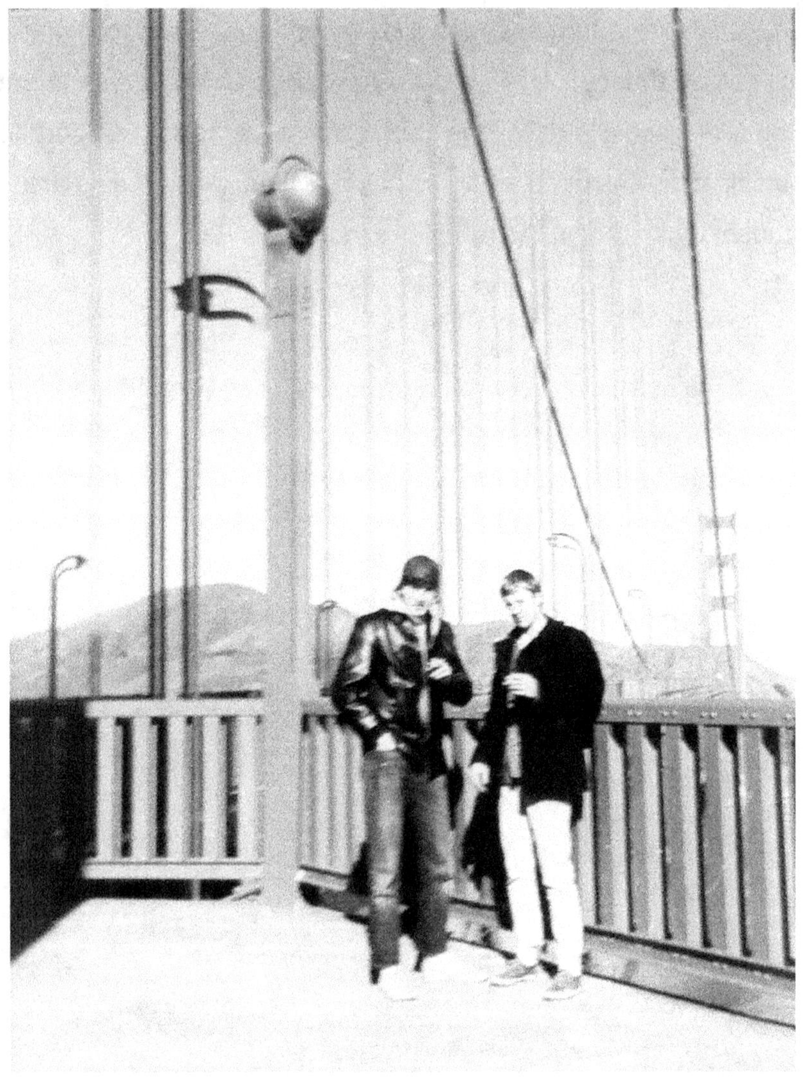

Figure 59: Dion Wright and Richard Remington III on the Golden Gate Bridge, ca. 1964. Photo by Chuck Everts.

Chapter XIII

Whatever It Was

Stewart Brand was one colorful and noticeable character coming and going from the USCO Church during its heyday. A tall blonde youth with his long Nordic face, crooked smile, blue eyes, and a perpetual uniform of white mechanic's jump suit, shadowed by his wife, Lois, an unemotive Navajo girl. They made some contrasty couple! Stewart made up for Lois' quietude by his own extroversion and jolly hail-fellow-well-met demeanor which, on close contact, proved to be wider than it was deep.

Stewart's role within USCO was dual: as a traveling, cross-country sometime photographer of slide imagery for the USCO media events. Folded into Carousel slide trays, they were projected during media events in a random way (allowing for unexpected serendipities of image conjunctions).

Gerd was doing an analogous function in more traditional collage medium with cut-up words glued in designed juxtapositions, thereby anticipating Bill Burroughs' later modus operandi, for which he received much applause from the literary peanut gallery. This part of USCO was made up of any weird symbolic imagery seen along the road, and not just by Stewart. He was the most peripatetic USCO-ite, being on the road more or less constantly, with NYC at one pole and Palo Alto at the other, dallying in Arizona and New Mexico in between. New Mexico played into the second part of the Brands' shtick, which was that semi-political, semi-spiritual movement called "America Needs

Indians," an action group energized by the Brands with silk-screened imagery by Steve Durkee. The group has disappeared so completely that there is not even an historical note to Google about it. Whether the movement foundered or not, America now needs Indians more than ever.

Stewart Brand, a product of Stanford, had always been au courant as to the expanding edge of technology and innovation. In this context, he heard a rumor that there existed a photograph taken by a satellite of the Whole Earth floating alone in space. Stewart knew the psychological potential of such an image to raise and change general human consciousness, so he started agitating to have this presumed photograph published. He created and wore buttons that said, "Why haven't we seen a photograph of the whole earth yet?", and handed them out others to whosoever might wear one. This was 1966.

In the fall of that year, Stewart exploited his academic contacts in California at the very liberal campus of San Francisco State College, to mount a media-educational festival there that was a development and outgrowth of USCO, in the wake of the collapse of that group. He called his media party, "Whatever It Is," in the hope, presumably, of setting the stage for novel enlightenment.

In it, he expanded the USCO notions by distilling the mélange of spontaneity endorsed by Gerd Stern into more discrete media aspects, which bore upon one another in a way that was mutually supporting, but less chaotic. *USCO Down by the Riverside* had been an encyclopedic exposition of media developments, while *Whatever It Is* also presented experimental and contemporaneous 'software' in the form of personalities sharing their systems and theories, from Yoga to technological philosophy.

Stewart Brand, the ringmaster, ran around in his white jump suit wearing a gold crash helmet shooting people at random with foos balls. It was an upbeat party atmosphere with a hard edge of political contention under it. Ken Kesey, a fugitive from justice presumably hacking his way through tropical jungles somewhere in Latin America, was mysteriously present. Also included was the always-dramatic presence at *Whatever It Is* of Neal Cassady, charismatic hero of the Beat Generation, and latter-day lieutenant/chauffeur for Kesey and the Merry Pranksters. Stewart Brand was also a Merry Prankster 'fellow traveler', as it were, but with his travelling feet in more than that one puddle.

Kesey was discreetly sequestered somewhere within the precincts of San Francisco State College with a public address microphone, intoning, "The head has become fat! The head has become fat! The head has become fat," over and over, in a deep and disembodied voice. There was no doubt in anyone's mind who the Fathead was, with Ronald Reagan a newly-elected governor and LBJ still in the White House (but rapidly speeding toward the denouement of Chicago in '68).

Within this general revolutionary atmosphere building up in America, Stewart Brand's extravaganza was exaggerated in its wake by authority as a menace to Society, when it was, in fact, anything but that. The upshot was that Ronald Reagan bid the State College Regents to crack down, and how. The Chancellor of San Francisco State was 86'ed and replaced by the ultra-right-wing semantics professor, S.I. Hayakawa, who proved so acceptable within Reaganlandia that he eventually became a U.S.

Senator from California. In the Senate, he dozed so much that he acquired the nickname, "Sleepy Sam." Yes, a soporific atmosphere was desired by Reagan and company, but not by Stewart Brand. Stewart gave up on showbiz as his vehicle, and went into journalism.

In 1967 the first *Whole Earth Catalog*: *access to tools*, was published, to instant and universal acclaim. It was so useful that everybody liked it. On the cover, there was that photograph of the Whole Earth. The designer J. Baldwin later remarked, "Stewart Brand came to me because he heard that I read catalogs. He said, 'I want to make this thing called a "Whole Earth" catalog so that anyone on Earth can pick up a telephone and find out the complete information on anything. That's my goal.'"

In 1968, the first Earth Day was launched, and it seems to me that Stewart Brand was the midwife for it. Stewart Brands' benediction: "Stay hungry; stay foolish."

Chapter XIV

John Griggs & Steve Durkee

USCO had broken into pieces. Steve and Barbara Durkee went to Taos to become founders of a new spiritual/psychological institute called "The Lama Foundation," originally an outpost of USCO. Steve liked the name as inferring Tibetan monks, and the little crossroads near the place chosen to build it actually was named "Lama"...but nobody seemed to know that "lama" is also the Spanish word for "mud." If you're going to make linguistic symbolic inferences, I thought to myself, you ought to make all of them, but I kept my cynical opinion to myself. Gerd Stern had remained in the East, where he was connected-up like a universal switchboard. He and Michael Callahan went to Cambridge, where they founded the Intermedia Systems Corporation. Stewart Brand ambled back across America to San Francisco, where he prepared to mount his own version of the psychedelic cultural extravaganza at San Francisco State College, "Whatever It Is," for lack of a language to describe it. I took my new girlfriend and my Mandala, and followed in Stewart's wake.

At a place called "Drop City" in Trinidad, Colorado, we stopped to check out a community there. It was derived from Timothy Leary's "Drop Out" injunction, and also because the people who were propelling the commune had dropped out of R. Buckminster Fuller's classes at Carbondale, Illinois. They decided to put Fuller's ideals into practice by erecting a bunch of small geodesic structures, to live and work in them. At Drop City, the pioneers encountered the several practical problems that plagued many other geodesic communes later. They were making their domes with two by four struts, and paneling them with sheet metal, which they got by chopping the roofs out of junk cars with an axe, flattening them out as best they could, and nailing the triangles to the wood struts, sealing them with roofing tar. The multi-colored domes looked quiltishly attractive, but the technique worked poorly, and leakage was a persistent problem, due to expansion and contraction in a climate where temperatures varied from over 100 degrees F to below zero. In such strenuous conditions, solutions troubled all the later experimental dome builders who proliferated in the Southwest over the next ten years. Drop City was a noble experiment, which tried to employ modern engineering with primitive technology. I didn't observe what the social structure was like, because we left in a day or two.

We stopped in to check out the Durkees in New Mexico along the way, and found them making plans while living at Mabel Dodge Luhan and Frieda Lawrence's ranch, no less, where D.H. Lawrence had lived and written. I wish I had known at the time that the Lawrence ranch was where Aldous Huxley had also once stayed, on his 1937 excursion across America. Lawrence was on his last legs and Huxley had yet to be submerged in Hollywood at that poignant lost moment, and they met in literature, and understood one another. There is always so much more to know that never gets into consciousness.

Now, in 1967, came Steve Durkee, marching to a drummer whom Aldous would have been able to comprehend, but who might have been too lurid for D.H. Lawrence. Whatever Steve was up to, it was structured, funded, and bursting with energy. Within a year, it would seem to me a good idea to have the merry cricket, John Griggs, meet the General of the Southwest, Steve Durkee, to assess whether these two latter-day heavy-hitters would commune as well as Huxley and Lawrence. But for the moment, we were still on the road and headed for San Francisco.

Once there, we had our participation in Whatever It Is, and then moseyed on down the coast to Laguna again. We moved into a flower-draped cottage on Woodland Drive, in the peacefully bucolic ghetto neighborhood from which the blacks would slowly be replaced by the hippies, and where peace and quiet among artists would be increasingly punctuated by hysterical screams and occasional gunfire.

The Woodland Drive neighborhood was re-named "Dodge City" by John Griggs, with whom we quickly became intimates. Johnny was a namer of names that stuck. He also named his fraternity of psychedelic buccaneers, “The Brotherhood of Eternal Love,” and the emporium that they were bent on opening in Laguna Beach at 760 South Coast Highway, “Mystic Arts World.” The Brotherhood moved wholesale into the Woodland Drive community, transforming it from black ghetto into an outlaw town that was short on cohesiveness or planning, while long on prophecy and idealism. The plan was to take shape later, when John intended to buy his island on which to make into reality the projected utopia of Aldous Huxley, imagined in his last book, *Island*.

In between came the Summer of Love, that colorful interlude in San Francisco, while the construction of Mystic Arts World proceeded back in Laguna at a glacial pace. It finally opened, thanks mostly to the energies of Mr. Joe Miller. I returned in

September to Laguna to run the Mystic Arts World Gallery. Mystic Arts World was up and running through 1968, it's classic, golden period.

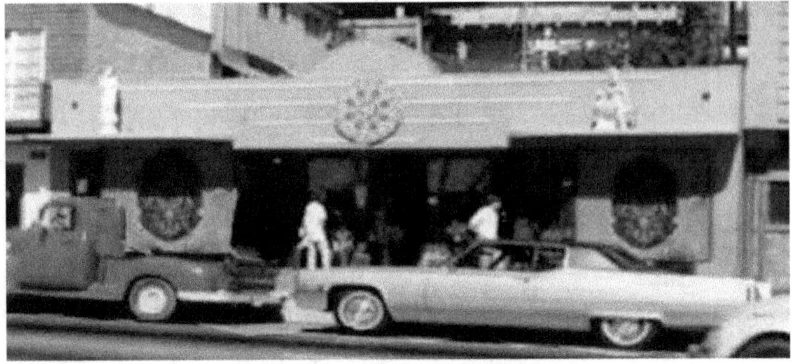

Figure 60: Mystic Arts World

One day shortly after Mystic Arts World opened, while minding my gallery and dealing with the many artists who wanted to be in there, I looked up to see the unusual sight of a cop. He was a sturdy little cop in blue uniform, and clearly putting some effort into his posture, which reminded me of a pouter pigeon. He looked cleaner than Paul McCartney's grandfather. It was quickly revealed that he was on the lookout for dirty pictures that might poison the minds of our clients, and he found a couple. He took them right down off the wall, and walked out of the store with them under his arm.

I quickly summoned John Griggs, who summoned the attorney, who started to raise hell in city hall. It was immediately decided that the seizure was completely out of bounds, and we might have back our Art work. The little cop, though, was not constrained to bring it back. I had to go down to the police station to retrieve it myself.

The two Art works were framed calligraphic studies in ink on paper by R. L. "Bob" Ross, who was having his one-man show at Mystic Arts just then. The cop who seized the Art was Officer Neal Purcell, making the opening gambit in his war on all things hippie. Purcell eventually reached the summit of the Laguna Police bureaucracy by busting Timothy Leary a couple of years later, after which he rose to become chief.

Were the pictures he seized Art, or were they smut? Judge for yourself.

Here they are:

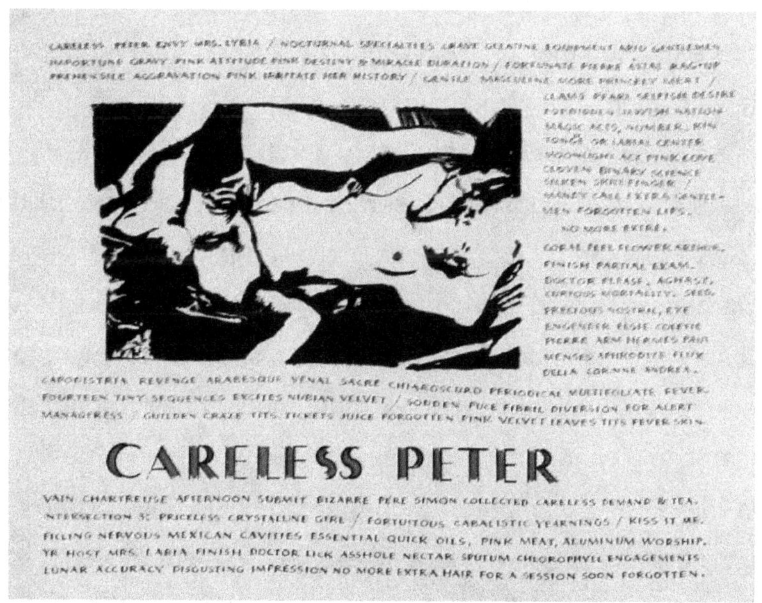

Figure 61: Careless Peter. R. L. "Bob" Ross

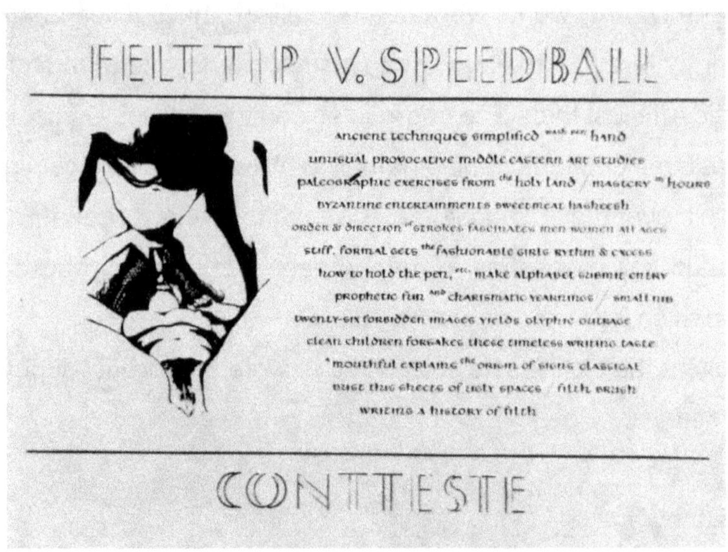

Figure 62: Felt Tip V. Speedball. R. L. "Bob" Ross

In the early summer of 1968, during the short interval between getting Mystic Arts World up and running, and the arrival in Laguna Beach of Dr. Timothy Leary and the Lady Rosemary, the Wrights and the Griggs families went on a trip. I had been talking-up Steve Durkee to John Griggs, naively thinking that these two powerhouses would like to meet each other. I touted Steve's visionary genius to John, and convinced him that we ought to go check out the Lama Foundation, then under construction, before he came to any hard decisions about how he wanted to define his own "drop out" commune. I wish that trip could have lasted a lot longer. It was the calm before the storm, "in memory yet green," when everything still seemed possible. We ambled to New Mexico, stopping at places like the Grand Canyon and Mesa Verde along the way, taking our time and saturating ourselves in the natural glory, accelerated by LSD. It was very primal stuff. We might have been the proto-humans leaving Africa, so deep and profound was our journey. Arriving at the Lama Foundation was a real shift of gears. The place that Steve and Barbara were building had a classic timeless quality to it, but it was most certainly happening in the present. We rose up out of the dawn mists of ancient consciousness, and got with the program.

The place was full of Indians. Steve Durkee had befriended and hired men from the Taos Pueblo as the work crew, who brought their own ancient roots into the scene as they made adobe bricks, and stacked them into walls cosmically designed by that Renaissance person, Steve Durkee. Steve and Johnny were fully appraised of each other at first glance. They were both alpha males whose nature was more rivalry than brotherly, as it turned out, despite my sanguine hopes for a powerful summit meeting. That is to say that lanky Steve was wary, because it was his scene, and he must have been somewhat taken aback by having a human spark plug such as Johnny suddenly zipping around his works like quicksilver.

Physically, they looked like Abraham Lincoln Meets Mickey Rooney, but spiritually it was more like Savonarola Meets Gandhi. Either way there was too much divergence of character for easy communication. Their similar idealisms failed to coalesce, because of LSD, which Steve continued to reject on the direction of Meher Baba. Johnny was nothing less than the prophet of LSD, and this made for the gulf between them, which was only widened by the fact that all the Indians fell in love with John at first sight. They regarded him with immediate and happy recognition, offering him a conviviality that Steve did not share. Steve was the boss over everybody, but it seemed that Johnny was the chief among equals. It was a natural. Johnny was doing his human monkey act of running along the tops of the high, unfinished walls, daredevil fashion, and getting all of the Indians chanting "Hare Krishna" as they worked. This was exactly the sort of thing Steve could not do, and it made for increasing awkwardness.

One Sunday morning a couple of laconic, smiling, raw-boned Indians named Tom and Jim came, got Johnny and me, and took us to the Taos Pueblo. They gave us a tour of that community, one of the oldest continuously inhabited places in America, which was probably more informative to us about social integrity, in a half day, than two weeks at Lama were. Tom and Jim barked short laughs, gave us a bag of chokecherries, and offered us dalliance with their frowzy sisters, which we declined with as much courtesy as we knew how to muster.

A few days later, we took off back to Laguna Beach, and on this leg of the trip, we flew low by the southern route, all the way down the Rio Grande River to I-80 west. Going through Yuma, we stopped to eat at a "plastic fantastic," as John called it. We were well-togged out in hippie garb, and seated at a table right by the entrance. Some Marines from the air station entered, making slurring remarks about us as they passed. John thought it over for a minute, and then arose and went back to the Marines' table, where he sat down and began to talk. Imagine! Invading the Marine Corps armed with love! We could not hear what he was saying, but within five minutes, he had those Marines adoring him as much as the Indians from Taos had. He had that golden gift of gab, and apparently, it worked on almost anyone. Except the likes of Neal Purcell.

We may have ambled casually to Lama, but we returned via the express mode. Johnny had things to do, while I, as usual, ambled into the future seeing what I could see, and awaiting the next lightning strike. In the meantime, the stately sequence of excellent shows took place at Mystic Arts World.

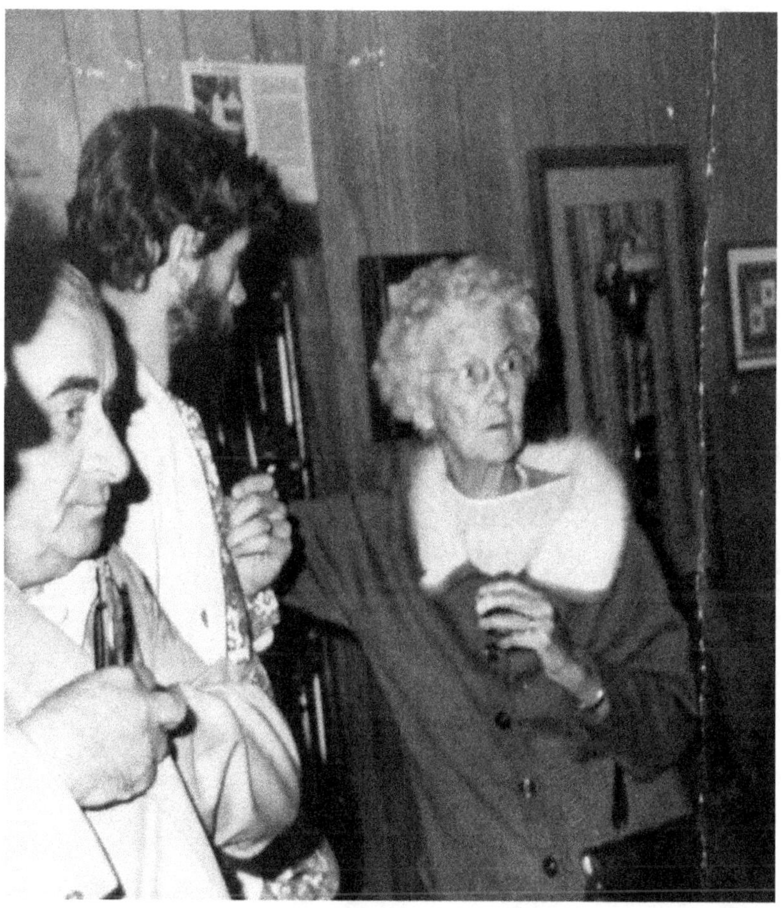

Figure 63: Assemblage artist Louis Goodman, Dion Wright and prize-winning poet Ruth Forbes Sherry at a Mystic Arts World opening. Photo by Chuck Everts.

Chapter XV

Fishing With Timothy Leary

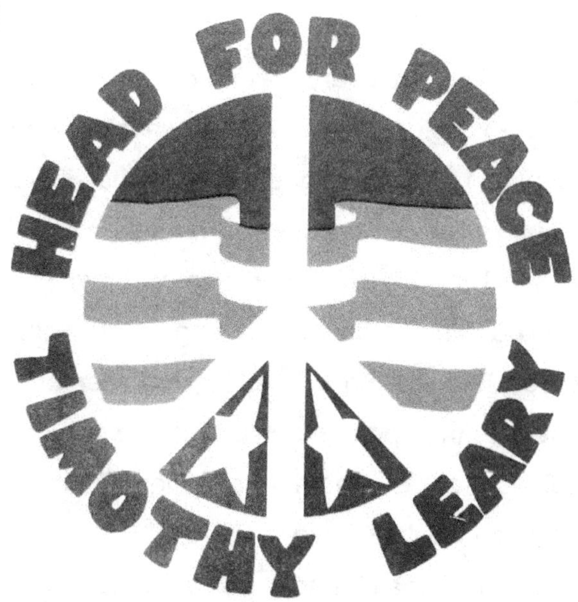

Figure 64: Bumper Sticker for Tim Leary's California gubernatorial campaign. His platform? More baseball, less football.

When Timothy Leary visited Laguna Beach in 1968, he was subjected to a rush campaign to live there by John Griggs and selected Brothers, by no means all of them, to which he soon yielded. God only knows why, but probably things were pretty hot for Tim on the East Coast, and Johnny and Company had plenty of good weed and acid. Not only that, they were also on the way of becoming a ready-made, built-to-order sociology experiment, on which Tim might tinker to his heart's content.

When the Learys were committed to Laguna Beach, Johnny Griggs pressed me into service as Tim's fishing guide. John could care less about fishing himself, but he knew that it was part of the local experience, and knew that Tim was adventurous. So, in his customary practice of plugging people into the places where an end might be thereby achieved, he cast me as Philip Percival to Tim's Ernest Hemingway, and we spent time "fooling around in boats".

Fishing with Timothy Leary was no different from fishing with anybody else, except for Tim's amazing knack of having Nature show off for him in a more exaggerated way than it did for others. We have all had grand experiences of Nature's wonders from time to time, but with Tim, every moment seemed to provide something extraordinary. Maybe it had something to do with expanded consciousness, and that Tim was so high so often that he just got more in tune with the operatic qualities of the natural world than average people did. It started right off when Tim moved into the cliffside house on Gaviota Drive.

Finding a house for a character as notorious as Timothy Leary might be thought a tough problem, but Johnny Griggs had a willing accomplice in real estate who had found many a place for the Brothers, and who was not daunted by The Great Man. This character was one Valentine, a baggy-suited, pomaded, jewelry flaunting, overweight, dark, middle-aged man whose office on South Coast Highway had a little red heart over the door.

On Valentine's wall within, there was a cartoon of a man lying across a desk with a knife sticking out of his back, the caption of which was, "Sorry, Charlie. Business is Business." Valentine came up with the house, and Tim and Rosemary moved in. A flight of wooden stairs descended through clumps of bunch grass and spikes of flaming Devil's Poker to the beach. When we first rushed down upon it, there was an exaggerated low tide.

At that point on the coast the beach was flat and long, sloping away gradually in a long shelf of grayish wet sand at low tide, remarkably featureless and free of objects, except for an occasional smooth boulder sticking up above the level of the sand. On the seaward side of each boulder, the retreating suction of the tide had scooped a hollow, which remained full of water. In one of these little pools a hundred and fifty feet out toward the receding, sighing waves, was an octopus.

I had captured thousands of octopi during the years when I collected biological specimens. In those days, I monitored the excessively low minus tides of winter, and haunted the tidal flats at San Onofre and Dana Point, hauling canvas buckets, and collecting as fast as I could while the normally inundated rocks were briefly exposed. There were always a few Portuguese and Japanese men after the octopi as well. They used copper sulfate, known as "bluestone," attached to metal rods which they inserted in crevices in the boulders. This toxic chemical, about to be outlawed, made any octopus in any such crevice quickly emerge. I found that I could accomplish the captures more simply with ordinary table salt. I learned to recognize the characteristic octopus holes in the sand. They were nigh impossible to dig out, but a little salt poured down one had the resident octopus come oozing out in a hurry. In this way, I always could get a hundred or more on any given afternoon, only stopping when the sun waned and the sea crept back in. Many octopi I collected were between six and eighteen inches in diameter across their outspread arms.

The one I found in company with Timothy Leary was at least five feet!

Tim didn't seem very impressed, nor did any of the others who were there. They were mildly interested, but not as excited as I was. I suppose Tim was just used to spectacular displays, but even in that case, he might have been a little more enthusiastic. I tried to drape the creature over my shoulders like a cape, but it was writhing and squirming too energetically, so I carried it out to the water and released it. It shot away in a cloud of ink.

Dick Aldcroft, the spaced-out inventor of a projection kaleidoscope, was in town to install one of the devices at Mystic Arts World. He and Tim had known each other in NYC, so we decided to go fishing together. I had a small inflatable boat that was big enough for three. We launched it through the surf in front of Tim's house, and paddled out to the offshore kelp beds. We tied up on the outside of the kelp and angled a little. Dick Aldcroft was a kind of techno-genius, but mentally he was somewhat like a loosely tethered helium balloon bouncing at the end of its string, collecting stratospheric thoughts, and only occasionally dipping down to the level of ordinary mortals to utter a disconnected phrase or two.

The talk was marginal and so was the fishing, but the day became dramatic anyway when a California gray whale abruptly rose right next to our boat, and blew a spume of vapor into the air that drifted over us. That animal had some severe halitosis! Gray whales are not the biggest whales, but this one was easily four times the length of our dinghy, and close enough to reach out and touch. The beast rolled over enough to cast a big, warm, curious eye upon us, and then it sank back into the sea without agitation.

This event did impress Tim, and even had Dick Aldcroft jabbering for a while.

The best fishing trip I took Tim on was an excursion on a sport-fishing day boat out of Newport Beach with Gary Paris, the dapper man who ran the clothing store at Mystic Arts World. I had been watching the reports, and noted that the bonito, a small tuna, were present in great numbers. Bonito are marginal fish to eat, but great fun to catch on light tackle. I was pleased to discover that the skipper of our boat was none other than Bud Brown, of the hunchback Brown Boys Twins, who had been my boyhood neighbors.

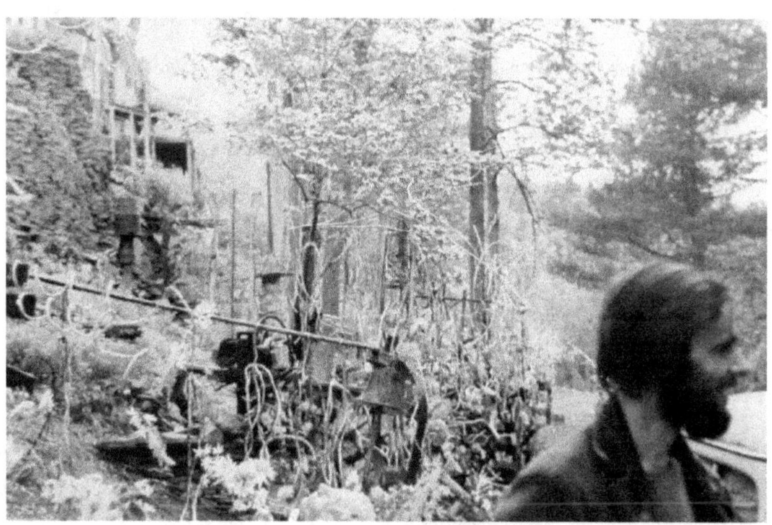

Figure 65: Dick Aldcroft, inventor of the projection kaleidoscope, at Clarence Schmidt's castle at Woodstock. All the trees and branches are wrapped in aluminum foil. Photo by Dion Wright.

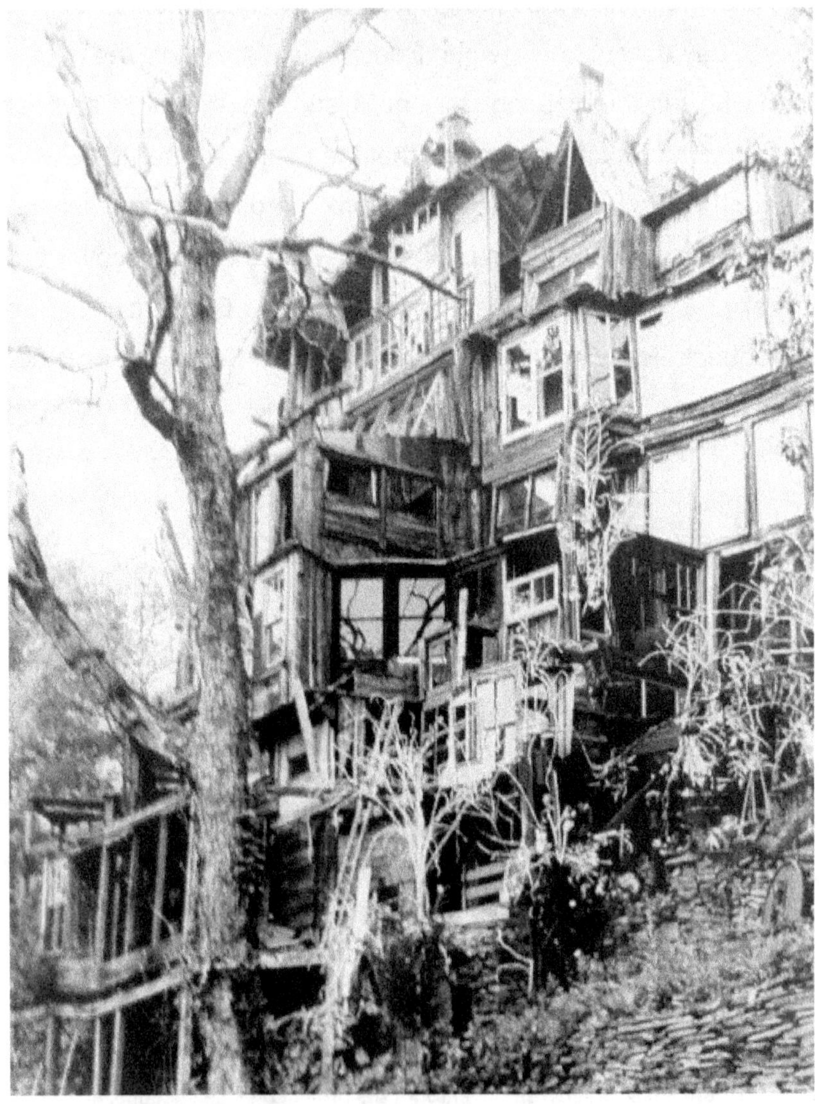

Figure 66: Clarence Schmidt's castle at Woodstock. He had a living room in it, made completely of dried Christmas trees, with the lights still in them. Of course it burned down. Photo by Peter Jones.

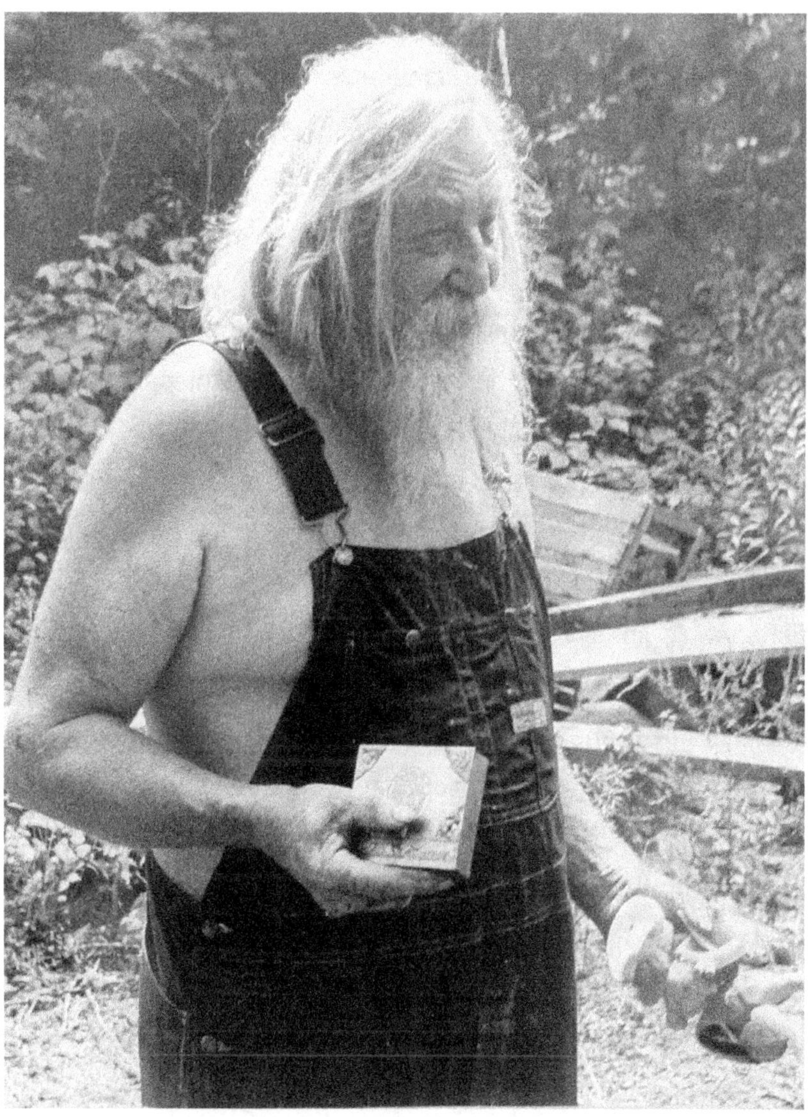

Figure 67: Clarence Schmidt at his castle in Woodstock. "Everyone has his own bag of delusions to carry on his back. Whomsoever calls me mad man shall learn to look upon the bag he carries behind him to be assessed." Photo by Peter Jones.

We exchanged a little light banter as the boat chugged out of the harbor. Bud was eying Timothy Leary closely, and finally said, "Say, your friend there is some kind of folk singer, isn't he?" I had a hard time keeping a straight face, as I told Bud, "Yeah, I suppose you could say that." The fishing was all that could be desired. Boats from miles up and down the coast gathered in a close flotilla off Dana Point, where several acres of the sea were boiling with large bonito of five or more pounds, which were hectically gobbling the millions of anchovies that were the focus of their attention. Anchovies have a permanent panic-stricken look on their faces, and who can blame them?

As the Bonito gorged on the anchovies, a huge hammerhead shark cruised back and forth, it's ominous shape passing under the boat at about ten feet deep, biting the Bonito whole off the fishermen's' lines, vulnerable as they were being hauled up to the boats by the wildly excited fishermen. It is a unique and impressive experience to reel in a fish head, with the fish's eye still glinting fiercely before clouding over. Everybody caught lots of the voracious Bonito which were bleeding and thundering their lives out on the deck by the dozens. Tim gazed upon them and said, "My God! What brutes we are!" No argument there. Poor Gary Paris lost his brand new rod and reel, which went over the transom while he was helping some guy untangle his line, so even the best day has something imperfect in it.

When Tim had engineered the purchase of the Idyllwild ranch in lieu of the Huxleyesque Island hitherto envisioned by Johnny as the "drop-out" commune, he and Rosemary moved to it, away from Laguna, and our fishing excursions stopped. I pretty much stopped fishing altogether from then on.

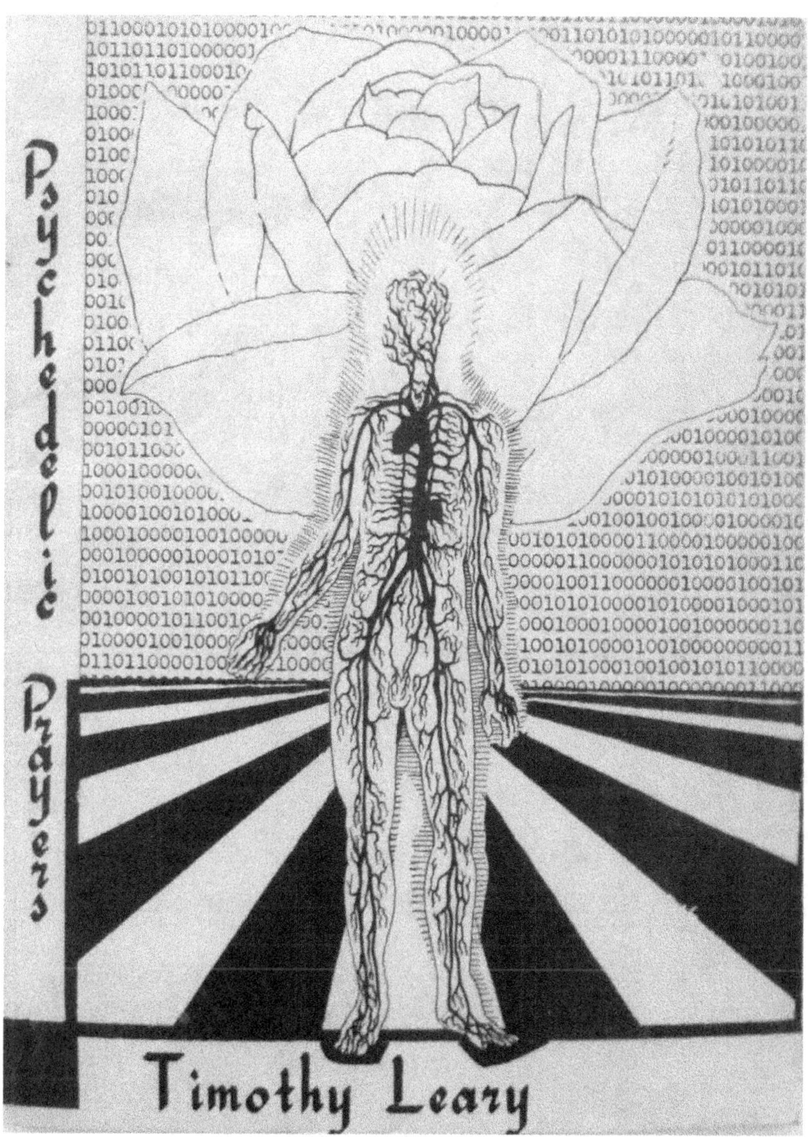

Figure 68: Dion Wright's cover for the Brotherhood edition of Timothy Leary's "Psychedelic Prayers," 1968. First graphic use of binary code as a design element?

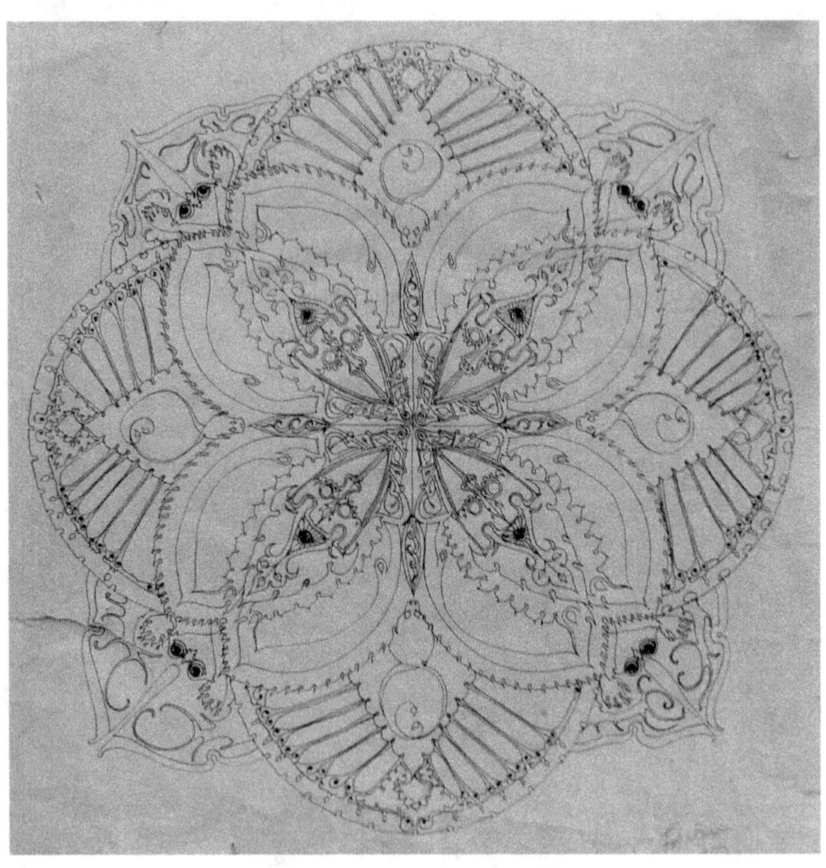

Figure 69: Freehand Mandala in ink on paper by Susan Frahm.

Chapter XVI

Dwight and Miriam

Dwight and Miriam Bulkley found themselves in the late '60s in Laguna Beach as the responsible but hip scoutmasters within the flood of zany youth. He had been in the diplomatic corps in Siam, and she was a rancher's daughter from the hot, dry, bare Arizona town of Buckeye. They were both excellent physical and intellectual specimens. They had come together in the Dianetics program of L. Ron Hubbard, before that group morphed into Scientology, and before Hubbard morphed into paranoia. When that happened, they exited the movement and set up housekeeping in Laguna Beach, CA, where they soon were interfacing with the lunatic fringe. They were solid psychedelic people from precincts separate from the Harvard group, and from the blue-collar Brotherhood. They set up their household on the hillside, and attracted a fiercely loyal set of friends who were not particularly special people. They were just the people among whom Miriam and Dwight landed, and it was clear that anybody whom they landed near would soon become their close friends.

Dwight Bulkley had the rational mind of a scientist, and was on an emotional even keel. He spoke many languages and was always in a mood to rival Santa Claus. Miriam was a fox who had the emotional nature of an amusement park ride. She was plenty smart, but not as intellectual as intuitive; almost a mind reader, but very close to the vest about her ability to have insight. They made an interesting couple, and they had sons, two older sons that Miriam had produced in two former marriages, and one of their own who was just a boy. The eldest of these thought only of flying, and how he could become a pilot. The middle one, Andy, became the most True Believer passionate disciple of John Griggs. The youngest one devoted himself to surfing.

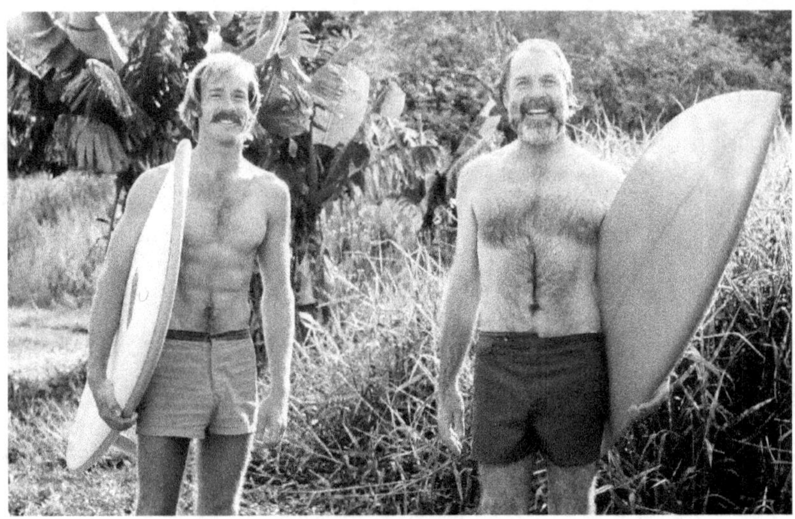

Figure 70: Son and Father. Brian Bulkley and Dwight Bulkley.

A big man, strong and fit, was Dwight Bulkley. He first wore his hair in a military-style buzz cut that lengthened as time went on. His eyes were blue and clear and open to everything in the universe, all of which he greeted with a huge habitual grin. The most unusual and interesting feature of his face was a small wen that was perfectly centered where his third eye would have been.

Dwight had been on many cosmic excursions, and he seemed to have the professorial élan of a traffic cop regarding the detours, sharp turns, pitfalls, and washouts along the highway of expanded consciousness. It worried him that youngsters might get into trouble entering the terra incognita of the psychedelic experience, so he published a little guide book called *Psycles* to help the wayfarer along the by-ways of random initiation. These *Psycles* may have been somewhat abstruse, but they had the undeniable value of assuring the pilgrim that, since this little guide book existed, there would likely be a way back. *Psycles* were in stacks, free for the taking, on the counter of the metaphysical bookstore in Mystic Arts World.

Warm and open Miriam loved to tell the story of how she and Dwight had once gone to the zoo, maybe in Portland or Seattle, and that there they had come upon a new child Asian elephant in its paddock, standing as far as possible from the people with its head pressed into the corner. Dwight called out to the little elephant in the Thai language of the Siamese mahouts, and the elephant straightaway turned and ran to the fence, its trunk extended, and tears pouring out of its eyes. Miriam said that tears were flowing across the board...but of course, they could not stay.

Timothy Leary was in Laguna with certain obligations that he intended to meet. He had to, if he was to get money. He was

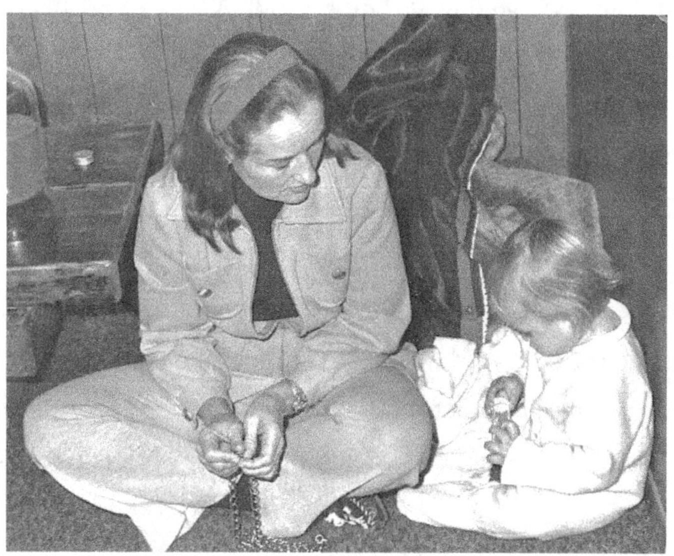

Figure 71: Miriam Bulkley and friend at Mystic Arts World.

contracted to write two books, *High Priest*, an autobiography, and *The Politics of Ecstasy*, a book-length treatise on how Tim anticipated the future, particularly the future of mind-expanding chemicals in the United States.

The environment at Mystic Arts World, and John Griggs' house, and at the Leary beach pad were all too roistering with groupies for Tim to have any peace for concentration on writing, so it happened that he became a secret house guest at the Bulkley home at Top of the World in Laguna, where Tim wrote *The Politics of Ecstasy*. *High Priest* was written at the Ranch.

Between hanging out with John Griggs in the big wide world, and having Timothy Leary working at his parents' house, Andy, who had the inclination and the disposition for it, soon became the most committed idealist in the whole Brotherhood, with the exception of the testifying prophet himself, John Griggs. Andy's enthusiasm was passionate, and it carried him through all the vicissitudes to come. It may be carrying him still. Andy and Candy, that euphonious pairing of names, happened when two sisters married two of the brothers, and went hopefully into the future.

Eventually Tim put together the deal to buy the Fobes Ranch up on Mt. San Jacinto, and talked John Griggs into it, thereby scuttling the Huxley-derived island plan and splitting the Brotherhood. Tim and John invited Dwight and Miriam to go and live at the Ranch, where there was plenty of room, with none of the buildings burned down yet. There was only one road in, of several dirt miles, which caused Dwight to smilingly decline. "I don't think it's a good idea to live on the center of a bull's-eye," said he.

Andy and Candy went there to live.

Chapter XVII

Tim & Rosemary

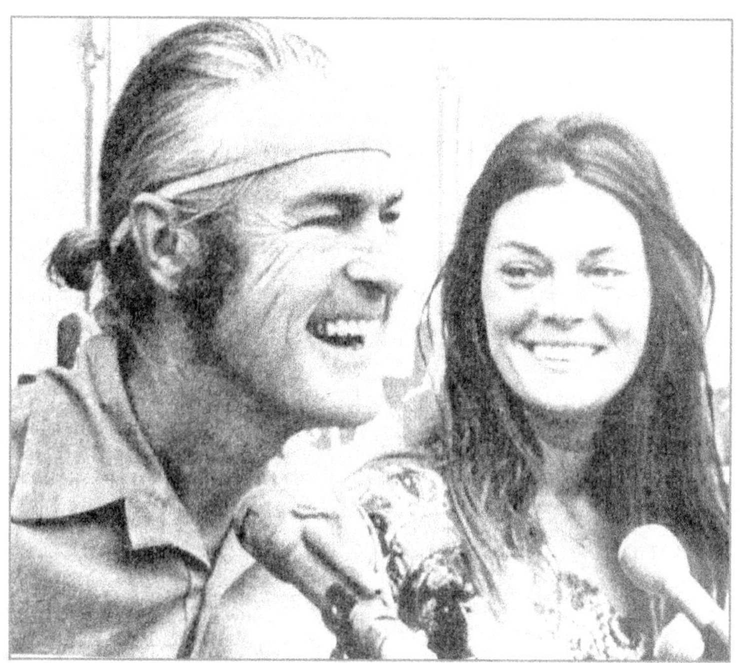

Figure 72: Timothy Leary and Rosemary Woodruff at the peak of their celebrity.

Soon after we returned to Laguna from that problematic excursion to the Lama Foundation in New Mexico, where Steve Durkee and John Griggs failed to reach a summit, Timothy Leary and the stately Rosemary became fixtures of our society. Margaret and I stood in a slightly different relationship to Tim and Rosemary than the brothers and their wives did. To John Griggs and his fellow travelers, Tim was like a sort of holy man, but to the brothers who were happy enough without a guru, he was beside the point. To me he was an intelligent academic who'd latched onto an interesting mode within which to steer his careening karma. The Brotherhood, it seemed to me, functioned as a private socio/anthropological, pharmaceutical experiment for Dr. Leary, who regarded them on hail-fellow-well-met terms that also had a sinister whiff of the mad scientist and his lab rats. As a scientific experiment, there were no controls, but it seemed, all the same, as if Tim was watching closely for results. This observation is mine alone, and certain true believers demur.

One time Margaret and I were over at Tim and Rosemary's house on Gaviota Drive for dinner, and Tim, always a laughing and joking raconteur, reflected, "Look there you are, Wright, and there is Margaret, a Lerner. And Rosemary is a Woodruff; two pleasant herbs. But ME? I'm all Leary!" and he began mugging and wriggling his fingers. God, that man could be charming good company.

Before he had actually been coaxed to Laguna, John Griggs had been annunciating Timothy Leary like John the Baptist touting Jesus, so the arrival of the Great Man in Laguna Beach was somewhat like the fulfillment of a prophecy. Tim knew perfectly well that he wasn't Christ, but he enjoyed adulation, so he came on like the reluctant virgin, or the secret guru, archly letting people believe what they wanted. Some Brothers, dazzled by Tim, lavished him with every indulgence they could provide, while other Brothers viewed him with the skepticism of guys who had bought used cars before, and wanted to look under the hood. The upshot was that Timothy and Rosemary stayed in Laguna, a watershed event, which changed everything. Their insertion into the Brotherhood body-politic worked for John, but didn't work as well for others, resulting in schism. The disaffected ones mostly went to Maui.

When the Ranch near Idyllwild had become the default place to establish the dropout Brotherhood commune, arranged by and for the benefit of Timothy Leary, Johnny went about setting it up on a basis he deemed workable. It was a very chauvinistic and tribal system, with the women and the men as distinctly separate as within any recondite New Guinea highland tribe. In my view it was problematic whether it was John's created community or Tim's private psychological experiment; probably both. Tim had clearly preempted Johnny's leadership role, at least within the balance between himself and John. Some of the other Brothers seemed less-than-convinced, and somewhat held their commitment back as they watched events unfold. I was most definitely a skeptic. Eventually there was a moment between John and Tim, where they had to be on opposite sides, and which had startling consequences. John had decided that in order for the community to function in a healthy way, all of the adult people who would live at the Ranch must be couples, as in nuclear famiies, or so he told me.

There were lots of big black rattlesnakes infesting the brush at the Ranch. They were killed as fast as they were discovered. A dog or two was bit, but no people, so I suppose the extermination was prudent, but all the same, I didn't much like the symbolism and esoteric implications of killing anything within a Buddhistic atmosphere, even poisonous vipers. I suppose they had to do it, kill the snakes, but it gave me the creeps, and felt to me like it was a crime against the spirit of the place. I mentioned it to John, but he brushed it off.

A confrontation between John and Tim came about over Tim's son, Jack. That little Ranch world of grown-ups living in couples, with assorted children, was compromised by young Jack Leary, who was there because of Tim, and neither a child nor an adult. He was grown up enough to up-end the balance of John's social arrangements, because he was a handsome young man whose libido was at first full flower. The Brotherhood wives and mothers were all in their early '20s themselves, and they were entranced by the romantic young Celtic. One young wife acquiesced to the lusty youth, perhaps partly explained by how their social roles had gone retrograde from the Women's Lib atmosphere that prevailed outside the Ranch, but was scarcely known within it. At least one of the girls wanted more freedom, and young Jack provided a fantasy relief valve. John couldn't tolerate it, and warned Jack and Tim that adultery had to stop. When it did not stop, John had to confront Tim. Despite Tim's position as the guru, John saw that, as the political leader, he had to do something to protect his little society from breaking up because of a loose sexual cannon. The eventual consequence of the dalliance was that the cuckolded husband eventually betrayed The Brotherhood.

Tim must have seen that the essence of the confrontation with John over Jack was a classic incident of church (himself) versus state (John), but it's almost certain that John did not see it in such terms at all. To him it must have been horribly wrenching to finally have to go to Tim and declare that Jack must leave the Ranch right away. That's how it happened that Tim and Rosemary drove Jack down off the mountain to Laguna Beach in their battered old black Plymouth, emotionally overwrought, and came to a stop illegally parked at "Dodge City" in the middle of the night. That's where their car was discovered by Detective Neal Purcell, the relentless policeman who shadowed Dodge incessantly, determined to catch Timothy Leary. The stories diverge as to detail, but agree that there was pot discovered, and that eventually Tim was convicted for it; the bust that sent him to the penitentiary, and sent Neal Purcell's career onward and upward into the position of Chief of Police in Laguna Beach.

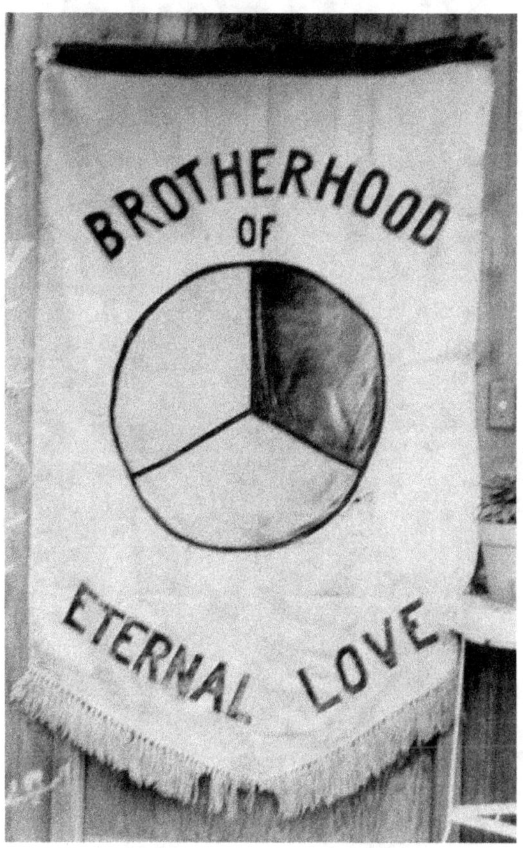

Figure 73: Hollywood parade banner sewn by Carol Griggs, 1967.

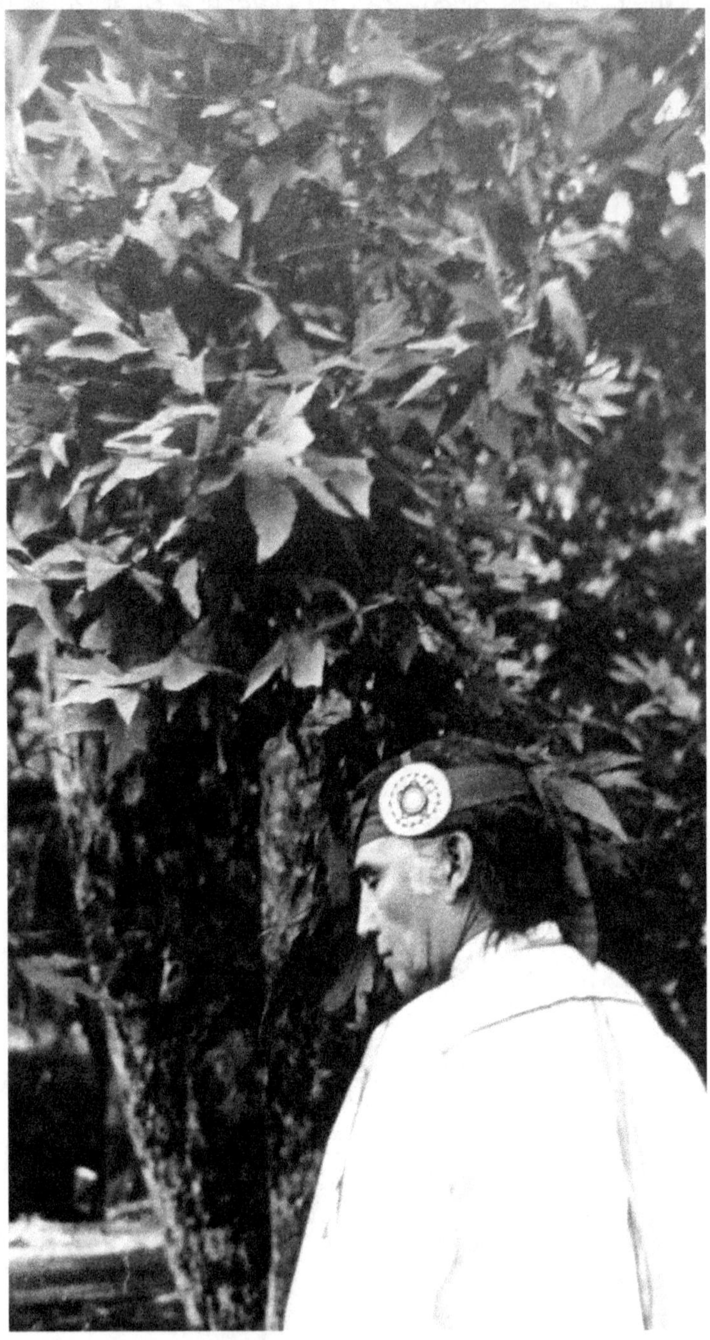

Figure 74: Cemu. Chumash shaman advisor to the Brotherhood. He was the traditional medicine man of the Chumash Indian tribe centered around the Santa Monica Mountains. Photo by Dion Wright.

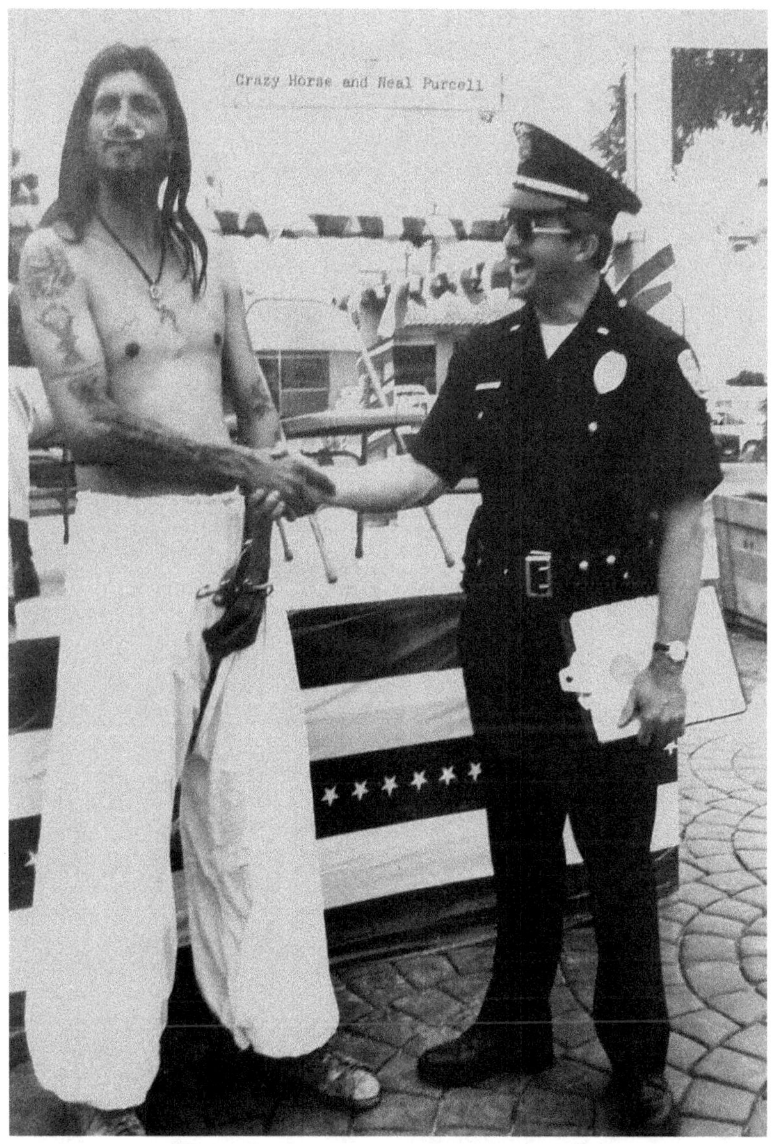

Figure 75: Cajun sword-swallower Crazy Horse, with Officer Neal Purcell before he became detective and before he became chief.

Chapter XVIII

Bathtub Chemistry

Human beings will pursue the light, and if the light comes through a chemical, they will pursue that chemical.

Psychedelic consciousness-expansion is the case in point. The chemicals that helped the pursuit of heightened awareness had been made illegal almost as fast as they had appeared. Apparently Society, being largely a conglomeration of historical privileges and vested interests, doesn't easily tolerate sudden and extreme consciousness expansion, maybe because it sometimes has the drastic effect of demonstrating how "the emperor has no clothes".

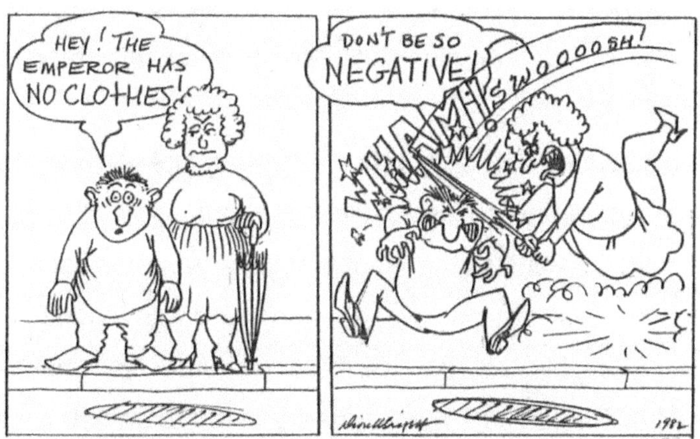

Figure 76: Illustration by Dion Wright.

Human beings will also pursue chemicals which make them feel good, but which dim the light, such as alcohol and opiates, one being legal and the other illegal. Why is there a distinction of this kind? Both are destructive.

All that is necessary to encourage a personal pursuit to bloom into a major social confrontation, it seems, is to prohibit it. People, being what they are, will test laws which deny them what they see as their innate rights. If the unfolding of their nature comes through the use of a substance, they will desire that substance, whether society forbids it, or not. Commercial exploiters will see profit in egging-on resistance to prohibitive statutes. In America, partly because of Puritan cultural roots, substance use is often characterized by some moralists as substance abuse.

Substance abuse is a real thing that does occur, but all substances are not the same, although many basically different sorts of chemicals are lumped together as unacceptable, while others are accepted, despite their obvious destructiveness, alcohol and nicotine being the most clear examples. No chemical groups could be more different than psychedelics and opiates, yet they are forced together within the social mechanics by definition as "drugs".

The stewards of proper behavior react to unlicensed freedom, especially in their children. Reaction comes in the form of repression. A culture of suppression takes shape, soon punctuated by all the excesses that go along with trying to control the uncontrollable, up to and including murder and mayhem. A bureaucratic machine emerges, and grows into an establishment with a life of its own. As such, it wants to survive, like any organism. Once the control mechanism has gathered momentum, the conflict between repression and resistance naturally gives birth to an illicit commerce. After that, it becomes almost impossible to get back into a state of balance. When economic forces are in play, the inertia becomes tidal. Reevaluation of the "problem" in the light of new knowledge, and reconsidering data once misunderstood, become next to impossible. The police function is concerned with its own survival, annual budgets need to be increased because of the momentum, and illicit commerce becomes concerned with maintaining profits, both for the malefactors and the police, locked together into a symbiosis where commensalism, mutualism and parasitism are all in play. The individual, as usual, is caught between titanic corporate forces.

The experiment of Prohibition in the American 1920s was our parents' and grandparents' case-in-point. The most otherwise well-behaved citizens went to "speak-easies" to have a drink or three. It became a fashionable behavior, associated with entertainment and being 'modern', to support a culture which was driven and made possible by gangsters. These gangsters set a deplorable mode of behavior, which, nonetheless, and through the very media run by the conservative element of society, became romantic icons of resistance. Thugs were willy-nilly embraced as Robin Hoods. This folly had echoing effects into the future, when bad boys later aped these worst persons in the history of the Republic as some sort of heroes. Prohibition, an experiment so profound that it was defined in a constitutional amendment, and then un-defined by a subsequent amendment of repeal, failed utterly, but the lesson of it was lost to subsequent generations. It was repeated in all its woes when the Consciousness-Expansion movement within academia blossomed into the Psychedelic Revolution, which was carried into the streets by blue-collar activists led by the novelist Ken Kesey and rebel academics like Dr. Timothy Leary, the Harvard University psychologist.

During the '20s, "moonshine", or "white lightning" was the firewater concocted in "stills", short for distilleries, which dotted the rural backwaters of the nation, producing alcoholic beverages utterly without quality control, and only inhibited by violent repression. Instead of regulation to ensure quality, anything went, and people sometimes died or went blind behind poison "hootch". The same mechanism of legal suppression leading to homemade liquor during Prohibition occurred four decades later with regard to psychedelic chemicals. The professional manufacturing controls on LSD, legal as it was before 1966, were stringent enough to be a bottleneck. Soon after entering government (CIA) and academic circles, where it was lavishly distributed as an "inside" marvel, a demand for chemical enlightenment had been created by turned-on citizens wishing to turn on all their friends. Because of the bottleneck it became a profitable endeavor for some entrepreneurial persons to start trying to make "bathtub" chemical LSD outside of the control of the pharmacological houses like Sandoz in Switzerland, far less the Food and Drug Administration of the U.S. Government. One of these new entrepreneurs was Bill Baldwin of Laguna Beach, California.

Bill Baldwin was a breezy, slender, button-down Ivy-League style young man who looked like he might be a car or real estate salesman, so toothy and wide was his perpetual smile. The last thing he looked like was the society's idea of a dope dealer. How could anyone talk like that and never stop grinning? He had the gift of gab, all right, polished and accelerated by chemistry. Bill

Baldwin had a constant air of expectancy about him, as if he were waiting for your signature on the dotted line, and sure he'd get it, too. It was an instance of Southern California controlled style. He was a salesman, alright, and what he sold was marijuana. The clientele was there, requiring no convincing. Bill was a slippery eel, and always managed to stay ahead of the Law, although the Law was well aware of him, and longed to arrest him.

Norm Babcock, our wholesome and rosy-cheeked cop on the Laguna Beach Police Force, often mentioned Bill Baldwin, and how his smooth operation was so frustrating to the folks down at City Hall. Norm, who was raising three boys himself, was always at pains to present a reasonable facade, however agitated he may have been underneath, commenting laconically and moderately in his mid-western twang, observations that might be supposed to have strong underlying emotions. His wife, Jan Peters Babcock, was the perky purveyor of in-your-face enthusiasms, which may have been, partially at least, a symptom of denial that her sons might be drifting into the fringes of expanded consciousness.

Bill Baldwin was not a raging criminal. In his own estimation, he was a public servant. When Bill decided there might be both some bucks and public service in the manufacturing of LSD, ca. 1964, he searched for somebody who could do it. Somehow, he found a sort of juvenile savant of chemistry, a pubescent kid serendipitously named Mike Moon. However Bill had managed to discover this pimply, bespectacled and overweight prodigy, he'd struck gold, because Mike Moon could definitely produce results. Bill set him up with a laboratory in the garage/basement of his large and charming white-framed house on the south end of

Glenneyre Street in Laguna Beach, where young Moon began turning out a lot of LSD in the form of electric blue liquid. Mike Moon was happy as long as he was provided with a constant supply of comic books and candy bars. Who knows if he sampled his own product? He must have. Bill Baldwin and his colleagues certainly did. New horizons were opening in all directions.

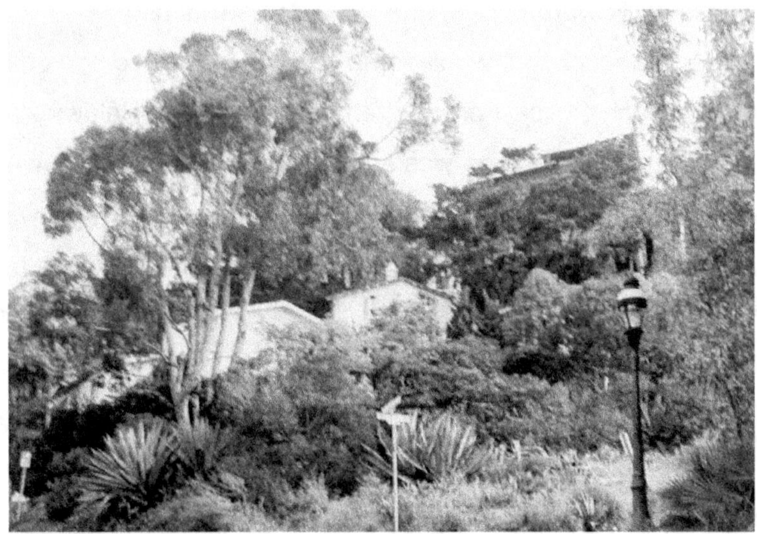

Figure 77: Bill Baldwin's manse and LSD factory on Glenneyre Street in Laguna Beach, ca. 1964. Photo taken years later by Dion Wright.

One day I looked up from welding on the giant brass serpent I was making in my driveway on the Big Bend of Laguna Canyon, for the facade of the Santa Ana Medical Arts Building. There was the smiling Bill Baldwin with his short, trim haircut, his button-down collar and his Sansabelt slacks, breezily offering me glass vials full of brilliantly blue liquid of a color that would please a neon tetra. "Try out this LSD," said he, "and tell me what you think of it." "OK," I replied, "but give me three. Chipmunk and Charlene will want to try it too."

We all loved it. It was 'da kine', as the idiom later went, despite its indubitable "bathtub" nature, being mixed up in a cellar by an adolescent, as if invented by Charles Addams. Janie Chipmunk liked it so much that she wheedled more of it out of Bill Baldwin, and started turning on the neighbors, including our morbidly obese landlady, Sally. When she came on, Sally fell on her back on the kitchen floor like a beached pilot whale, waving her arms and legs helplessly in a swoon of ecstasy as her energetic brats stared on, non-plussed, at the strange spectacle. She soon afterward started losing weight, the sort of positive consequence often seen in turned-on people before the demonization of psychedelics had kicked in. Baldwin was truly The Candy Man, taking up where the LSD "therapist", Dr. Frank Dunne, had left off, and increasing the effect on the artist community exponentially. The police were frustrated, because LSD was still legal, even if it's manufacturing in a garage was not. Apparently, the police hadn't figured that part of it out yet, for Mike Moon continued to produce in high gear for many months.

Into this milieu came the artist, Tom Blackwell, and his hip little wife, Rosalie. Tom and Rosalie were early psychedelic hands, as befitted genius artists. Rosalie was a small, dark, acute girl with one eye disconcertingly larger than the other one. She was a fine artist in her own right, producing excruciatingly sensitive spidery drawings that were of unique character, suggesting Morris Graves, Edward Gorey and Goya.

Tom was a serious and sober-sided young redhead with zero sense of self-irony, a big nose, and a humorless conception of himself as an important artist, which he actually was. He had an intense talent that burst out whenever he used paint; that caused every gesture he made on canvas to be naturally compelling to look at. Yes, he was a stunningly talented painter, but his grave attitude of self-importance was quite undone by his unfortunate resemblance to the TV puppet, Howdy Doody. That popular puppet wore a permanent smile, but Tom's signature expression was a dignified scowl, which did nothing to reduce the comedic essence of his face. Tom further, if unconsciously, emphasized the comic aspect by his bouncing gate, his heels seemingly never touching the ground.

The Blackwells had been living down on the cliffs overlooking the beach in South Laguna. With the burgeoning of the LSD plenitude, they moved into the fold of Baldwin's establishment on Glenneyre Street. For Bill Baldwin, Tom was a sort of iconic emblem of great creative respectability, which reflected well on the whole scene. That's what they thought. How Tom appeared to the rest of the town is a moot point, although cultural cover was no doubt a part of it.

One of the effects of LSD enlightenment is an emphasis on healthy living. All of the habitués at Baldwin's place became vegetarians. They were fanatical consumers of carrot juice, which they kept flowing through an Acme Juicer that was running constantly. In the back yard was a large mound of compost that was solid carrot pulp. In my mind is burned a memory of Bill Baldwin's spacious kitchen. Large plastic bags of carrots are leaning against the counter cupboards while Rosalie feeds one after another into the humming juicer. Once in a while, she adds a beet or a stalk of celery. On the floor against the wall is a collection of one-gallon glass jugs, at least three dozen of them, half of which are full of opaque orange carrot juice, and half of which are full of dazzlingly blue, transparent LSD. Tom Blackwell is tossing back one glass of juice after another. His pale complexion has actually turned orange from so many carrots; almost as orange as his hair, and the riveting effect is enhanced by his chartreuse-sprayed Little Abner boots.

Low-profile he was not, as he bounced around town like a technicolor wizard, his high profile all the more exaggerated by his habit, for a while there, of grabbing people by the lapels and telling them in no uncertain terms about how his next project was going to be a "Fuck Death Machine!!!"

By the summer of '64 I completed the daunting Medusa sculpture, took it to San Francisco, broke up with Charlene, and stumbled back to Laguna in the early fall. At this point I left Laguna for an abandoned cabin near Woodstock, New York, hitch-hiking across the country in need of a change of scene, and also on the track of "where it was at", having paid enough attention to know about Timothy Leary in Millbrook, New York. At Woodstock, I became socialized with the USCO experimental mixed-media Art group of supposedly egoless makers, including Bob Dacey, The Hip Leprechaun, who held forth engagingly in his home on Byrdcliffe, a mountaintop overlooking Woodstock.

Meanwhile our old buddy, the foxy Xandy Xhaw, had entered a new incarnation, and was living in South Laguna with Bill Baldwin's somewhat sinister partner, Bill Grimes. They were feeling increasing heat from the police, and were soon busted for dealing marijuana.

Breezy Bill Baldwin always knew when to disappear, so when his sense of imminent catastrophe became pointed, he liquidated his assets, jumped into his nice new Jaguar XKE, and split town. Rosalie Blackwell went with him.

In synch with the curious incidence of names which were uncannily appropriate to their owners, when Tom Blackwell was fallen into the depths of his endemic depression, he was indeed a 'black well'. After Rosalie had taken off for parts unknown with Bill Baldwin in his XKE, Tom was really down in the pits, broke and homeless. He was taken in and encouraged by none other than Jan Peters and Norm Babcock. Jan loved Tom for his artistic chops, and Norm saw him as the potential key to the success he needed in order to score a win in the drug-enforcement arena, after his recent demotion from detective back to uniformed officer. Norm tried not to bust his friends, unless he had to, but Bill Baldwin was fair game, and big game, too.

Being activist liberals in a reactionary town was never so easy for the Babcocks, who should have known better than to let themselves be as vulnerable as they were. They were stung by their own inattentiveness to legal protocol, and it happened like this: They sponsored a fund-raising event in their home for the NAACP, which was not a universally respected outfit in 1960s reactionary Laguna Beach. They committed the folly of raising the money, in part, by selling mixed drinks. They had no license or permit to do this, and were busted for it. Of all people, one would think that Detective Norm Babcock would be aware of this well-known law, but he somehow allowed himself to be caught with 'his pants down', and suffered demotion back to uniformed patrol officer because of it.

When Tom Blackwell defaulted into the gracious Babcock home, an opportunity to make a restorative coup must have been on Norm's mind. If he could arrange to nail Bill Baldwin, he might once again become a favored cop on the force. Norm and Jan set about turning Tom Blackwell into a secret agent, and they succeeded. Tom was simmering in bile after Rosalie had run off with Bill, so he was vulnerable to a revenge screenplay. Apparently, he was also ambivalent about reversing his idealism, for he let it slip to Xandy Xhaw what was in the wind: that he was going to New York to try to set up Bill Baldwin.

Xandy reacted with appropriate alarm. Her paramour, Bill Grimes, the erstwhile colleague of Bill Baldwin, had been convicted, and sent away, but Xandy had been acquitted, so she was enough at loose ends that she was able to pull up stakes and

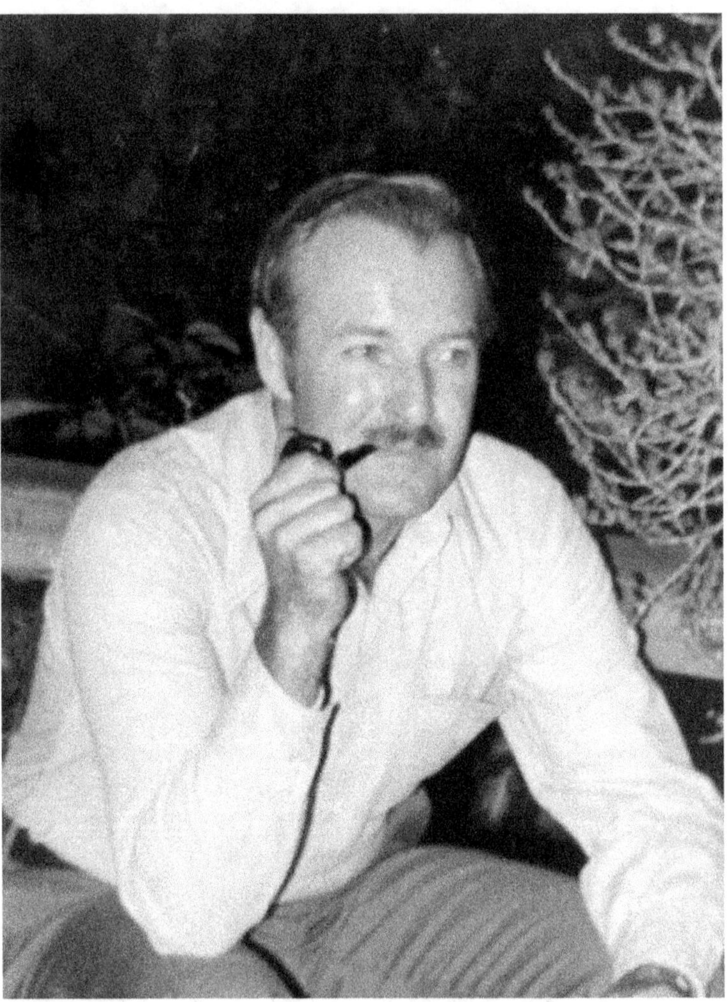

Figure 78: Detective Norm Babcock on his deck at Dunning Drive, Laguna Beach, around the time of his hospitality to Tom Blackwell. Photo by Dion Wright.

rush to New York ahead of Tom Blackwell, to sound the alarm. She had no more idea of where Baldwin and Rosalie actually were than I did, or Tom did, so she came to Woodstock, the magnetic scene where we, whom they knew, actually were. It was all a sudden crisis to us, but a somewhat academic one, since we were not directly threatened by anything. It really seemed that Tom was endangering himself. We awaited his arrival, which was immediate. His deep-set, close-together, suspicious little blue eyes were darting uncontrollably from side to side when he arrived. He had dark bags under his eyes, and looked so obviously like a person who was up to no good that it was almost amusing to see, but we knew the gravity of his situation and dealt with it the way we knew how. We all; Chipmunk, Dacey, Xandy, Tom and several others; experienced together on good Sandoz LSD, sitting down at a big round table in Dacey the Hip Leprechaun's house, eating bowls of brown rice. As we came on, all our feet melted together, and we turned into one large organism. "I don't believe what's happening under this table," cried Dacey in his radio-announcer, Brooklynese voice. Coalesced as we were into a single unit at our nether regions, above the table our heads continued to operate as individuals. Bob Dacey checkmated Tom Blackwell with a reminiscence. With the great and droll good humor he always had, Dacey reminded Tom of how they had been friends years earlier, how Tom had been a sailor who came to visit Dacey in San Francisco upon his discharge, and how he went bonkers over Dacey's girlfriend...Rosalie! He, Tom, had run off with Rosalie! How, asked Dacey, could Tom now be seeking revenge against Bill Baldwin, when Baldwin had only done to Tom what Tom had done to

Dacey? He, Dacey, was never vengeful, was he? Tom melted and morphed back into a relaxed and self-deprecating human being again before our astounded eyes, and no more was heard about plots. Neither Rosalie nor Baldwin were ever heard from again, either. Tom became a famous artist.

The USCO period elapsed, with Tom holding himself aloof from such idealistic scorning of individuality. When USCO fragmented, I took my Mandala to San Francisco, following in the wake of Stewart Brand. It was the fall of 1966.

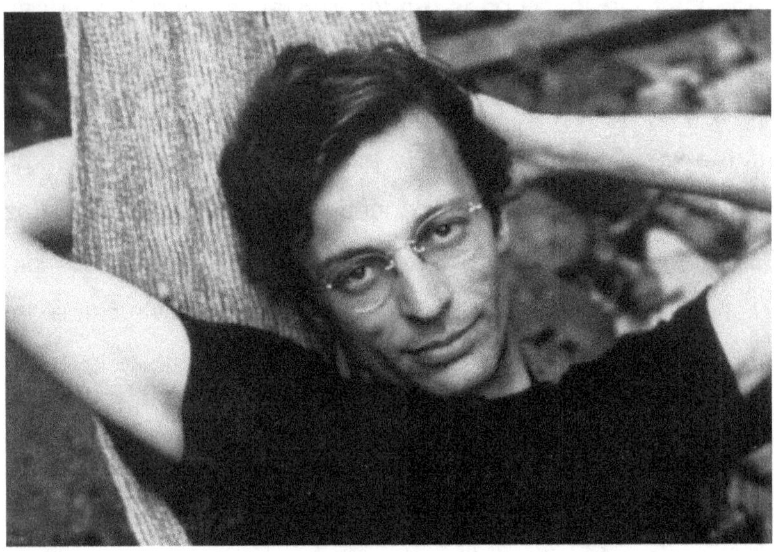

Figure 79: Bob Dacey, "The Hip Leprechaun" ca. mid-'60s.

October 6, 1966 (10/6/66) was the day that LSD was made illegal. Mavens of the occult were making much of the symbolic "Number of the Beast: 666". I was in San Francisco that day (serendipity again), and went to the Golden Gate Panhandle, where the psychedelic/liberal element was staging a protest. The action was the preamble to the so-called "Summer of Love" which would overwhelm San Francisco the following year. I passed a few non-sequitur sentences with Neal Cassady, who was there, dripping sweat, his eyeballs popping from his face, chin tucked down, wearing a tight t-shirt with the sleeves rolled up, and tossing that little sledge hammer into the air over and over, like the neurotic repetitions of a confined bear.

If I'd known a little more, I would have realized that Neal's presence was a herald that Ken Kesey could not be far behind, despite Kesey's fugitive status just then. It was a very idealistic moment. At that time the "movement", which was really the natural political consequence of expanded consciousness, was still uncorrupted by very much of the nefarious cops-and-robbers type of action that came later. No cynicism had set in yet. The huckster thrust, so painfully obvious a year later, had not yet gone into gear.

We left the San Francisco turmoil, and went back to Laguna Beach, which was still laid back and sleepy. We took a house on Woodland Drive in the Canyon. I met John Griggs. Mystic Arts World was on the drawing board. The Brotherhood of Eternal Love was swinging into high gear, super-charged by the illegalization of LSD. The gates of opportunity swung wide open, and the zany banditos rushed through, doing whatever they could to encourage new sources of LSD. Repression had its common effect of accelerating what it sought to squelch. Chemical savants flourished, and "bathtub" psychedelics proliferated as the only

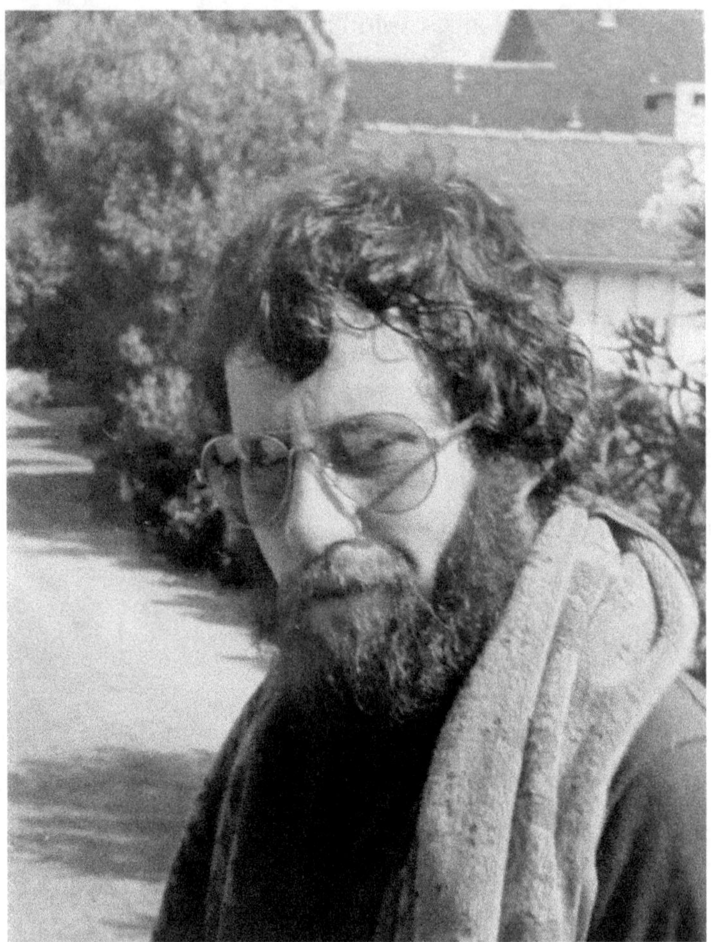

Figure 80: Tom Blackwell in Laguna in the '70s. Photo by Dion Wright.

game in town - any town in America. Psychedelic evangelism was in flower, and John Griggs was its prophet. The demand exceeded the supply, allowing the Brotherhood to flourish mightily. They weren't the only ones. "Bathtub" chemistry was practiced in many places, and yielded many different results. The will to produce the real sacrament motivated everybody, and there were chemists of great talent pursuing success at it, but with uncertain results. The problem was that the consumer in the street never knew what the true origin or nature of the substance of the moment was. It's built into individual initiative that the ego of a chef will be part of the production, ergo: inconsistency at best. Many "brands" of LSD came and went until The Brotherhood developed a substance they called, "Orange Sunshine"

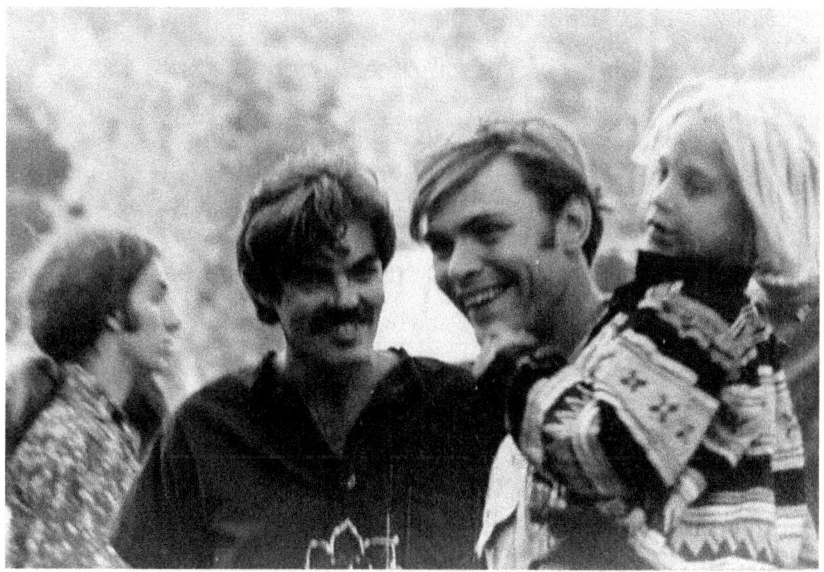

Figure 81: Brotherhood authenticity: L to R, Doyle, Russ, Chuck and Jerry Griggs

Orange Sunshine became #1 on the top 40 list of hit psychedelics in 1968 or so. The folks who made it said it was LSD. I never had a good experience with Sunshine. (God only knows what is being sold in the street nowadays, as LSD, since we see no public symptoms of spiritual revival, such as were constant signatures of the movement in the late '60s).

My opinion about "bathtub" chemicals is strictly subjective and only based on my extended experience with a large variety of consciousness-expanding substances. I perceived Orange Sunshine as an unreliable chemical, which stimulated definite and more than occasional inclinations toward craziness. I'd love to know the comparative statistics of how many experiences of enlightenment there were, as opposed to excursions into the "territory of Sammy the Butcher", as William Burroughs put it. Potential "bad trips" or "bummers" were always a possibility when taking any psychedelic. These usually had been the result of individuals' ego-armor resisting meltdown into universality, but now they became commonplace, even among seasoned veterans.

Chemicals cooked-up by artistes working as impresarios may be this or may be that, but they will always have to be accepted on faith and not as reliable Science. That's one of the reasons why the mean streets of America are currently awash in a confusion of chemistry of unknown and unknowable provenance.

The consequences of governmental meddling in matters of individual spiritual evolution are incalculable. Making pharmaceutical-quality visionary chemicals illegal was bad enough, but there was an even more sinister shift from pharmacology that opened the mind, to pharmacology that addictively indulged the body. I can't help but wonder what the government and the Fat Cats who rule it stood to gain from a tidal wave of cocaine washing over American society? Such a complete dislocation of orientation from perceptions of the mind to somatic body indulgence can't have happened so enormously without a policy in place to expedite it. Who has profited from this?

The arm of repression can only ever have temporary and occasional successes fighting an evil that reflects a hunger in human nature. The more stressed, pressured and anxious the population feels, the more and larger a segment of it will seek escape valves as available. Such craving will always continue to be exploited. Today's exaggerated drug enforcement successes do not balance tomorrow's failures, proven by the fact that the drug wars go on and on, and get worse and worse. Bad chemical products will enter the system forever, until common sense replaces venality, and the availability of pharmacologically reliable substances is restored.

Real life, and the literature which derives from it, is chock-full of absurd irony, whether the form is urban legend, or not. We are always only a cell wall away from eternity, and we ought to conduct our lives in the light of that precarious reality. Looking around, it seems that not everybody is in the same state of mortal awareness, which has something to do with the panicky reaction to the sudden immanence of some latest catastrophe or another. Un-philosophical, and lulled into soporific unconsciousness as they are, a looming threat sends ordinary folks off pell-mell after the current pills reputed to cure it, like startled chickens, thinking this buzzword anodyne will preserve them, and allow them to slumber anew. Chemicals will save us! What a way to work off karma.

Chapter XIX

Howard Warshaw

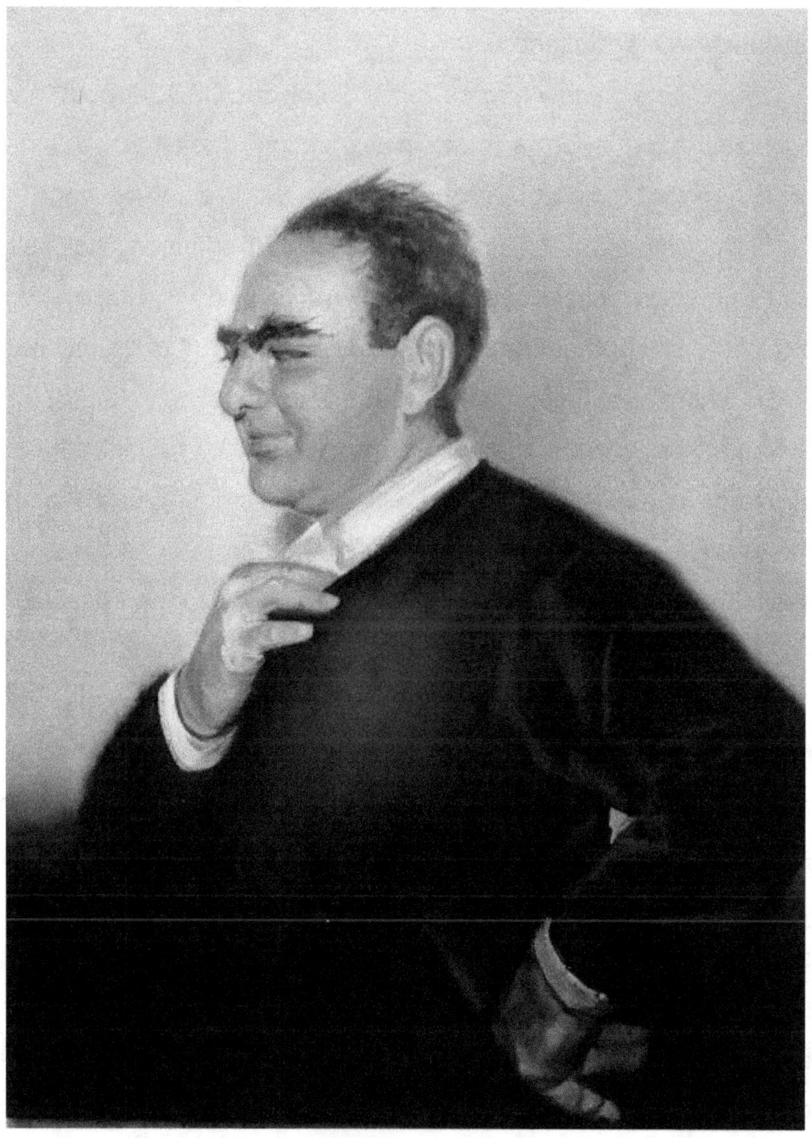

Figure 82: Howard Warshaw, painter and teacher. Rendered in oil on canvas by his student, friend, and colleague, Michael Dvortcsak.

In the 1950s there was a great man teaching at UCSB who made a terrific impression on his brightest students. He was the painter Howard Warshaw, one of the few professors at UCSB who did not have a PhD. He was there through his achievements as a painter, and his sponsorship by Rico Lebrun, and not least by the brilliance of his intellect.

In the time I knew him as a professor at UCSB, nobody had had any experience with mind-expanding chemicals. *Almost* nobody had, outside the pharmaceutical world and the world of the CIA, which was turning-on incarcerated criminals, soldiers, and their own colleagues without warning. Aldous Huxley was one of the first humanists outside the establishment to be initiated, by Dr. Humphrey Osmond of Canada.

Later, Mr. Warshaw thanked the student who had introduced him to psychedelics with the remark that this student "had caused me to raise my eyes higher than I had ever before done." His one eye, that is, since the left one was glass, a cyclopean limitation he shared with Aldous Huxley.

Howard Warshaw and Rico Lebrun were colleagues who forged their relationship working for Walt Disney. Warshaw, a graduate of the Art Students League, had been working as an animator. He told many stories about the less-than-perfect world of working under the thumb of Walt, one of history's most overbearing and egocentric prima donnas. Howard was about twenty years younger than Rico Lebrun. Lebrun's position at Disney was more elevated. Walt had hired him in the early stages of producing *Bambi* to teach the animators how animal anatomy actually worked, so that their renditions of *Flower, Thumper* and *Bambi* would carry conviction. Since Lebrun and Warshaw were both intelligent humanists who derived their methods from similar sources, and held the same heroes, they fell in with each other, and soon carried their association beyond the benighted precincts of the Disney studios.

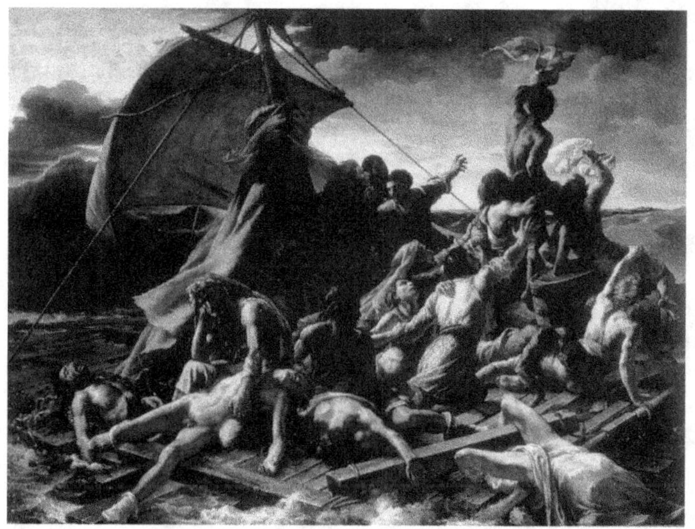

Figure 83: ***The Raft of the Medusa*** **by Gericault. Le Louvre.**

Howard Warshaw had started out as an artist being influenced by Dali, Kandinsky, with Eugene Bermann as his teacher in NY. He grew past all of these influences, retaining what was good: draftsmanship from Dali, color and composition from Kandinsky, and from Bermann, the drawing strategy of beginning from a neutral ground, tan or grey paper, and then working simultaneously toward the light and toward the dark. He was propelled more toward Humanism by Rico Lebrun, a passionate soul horrified by the excesses of Man's Inhumanity to Man that he saw in his own century, and resulted in his daunting series of figurative works about the death camps. A line of descent from the Ice Age cave painters through Goya and Rembrandt's etchings, Gericault's *Raft of the Medusa* to Picasso's *Les*

Demoiselles d'Avignon and culminating in *Guernica* were the underpinnings of the Lebrun/Warshaw posture toward what Art should be.

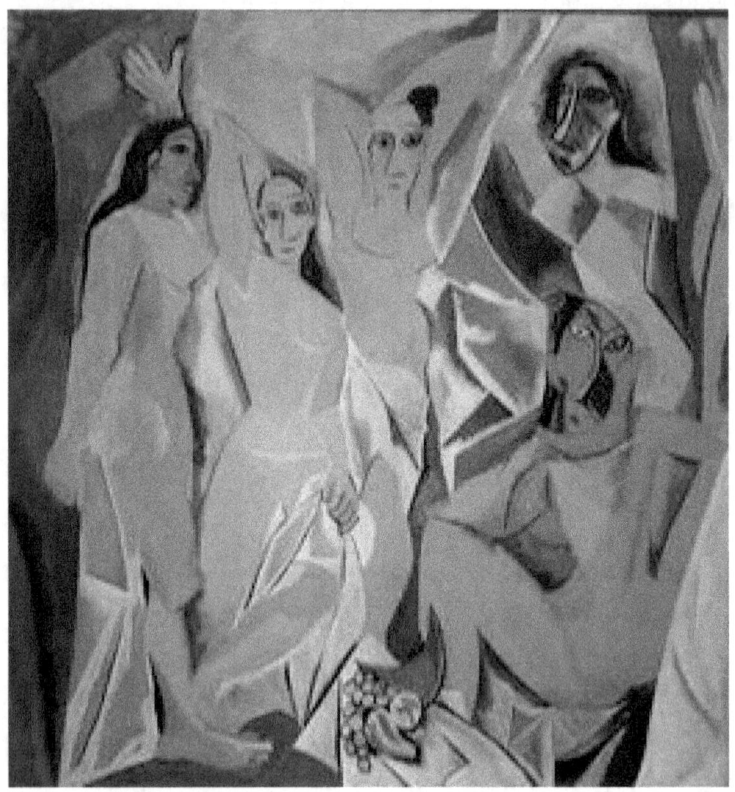

Figure 84: *"Les Demoiselles d'Avignon"* by Picasso.

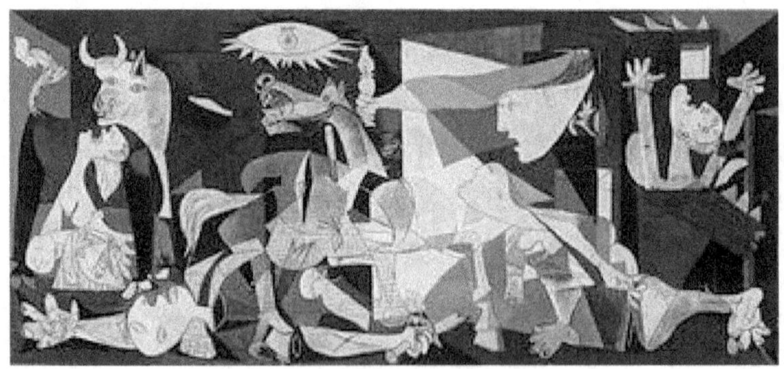

Figure 85: *"Guernica"* by Picasso.

Legend has it that one summer around 1950, give or take a year or two, Lebrun and Warshaw spent the season at Ensenada in Mexico, where they discovered a concrete sea wall along the beach of some several feet high, and many yards in length. On this wall, they commenced a painterly dialogue, drawing and painting their way along in poste and riposte all summer long until they reached either the end of the wall, the end of their finances, the end of their paint, or the end of their vacation time. The wall itself was lost. I went looking for it, and never found it.

Warshaw occupied the position of campus legend by the mid '50s. Art students wanted to be in his class, and his lecture/bull-session events drew large audiences. He could and did talk with more erudition than most of his listeners could comprehend. He was certainly the most articulate, spontaneous and educated man among all of the Art professors, who were mostly narrow specialists of one kind and another. He was also the only one splattered with paint. Warshaw roved freely through the entire history of world Art citing examples right and left to illustrate his themes, which were: Art is a noble and dignified calling; Man is a magical animal who can reach farther than he thinks he can; The shallowness of contemporary culture can be overcome by idealism and intelligence.

Since Howard Warshaw was a muralist, his principles played out in front of all his students, as his ideals and practical intentions ran into the egoism of a high and mighty architect. The architect was William Pereira, who had parlayed his successes within the growing number of campuses and their attendant buildings of the University of California into a Juggernaut of style over culture. Pereira was the fair-haired boy of the University President, Robert

Gordon Sproul, and Pereira's star was mightily in the ascendant at UCSB, a campus which was just then evolving from a WWII air base into a faux Spanish cum Japanese cum Babylonian group of monuments to the architectural syntheses of William Pereira.

All of this was to the good, inasmuch as the Pereira buildings were gracious and workable, and fit into their landscapes nicely, and functioned for the purposes intended. Unfortunately, however, Mr. Pereira seemed to have a precious conception of architecture, his architecture, at least, as being so pure and good that it could not abide the intrusion of the other Arts into its (Pereira's) sanctified precincts. This was not a good situation for a muralist to inhabit, and especially a great one like Howard Warshaw. Any half-alert Art student who knew what the Renaissance was all about was flabbergasted that the stage-setter of the new millennium, namely the Regents' anointed architect, could be so block-headed as to resent painting and sculpture.

Obviously, Howard Warshaw's closest students also wanted to paint murals, and we were all treated to a discourse of several years duration in which Howard Warshaw contended with William Pereira for walls on which to paint murals. To say that there were such walls begs the obvious. There were huge and pristine walls everywhere, and all of them were defended like the Pass at Thermopylae by the Pereira faction. Their resistance was supposedly aesthetic; that the purity of the large expanses would be diluted by the intrusion of painting. The Pereira faction never perceived for an instant that murals could enhance the walls, or give them an added (and intellectual) dimension.

Howard Warshaw prevailed, to a degree. Some walls were allowed to become murals by him and his students. But the University had to be badgered into it, and never really rose to level of the Di Medicis.

This struggle between Pereira and Warshaw may have been an early blip on the screen of the split between Art that has traditional form and content, and Art that only has form.

Mr. Warshaw could not abide mindlessness in Art. One day, a group of us were in his second story classroom, held in one of the old barracks buildings next to the scenic lagoon. It looked down on a large rookery of blue herons, who croaked primitively all the livelong day, nesting in the old eucalyptus trees. From the landing of this building, we were throwing paint down onto a canvas below in shallow amusement at aping the approach of Jackson Pollock, who was big news just then.

Howard Warshaw came upon us having this brainless fun, and hit the ceiling. If we had been in any doubt about how serious he wanted us to be before that, we were in no doubt afterward.

As it happened, Richard Serra, the fair-haired boy of monumental sculpture nowadays, was one of Warshaw's students. Later Mr. Warshaw had a dismissive and ironic attitude toward Serra, alluding to something irregular that had happened, which he would not define, and dismissing Serra as one of those minimalists who ought to know better. When Serra made the cover of Time, with his pigs in crates as sculpture, Warshaw remarked, "At last Richard has learned how to cage volumes."

Aldous Huxley came to lecture at UCSB in 1959 and '60, near the end of his days. He looked at the faculty and characterized them as “Mesozoic reptiles,” except for three men he could talk to: Dean Noble, Douwe Stuurmann, and…Howard Warshaw.

Chapter XX

A Counter-cultural Art Festival

At a loss for what else to do in the wake of the diaspora of USCO, I decided, as if by default, to follow the dictum of Dr. Timothy Leary, and to return to whence I came, bearing such knowledge as I had gleaned, to share for the improvement of the provinces. This was little enough in my case. The shutters had been ripped off and the doors blasted away so that I could see the possibilities, but my expertise was at low tide compared to such monsters as Gerd, Stewart and Steve. I moved into the Woodland Drive neighborhood of Laguna Beach, where I met John Griggs.

I had my show in San Francisco, experienced the "Summer of Love," and then returned to Laguna to monitor the slow construction of Mystic Arts World at 670 South Coast Highway. Mystic Arts World grew with a momentum like the flow of frozen molasses until Joe Miller appeared on the scene. Joe, an ex-marine artilleryman, was a jack-of-all-trades. He moved like a force of nature, whipping the languishing construction into shape efficiently, even if he sometimes left out things, and jury-rigged solutions for expediency.

We hit it off famously and made up a sort of triune aspect with John Griggs, who was no artist, but had a love of creative effort. Joe was an artist and we sort of whipped-up each other's enthusiasm. Joe got behind my tales of USCO big time, and we anticipated what the next act might be of our own creative efforts, as Mystic Arts World finally was up and running and offering monthly shows scheduled by me according to what I had sense enough to apprehend, and luck enough to sift out of the limited artistic resources available.

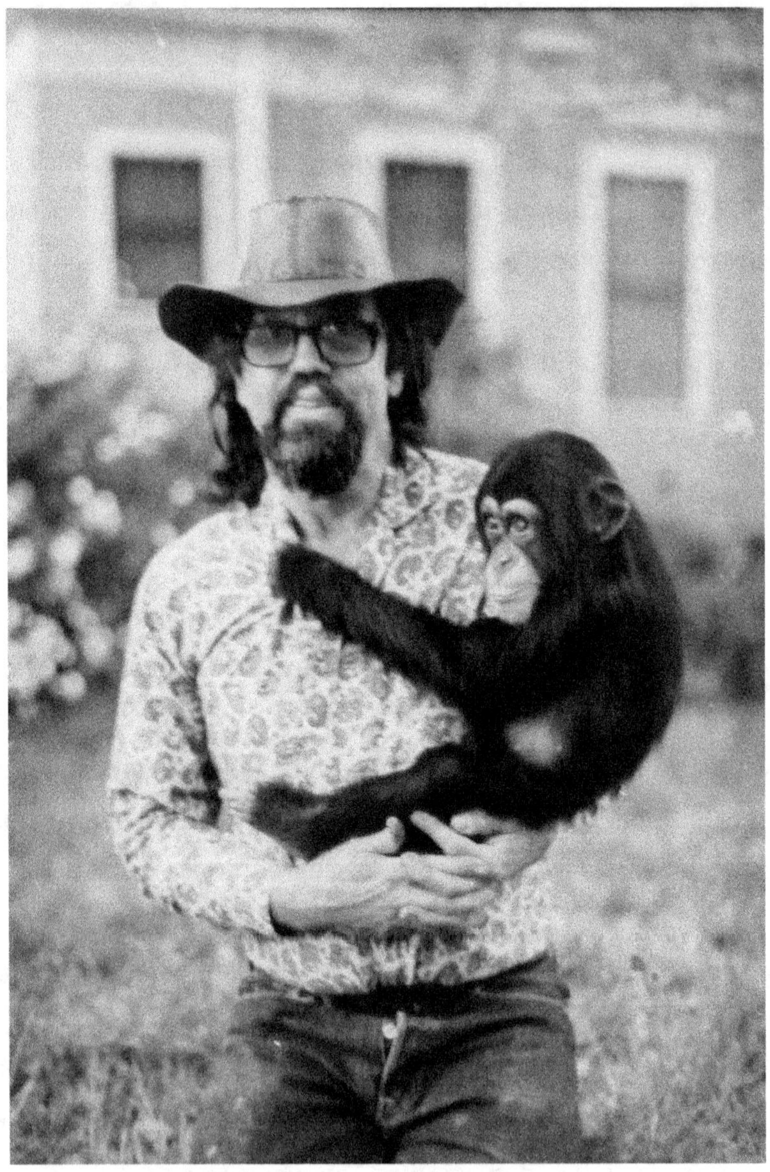

Figure 86: Joe Miller and friend in Apalachicola, FL, 1972.

When I started programming exhibitions for Mystic Arts World, I took as my philosophical ideal the qualities of Howard Warshaw.

In the spring of 1968, an intense little bulldog of a woman named Dolores Ferrell accosted me on the street, knowing that I was part of the radical creative fringe, such as it was in Laguna, touting a new, free, Art show. The new festival was to be called "Sawdust" to distinguish it from the cement floor that had been established at the Festival of Arts across the street, and to hearken back to a more nostalgic, organic, and less rigid time. This new Sawdust Festival was a reaction to the Festival of Arts by people who mostly couldn't get into it, and who vowed to nourish creative freedom, as they saw it, by not having a jury system. This begged the issue of quality control, but the rationale was that with a completely open forum, artists could develop and flourish in freedom. The premise may have been correct, for the Sawdust Festival is approaching its fiftieth anniversary, and still going strong, if radically different from the future Joe and I had imagined for it.

As an independent artist, I had learned the necessity of staying away from any group that I could perceive, and possibly avoid, including Art associations. That posture had been hammered into my soul by the San Francisco Beats, who certainly had plenty of flaws, but were dead center on this issue. All the same, Dolores was compelling, and the direction in which she was moving suited my already rebellious nature just fine, so I thought about it.

I had no "group", whatever Dolores' perceptions may have been, but I decided to concoct one; an ad hoc conglomeration for the purpose of launching the new Sawdust Festival on its trajectory with as much creative chops as it might be possible to ram into it at the get-go. I went around dragooning my more avant-garde friends of the community into joining hands, temporarily, as "The Experimental Artists of Laguna Beach".

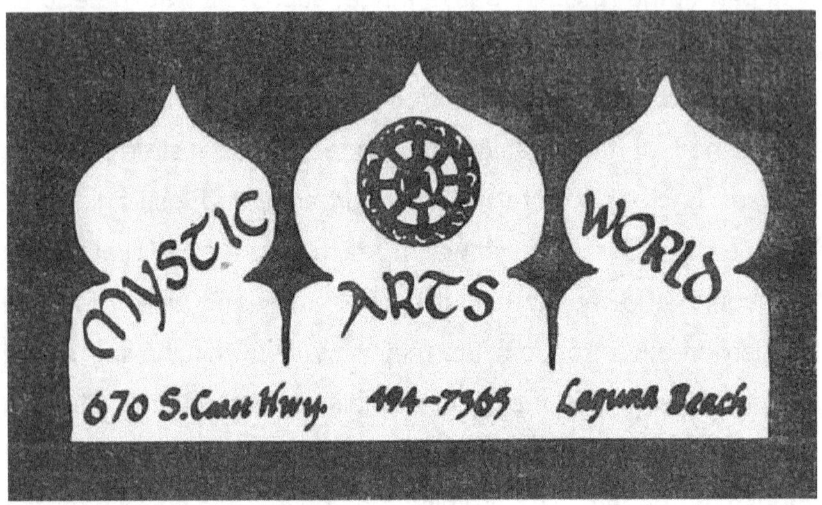

Figure 87: Business Card for Mystic Arts World.

Experimentalism in Art was revealed to me in NYC by the aesthetic juggernaut association of USCO." We were pressing every envelope of every medium in every direction in 1966-67, culminating in the psychedelic Art show, "USCO Down by the Riverside." I imagined a forum in the new festival where artists could let reign their creative imaginations without restraint. I failed to suppose the real limitations of those imaginations, and how they would too often be turned to scamming and manufacturing. Still, the Art kept improving.

Having found out, largely through USCO, far more than I could ever have anticipated in my wildest imaginings, I came back to Laguna and settled on Woodland Drive. I ran into the ferocious Dolores on the boulevard; urging me to join up with this "Sawdust" effort, i.e. back to a simpler time such as obtained in the early days of the Festival of Arts. Such nostalgia as this was romantic and unrealistic, because times had changed, but, the property was there and the opportunity to do something beckoned, so I formed that ad hoc group and away we went.

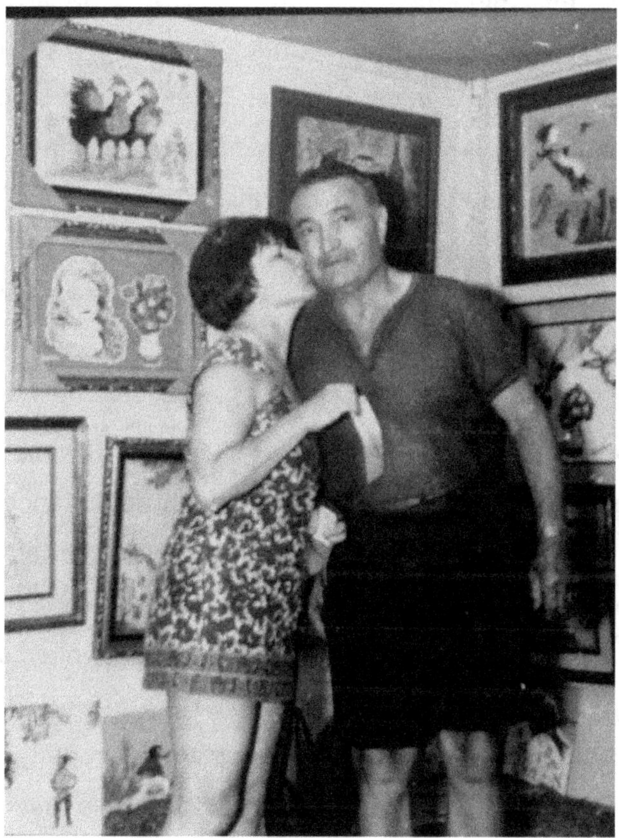

Figure 88: Sawdust '68. Delores Ferrell plants a buss on the cheek of prizewinner Pantaleone P.P. Zemoz, painter of the three-legged chicken (upper left). Photo by Dion Wright.

Now, my ad hoc group, The Experimental Artists, was at polar opposites of many of the inept Sunday painters and sundry limited malcontents that made up the population being fronted by Dolores, and her paramour, Edmund Van Deusen (an amazingly brilliant and canny businessman, but also a rebel who had rammed through the then-new Laguna Playhouse). Dolores dragooned Van Deusen on board by use of the vaginal wrench.

He was smarter than anybody else, and yearned to be an artist. Balancing Van and Dolores was another couple, the Tauriellos, motivated mostly by the ego of Mrs. Tauriello. They formed a sort of competing axis that extended into the first half dozen years of the Sawdust Festival. Those four persons, Frank & Marilyn, Dolores & Van Deusen, had quite a lot of talent among them, but they could scarcely be called "experimental," except Van. The experimenters, such as they were, were Bob Young, and me, the really active players from The Experimental Artists, most of whom were along for a fun ride which nobody, including us, expected to last more than a year or two.

Of those inept and archconservative early Sawdusters who were appalled and shocked by the sudden appearance in their midst of The Experimental Artists, a large segment of same bolted from the new show, citing "filthy hippies, and their big light show". As it happened, the majority of the first board of directors went with them, taking the treasury.

So there we were, with the Walter Funk property, and no money. Bob Young performed miracles to get the first Sawdust Festival up and running on a budget of a few bucks. He acquired some items nobody ever imagined could be "booths." including a chuck wagon, a dead fire truck, and a tall crane preempted by Joe and me.

The reactionaries who bolted dubbed themselves "The Sawdust Splinters", went on up Laguna Canyon to Vernon Spitaleri's lot at Canyon Acres to begin yet a third festival, which would feature mind-numbing conservatism, and a reinstated jury system. That group morphed into the Art A Fair, and all the founders of it were soon eliminated via their own jury system.

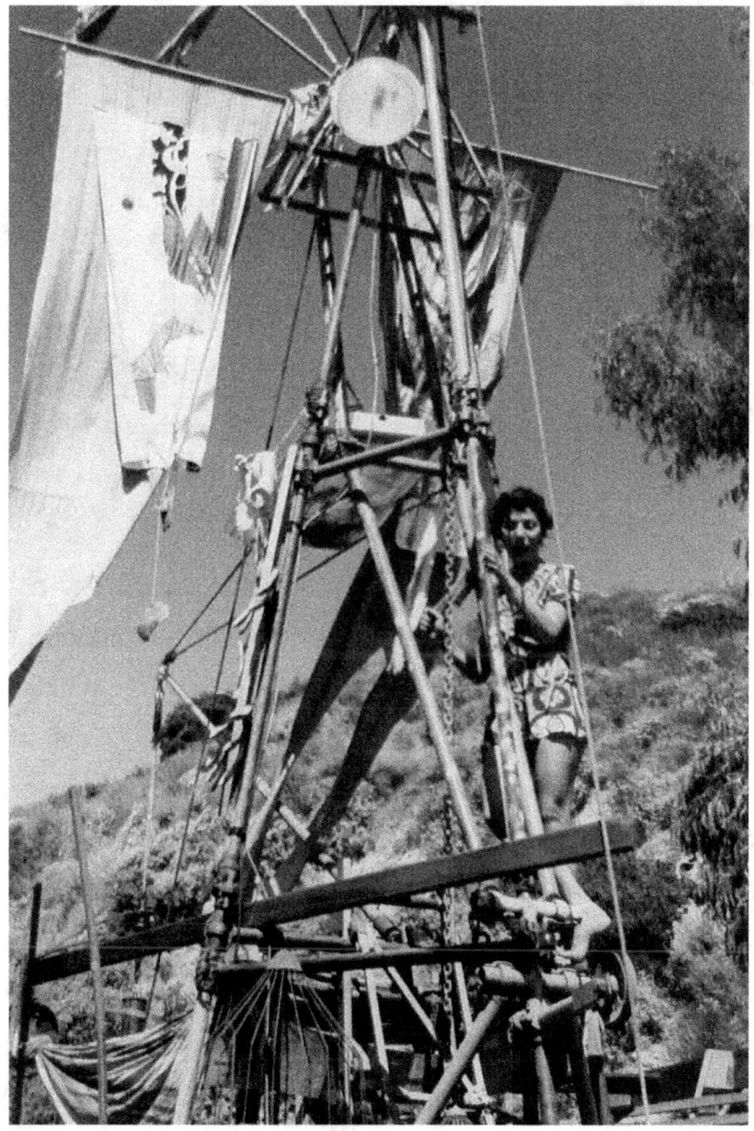

Figure 89: Julie Kahn on the Sawdust Tower. Photo by Dion Wright.

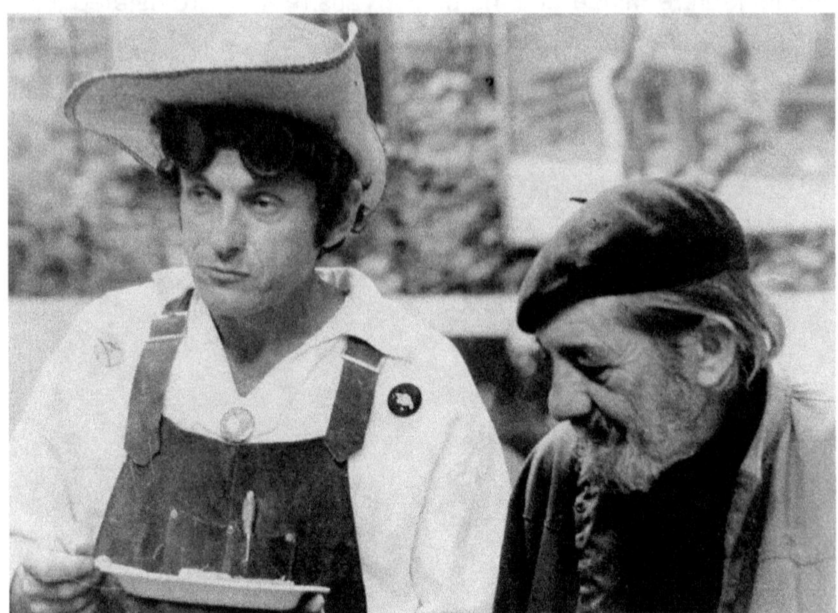

Figure 90: Dion Wright and Italo d'Andrea at Sawdust. Survivors united by common denominator of cynicism. Photo by Doug Miller.

The lively place was the new Sawdust Festival. For all its financial poverty, there was a torrent of creative energy on the loose there, and the whole community felt it. The restrictive elements of the body politic were terrified by it (read "Festival of Arts"), and its minions. The City Council, in a move that was as repressive as anything in history, decided to judge what Art and creativity legitimately might be, and they tried to squelch the use of non-traditional media (read "light show") from ever getting off the ground, by the simple expedient of refusing a permit. Whether such a permit was legal or not in the first place was beside the point, for we had no assets to fight the case. So, from a creative point of view, we got off to a somewhat crippled start.

The crippling might have been avoided but for a boo-boo by Joe Miller. Some of the City Council was willing to look at a preview of what we may have had in mind as a light show presentation, and so a demonstration was set up, where our media was to be shown on the concrete block wall of the adjoining body shop. We were impoverished as to technology at that early moment, but we managed to put together a bank of four carousel projectors, a Strobe light sent to us by Gerd Stern, Richard Aldcroft's projection kaleidoscope, tape sound equipment, and a light organ invented by John Forkner.

The programming and overlap of these effects was random, in the spirit of USCO, and besides, we were a confederacy which had little clue as to what we were trying to do. Joe programmed the slides into the carousel trays for their spontaneous projection and overlap upon the block wall, and that's where the problem occurred. The City Council showed up at the appointed hour, and we commenced to inundate their senses with our stuff. In short order it was obvious that Joe had inserted the wrong tray into one of the carousels, and instead of prosaic imagery, the City Council was treated to close-up slides of Cathy Solmes' natural childbirth. Disaster! Consternation! No permit.

We went for it anyway, as far as we could without getting shut down. Everybody from what the burghers regarded as the lunatic fringe showed up to partake in one way and another, including our old pal from Mazatlan, the erstwhile Viking, Eldon Setterholm.

Joe Miller married Julie Kahn. Ed Van Deusen broke up with Dolores, and hired a new teen-age wife, Janice Costello, with whom he eventually wrote the book, *Contract Cohabitation*. Ed's fiberglass and resin sculptures got bigger and more hideous year by year until he finally lost interest and moved on. All of these sculptures were renditions of flagrantly naked women wearing boots. Take that, City.

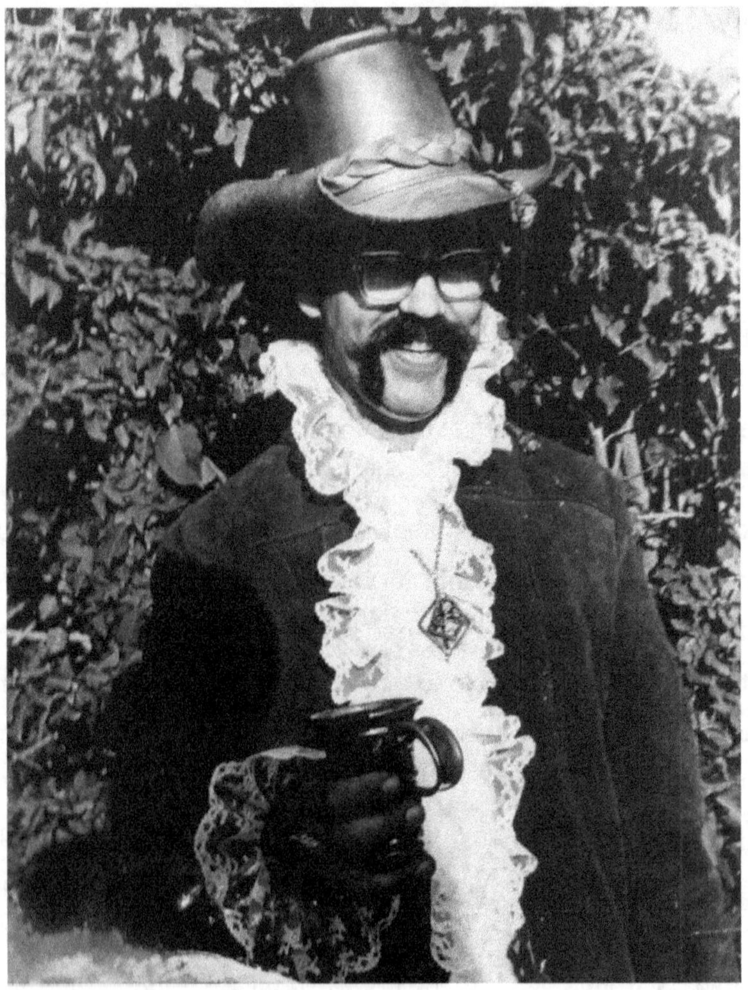

Figure 91: Joe Miller: Bridegroom. Photo by Dion Wright.

Chapter XXI

A Set of Twins

When Timothy Leary arrived in Laguna Beach in 1968, a wave of colorful, hip and sophisticated riffraff came in his wake. The first lot of these characters, many of whom seemed to me like the wee-hour denizens of an amusement arcade, were connected to Tim in one way or another. After the initial influx, other self-promoters followed, who were new to Tim's scene. Among these were the Martino Twins, perceptively called "Heckle and Jeckle" by one hippie who was on the Mystic Arts World scene. That psychedelic emporium was the stage for endless exaggerated soap operas.

Perhaps it was just my xenophobic flush of provincialism, but it seemed that there was a qualitative change in the sociology of our situation from "before Tim Leary" to "after Tim Leary". There was something MGM-wholesome about John Griggs and his original circle of wild men. Despite their buccaneer activities, their naive presumptions, and their nefarious adventuring outside of the law, they were examples of the best kind of romantic American revolutionary idealism. They saw the future, and it was good. They went for it with the pedal to the metal, a confederacy of equals with John at the wheel.

It was a Utopian goodness that the Brotherhood tried to bring into the world, but they couldn't prevail against the culture of blood and money which was the Establishment in those days...and only marginally less so, if at all, these days. The Viet Nam War was the counter-spring to the idealism, which had an idealism of its own, albeit a violent one. Dr. Timothy Leary brought in a different, more world-weary atmosphere when he came onto the Laguna scene. The fact that he was leveraged into Laguna and the Brotherhood by the determination of John Griggs piled on the irony.

The foremost quality that came with Tim Leary was the glare of media attention. Tim was notorious. He was well versed, by 1968, in his self-produced and self-promoting chapter and verse, all of it cogent, brilliant and compelling. But, somehow it rang counterfeit. Maybe that was because of cynicism. One thing John Griggs never was, was a cynic, but the Messiah he imagined so enthusiastically in Timothy Leary actually was a cynic. It's just my informed opinion, but I saw Tim as a shallow hedonist talking a deep game, while Johnny was a deep idealist with a shallow worldliness.

Upon Timothy Leary's arrival, the organic cohesiveness of the original Brotherhood became divided immediately, between those who thought of Tim as a guru, and those who did not. The fragmentation of Brotherhood society once begun, continued. Into the breach started to arrive Tim's minions from the defunct Castalia Foundation at Millbrook, NY, and other places where Tim had formerly held the catbird seat. It would be very difficult to define this influx of persons in a comprehensive and general way, except possibly by the occultist's reference to "familiars," but the tenor of the feeling given off was certainly less idealistic and less innocent...if "innocent" can be a fair and just word to use describing the Brotherhood of Eternal Love. It works by comparison.

Those Martino Twins, Dennis and David, were rude, sandy-haired, energetic, wise-cracking, short, nattily dressed, intrusive, ambitious, noisy, ubiquitous and generally irritating. I saw them careening around Mystic Arts World like a couple of coyotes looking for an injured squirrel. In short order David Martino had wooed and won the drab and introverted little Susan Leary, Tim's daughter. All of the foregoing I know because I was there and saw it. What follows is grapevine hearsay, most all of it from printed sources.

Who knows what sort of marriage David and Susan Martino had? All that I know is that Susan eventually ended her own life by hanging herself in a jail cell.

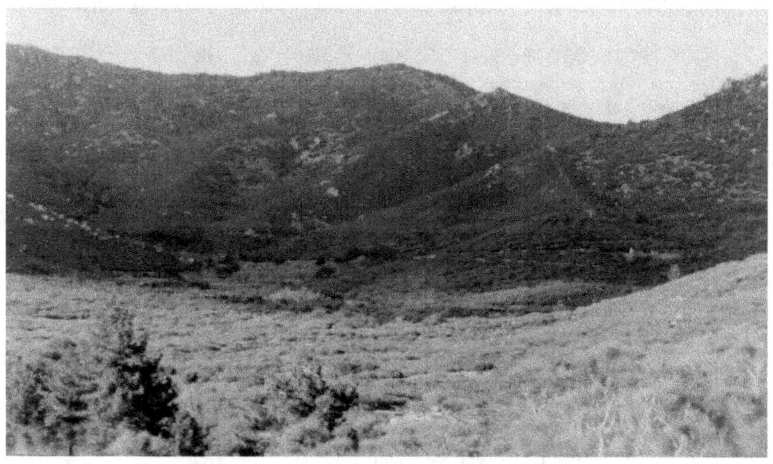

Figure 92: The physical setting of The Ranch on the southeastern flank of Mt. San Jacinto. The Pacific Trail follows the ridge. Photo taken by Dion Wright in later times.

I know that Timothy Leary influenced and engineered the shift in John Griggs's utopian plan away from the goal of setting up an ideal psychedelic community on an island, to the purchase of the infamous ranch in the San Jacinto Mountains above Palm

Springs, where many people, including Johnny, went to their doom.

Timothy Leary started running out his slowly unraveling karmic string: into the penitentiary, the hair-raising escape, and a flight that plopped him and his wife Rosemary, down in Algeria with Eldridge Cleaver and the Black Panthers. Cleaver may have thought that Tim would be a chip of political capital, but he soon learned that the silliness attending Tim was not worth his value.

He kicked Tim and Rosemary on down the road to Switzerland, where Rosemary left Tim to his unwinding parade of folly. In my view that was an irreparable catastrophe for Tim, whether he knew it or not. He was always good at casual disregard of negative realities. Tim started to have affairs, make deals, get high, remarry, and flee again, at last to Afghanistan. There he was involved in stillborn schemes with his new wife and none other than Dennis Martino, his daughter's brother-in-law.

The game was up when Interpol busted Tim on the tarmac at the Kabul airport, and thrust him back into shackles for his return trip to penal custody, where he testified against everybody who had helped him over the years. It was later revealed that Dennis Martino, who died under obscure circumstances, was the undercover agent who had set up Tim for his fall.

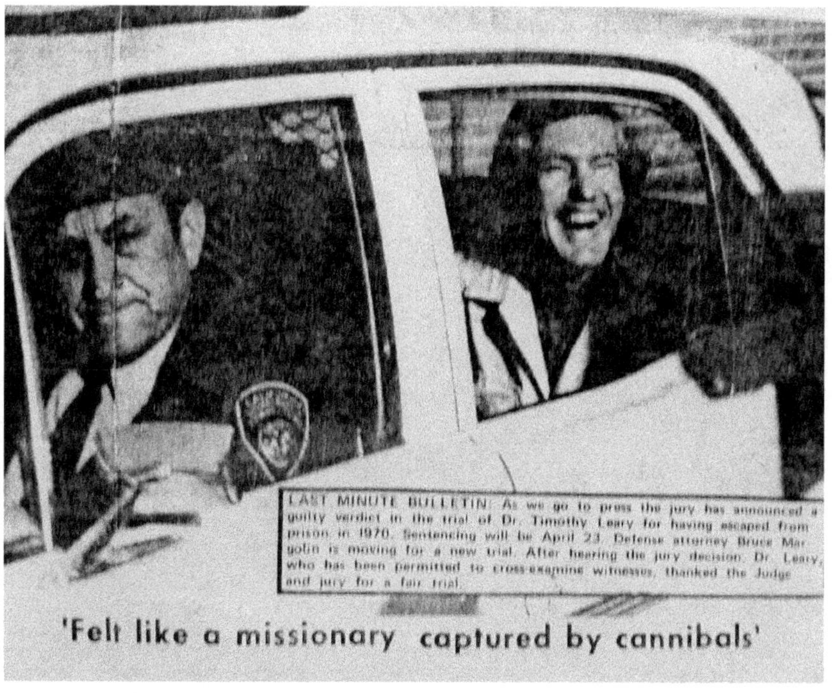

LAST MINUTE BULLETIN: As we go to press the jury has announced a guilty verdict in the trial of Dr. Timothy Leary for having escaped from prison in 1970. Sentencing will be April 23. Defense attorney Bruce Margolin is moving for a new trial. After hearing the jury decision, Dr. Leary, who has been permitted to cross-examine witnesses, thanked the Judge and jury for a fair trial.

'Felt like a missionary captured by cannibals'

Figure 93: Press clipping of Tim Leary being hauled off by the cops, still happy as ever.

Chapter XXII

Killings

"All true stories end in death."

- Hemingway

If Papa was right, then the 1960s melodrama was true by that measure, since there were more dead people on stage at the end of the saga than at the closing curtain of *Hamlet*. The Brotherhood story in particular staggered on for a while after the Gotterdammerung, but by all practical measures, the visionary Utopianism was in intensive care. To cite mortality by the numbers:

After the inundation and collapse of "Little Rome" in 1963, I took my stunning, but not-too-hip, bride and moved into the old d'Andrea apartment upstairs at 703 Browncroft, shoveling debris into the trash. We commenced to learn what sort of mutual fix we'd got ourselves into. One morning we turned on the TV and the world had changed, never to be innocent again. President John F. Kennedy had been shot. It was November 22, 1963, and few people noticed that Aldous Huxley had also died that day, dropping his body while on a double-dose of LSD.

JFK's murder was the first of the series of political assassinations that occurred with bloody frequency during the '60s, punctuated by a string of immediate disasters closer to home. On February 21, 1965, the reformed criminal, Detroit Red, his name changed to Malcolm X, became a victim of Muslim internecine rivalry over leadership of the Black Nation of Islam, which was just then trying to mature, while the Civil Rights Movement was barely getting off the ground.

Malcolm X was nothing if not an inspired orator. It turned out that he was too inspired for his own good, because his forensic prowess put his erstwhile guru, the Reverend Elijah Mohammed out of the center stage limelight, a disarrangement he did not like. It was black men pulling the triggers that killed Malcolm in a fusillade at a public lecture, but at whose behest?

Malcolm X was uttering all sorts of immoderate anti-white rhetoric, while he was simultaneously enraging his political/spiritual leader, so it might have been either the white establishment or the black establishment that did him in. Either way, both sides were relieved to be rid of such a loudmouth. Little could they anticipate the emergence of such a group as the Black Panthers a few years down the line.

If not for Malcolm X, so extreme a group as the Black Panthers might not have emerged. Meanwhile, I broke up with my first wife and went to New York to encounter USCO and the Castalia Foundation, and got enmeshed with a new wife.

After the USCO interlude, I returned to California with the new bride, Margaret Lerner, and my just-completed Mandala of Taxonomy and Evolution. I showed it at "Whatever It Is," Stewart Brand's 1966 media festival at San Francisco State College, and then we proceeded to Laguna Beach again, where I took a charming fairy-tale cottage on Woodland Drive, where my intention was to follow Timothy Leary's advice to "go back to where you came from, and share what you've learned". I soon met John and Carol Griggs when they came over to "experience" in front of the Mandala.

Johnny was the spark plug of his tribe, a group of psychedelic buccaneers whom he dubbed, "The Brotherhood of Eternal Love." He'd heard about my Mandala, and one day I answered a knock on the door to discover John and Carol, dressed in their finery, asking permission to take LSD in front of my painting. I of course agreed, and the upshot of it was that John adopted both me and my Mandala as icons of the Brotherhood of Eternal Love. He generated a momentum that was hard to resist, even if one had wanted to.

He made the Mandala central to the emporium the Brotherhood was putting together, very slowly, on Coast Highway, to be known as "Mystic Arts World". This sensational nomenclature was also an appellation by John, who also coined a new name for the Woodland Drive neighborhood: "Dodge City." His namings, for all their corniness, stuck. John was unashamedly lurid in the way he dispensed names. There was some debate about who had come up with what name, and when, but the prime user and popularizer of these melodramatic names was the unabashed redneck, John Murl Griggs. (In its Shetland/Orkney Island origin, by the way, a "grig" is a "merry cricket," a most fitting symbol for the man).

With John's energetic and upbeat help, I took the Mandala to San Francisco again for a summer-long one-man show at the Canessa Gallery on Montgomery Street. I stayed there in a flat on Shrader Street overlooking Haight Street and the Golden Gate Park Panhandle, for the 1967 "Summer of Love." Serendipity was operating big time. At the end of that summer, I returned to

Laguna for the opening of Mystic Arts World, where the news of "Hippie's" demise, as announced by the Diggers, had not yet been absorbed, and seemed instead to be going into high gear. When I took my friend, the writer Ward Bowers, in to show off Mystic Arts World, he observed everything with close attention, sniffed a couple of times, and pronounced, "It's a tent revivalist's dream of respectability." The perspicaciousness of this quip irritated me mightily for its penetrating bulls-eye.

The Brotherhood was idealistically trying to turn on the world to LSD, and moving a lot of marijuana at the same time. This activity was the cause of huge reaction by law-enforcement, to nobody's surprise. It was widely believed among the conservative parts of local society that Mystic Arts World was a hub of drug dealing, which it was not. The place certainly touted expanded consciousness through whatever means that could be achieved, but illegal activities that may have happened there were not part of the establishment mission. The Brothers knew perfectly well that in order to flourish, Mystic Arts World had to stay within the law. All the same, many of the people ricocheting around that environment had illegal operations going on elsewhere in the community. There were unfortunate incidents.

Many years later, Norm Babcock, the Laguna Beach detective who had been my long-time friend, and was also uneasy partners with Neal Purcell, the detective who had busted Timothy Leary, and consequently became Police Chief, heard that I was going to write about the death of Peter Amaranthus in late 1967. He gravely urged an excess of caution. Norm said that the Amaranthus killing was a taboo subject buried in a shallow grave, and that I would be stirring up dangerous forces by talking about it. But we have to talk about it. Once one begins to leave stuff out, particularly under threat, the truth of the narrative is compromised.

"Amaranthus": the preferred definition of "amaranth" in *The Oxford English Dictionary* is, "An imaginary flower which does not fade. Poetic usage". This is another example of that serendipity that cropped up all the time during the psychedelic era. This instance of it I only uncovered just now, when I thought to check out the origin of the poor kid's name. Let us try to imagine the crime scene:

A group of youngsters gathered one afternoon in a Laguna Beach house. They were typical rebels and prophets of the coming Golden Age, and some of them were still teenagers. Peter Amaranthus, a dark-haired boy, was one of these. He was less careful than he was enthusiastic, as he took part in a commercial exchange of forbidden fruit, probably marijuana. It must have seemed exciting to be a romantic bandito outwitting the repressive John Law. All of the young conspirators gathered around doing their business when the doors burst open. It was a bust. It was a set-up. Confusion ensued, with narcotics officers togged-out as hard-hatted workmen shouting orders and throwing kids down on their faces. Peter Amaranthus made a break for it. He jumped through a window, jumped over a hedge, and here speculation gives way to the harsh reality of Agent J. D. Green's bullet tearing into Pete's lower back , severing an artery and causing him to quickly bleed out. The scuttlebutt is that the police moved the body, and tried to make the scene look less like an assassination. Hush, hush. Let the boy get lost in the onrush of events, and become obscured in the unfolding of time. But poetically he is "the flower which does not fade", so here he still is, on the page, living forever; a testament to the martyrdom of idealism, however illegal.

In 1967, we were vouchsafed the ambivalent blessing of the arrival in Laguna Beach of Dr. Timothy Leary, the LSD guru, which put the quantum spotlight on the town, thank you very much. At least he brought the lady Rosemary with him. In my

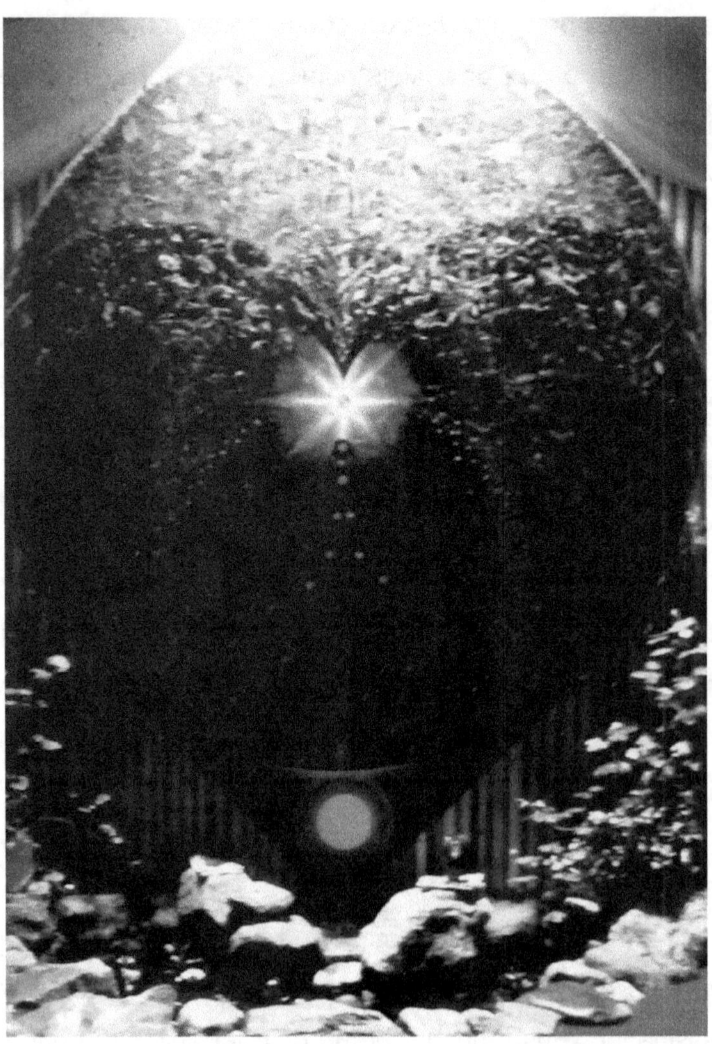

Figure 94: Evolution Mandala in the meditation room at Mystic Arts World. A persuasive presentation...photo by Dion Wright.

humble opinion she was the very best thing about the megalomaniacal ex-professor. John Griggs, more than anybody else, regarded getting Tim to Laguna as a coup, but the rest of the Brotherhood were by no means uniformly enthusiastic. Half of the Brothers were vying to roll out the red carpet for the erstwhile academic, the other half couldn't care less. Within months, a schism divided the Brotherhood into pro-Tim and who-cares-about-Tim wings, the latter drifting off to the Hawaiian Islands, while the mainland faction slowly morphed away from their vision by the wishes and needs of Dr. Leary. Life careened apace in "Dodge City" as all sorts of wild behaviors punctuated the background serenity of the bucolic neighborhood.

One night while my wife and I were still living on Roosevelt Lane with Carol and John Griggs, the tranquility of "Dodge City" was shattered by gunfire and the angry shouts of men. Johnny and I tumbled down Roosevelt Lane to Woodland Drive to see what was going on. All the other residents of "Dodge" were also emerging onto the street. Under the streetlight, a couple of guys were waving pistols and yelling into each other's faces. They turned out to be discomfited undercover narcotics officers.

There was a hotshot kid hanging around "Dodge" who wanted nothing more than to be just like John Griggs. He was John Gale, a slavish disciple of "The Farmer," who yearned for John's approval, and went out of his way to get it. John Gale knew he was being set up by some narcs. Instead of making himself scarce, he agreed to sell them an ounce of hashish. They were to meet on this particular night in a car in "Dodge" to complete the deal. The narcs handed over the money to John Gale, who gave them the contraband, but immediately leaped out of the car and disappeared onto the brushy hillside. The gunfire was the infuriated policemen firing their service revolvers wildly into the hillside after the vanished felon. Then they discovered that John Gale had sold them not hashish, but a lump of dog shit. That's when they started to screaming blame at each other, and all of us residents came out to see what the uproar was about.

Complicating the entire issue was the fact that *another* police agency was conducting *another* sting at the same time on the other side of "Dodge City"; a sting that went south upon the sound of the gunfire. That set of narcs came barreling around the corner and started in to castigate the first set of cops for ruining their bust. Just then, the local cops, led by Norm Babcock, drove pell-mell into Woodland Drive to find out what the hell was happening. The functionaries of three police agencies were all shouting at each other at the top of their lungs, much to the amusement of the residents, who all started in to chant "Om" in a hundred voices. This chanting made a couple of the detectives go completely bonkers, and they ran down the line of chanters, whacking them over the head with flashlights and billy clubs. Half a dozen people were injured before sense finally prevailed. In the usual mechanism of the times, the injured parties were taken into custody for "resisting arrest." Johnny Griggs and I watched this amazing scene unfold, until we were tapped on the shoulder. There was the smiling John Gale behind us, riffling the handful of cash he had bilked out of the undercover detectives.

John Gale lasted into the early 80's, an exaggerated and insincere lampoon of the man he modeled himself upon, John Griggs. He ended up dead under his own rolled-over Mercedes amid a swirling storm of rumor.

Then, John and Carol's high-spirited elf of a little boy, Jerry, saw somebody bury an unknown stash in a Dodge City back yard. He dug it up, and swallowed whatever it was, taking a dare from some other kids. The reaction was a neurological meltdown that left the little boy barely alive. He recovered slowly and incompletely over many years, and finally died decades later, another casualty of the Psychedelic Revolution. John didn't reveal his feelings to me about it, but he never slowed down his efforts to turn on the world and create utopia.

In the spring of 1968 our friend Jay Thelin, co-owner of the Psychedelic Shop on Haight Street in San Francisco, came to visit us in our artist-pad house on the Street of the Blue Lantern in Dana Point. We went off for a jaunt into the desert around Anza-Borrego. We were soon lackadaisically falling back in the sun, lazing on the hot rocks in a palmy canyon, and listening to music on a transistor radio, when the program was interrupted by a bulletin. Martin Luther King Jr. had been assassinated in Memphis, Tennessee. It was April 4, 1968. Catastrophe was piling up.

More-or-less at this time, Timothy Leary managed to re-direct John Griggs' visionary goal. Johnny had been supercharged by Aldous Huxley's idealistic utopian book, *Island*, and had set the Brotherhood of Eternal Love's goal in that direction. John's strategy was that the Brotherhood would establish Mystic Arts World as a going concern, then turn it over to another generation of youthful enlightened hippies, so that the original group could devote itself to following the lines of Huxley's utopian fiction. Timothy Leary's influence would carry it forward. At that point the

Brotherhood would acquire an island in some tropic place, and "drop out" there to develop a community.

John Griggs had become stronger by the summer of 1968, and Timothy Leary did not *want* to move away from the center stage of publicity to play Wise Man on some remote island. He wanted to stay accessible to the lime light of publicity, and so he

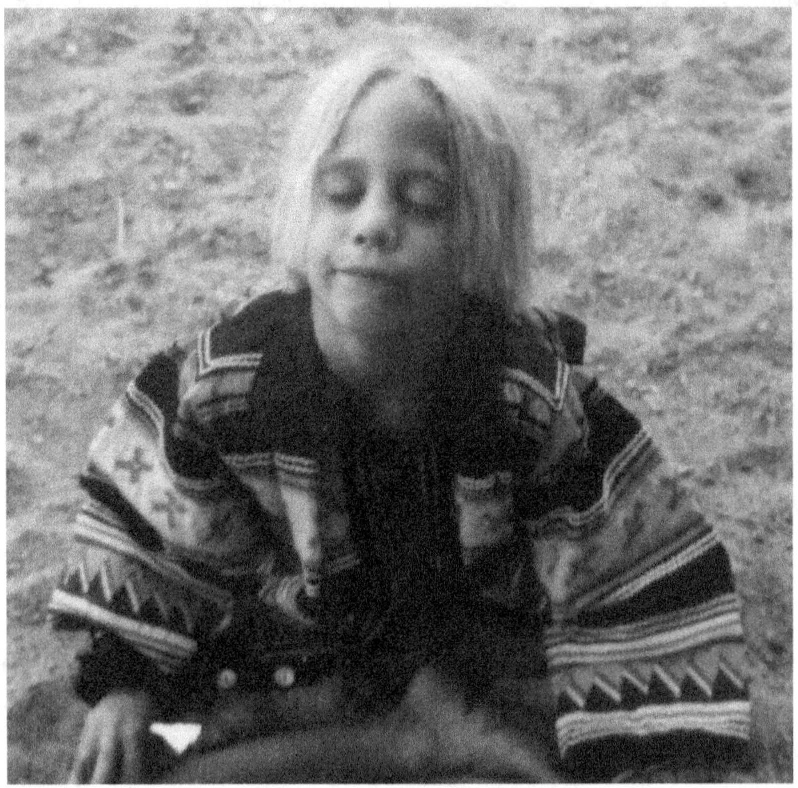

Figure 95: Jerry Griggs. Closest to the Buddha.

instead managed a potential deal for the purchase of a ranch in the San Jacinto Mountains high above Palm Springs, with the help and influence of "Jesse", one of the Brothers, and talked John Griggs into the idea. The island was a pretty literal idea as John first told it to me, but that changed into a metaphor when

Tim became involved. I can just imagine Tim persuading, "Oh, you don't have to cross the sea to drop out! (Let's drop out where I can still get to Hollywood easily)."

The deal was sweetened by the fact that John had helped "Robby," the son of the seller of the ranch, to get off of heroin through LSD. The purchase of "The Ranch," instead of an island, caused the Brotherhood to drift further out of unity. Some of the brothers were less than impressed with Tim in the first place, and some of them were barely sold on Utopia in *any* form, and were only carried along by John's passionate enthusiasm. A number of these core people broke away and went to Maui, as The Ranch became a reality.

The worst tragedy so far happened on June 21, 1968, the *summer solstice*, God help us. Robert F. Kennedy, the political hope of the generation, was assassinated at the Ambassador Hotel on the night of his victory in the California presidential primary, assuring the election of Richard M. Nixon, and a long continuation of the Viet Nam War.

The conspiracy theorists have been reduced to nut status at this late date, but...but...but, can anyone of normal and common perception really believe, without some nagging doubt, that there was no thread connecting these assassinations? It wasn't over yet. 1969 was coming over the horizon, to finish-off the idealism of the Summer of Love, once and for all.

It is an unsolved mystery, the matter of Robbie and Gretchen and their baby. Robbie was the junkie kid whom John Griggs had tried to cure, and whose father was the seller making the deal for the Ranch with John and Timothy Leary. Robbie and his young wife, Gretchen, had been absorbed into the Brotherhood-at-the-Ranch society, where they were background figures, as far as I could see. There was considerable traffic between the Ranch and the Island of Maui, where Gretchen and Robbie and their new baby eventually went to vacation. One of the attractions on Maui was to go up into the extinct caldera of the dead volcano, called Haleakala Crater, a weird, unearthly and beautiful spot, to "experience" as the euphemism had it, which meant taking LSD, in the glorious lap of nature.

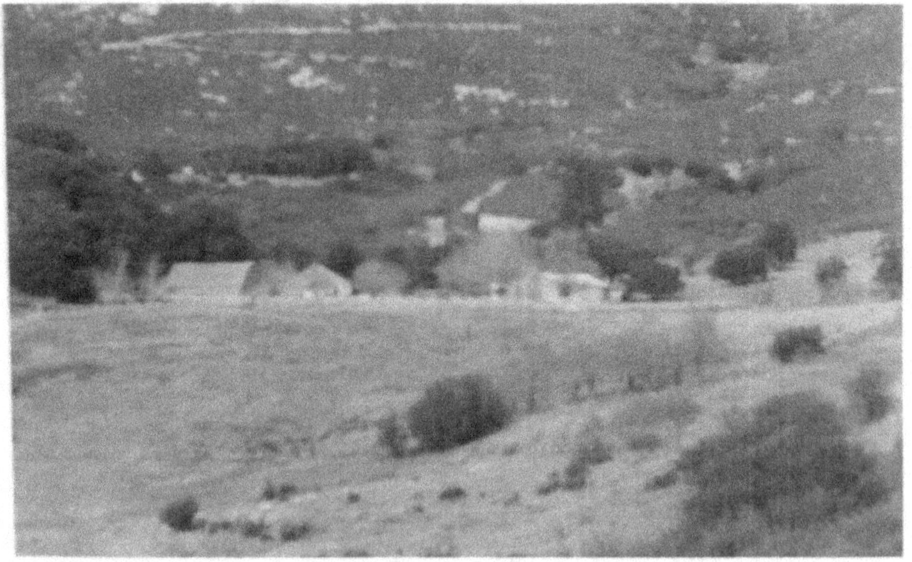

Figure 96: The Ranch, as it appeared three decades later.

One of the features of the Haleakala Crater is a deep fissure in the lava called "The Bottomless Pit". The young family went to this place to watch the rising of the sun, but when the daylight came, park rangers found their three bodies, broken and dead, down on the rocks in the Bottomless Pit.

The ranger who found them said his attention was drawn to the scene by something yellow fluttering on the rim. When he went up to investigate, he found a copy of Timothy Leary's Psychedelic Prayers on the lip of the crevasse, its pages riffling in the breeze. No explanation was ever forthcoming. It was another desperate tragedy to absorb into a stressed attempt to continue optimistically, asserting that all was well, and the new dawn would still prevail. Meanwhile, back at the Ranch, poor young Charlene Almeida, fiancée to a Brother, drowned in the muddy cattle tank, which the Brotherhood women euphemistically regarded as a "swimming hole". "Charlie" wasn't killed, but she wasn't saved, either. As it happened, Timothy Leary was a couple of hundred feet away in his tipi as the women cried for help as they pulled the drowned girl from the brown water. He said he hadn't heard the cries. His consciousness wasn't expanded enough, I suppose.

Then Charles Manson launched his murder spree, further drenching the tattered hippie image in innocent blood. The already drunkenly staggering idealism of "the movement" came crashing down at that, heralding the final nail in the coffin of the "Psychedelic Revolution."

Next, the chasm between our government's statements about Viet Nam, and the reality of it on the ground, came into brutal focusEx-GI Ron Ridenhour and journalist Seymour Hersh exposed the massacre at My Lai and My Khe, where the entire populations of more than 425 souls, men, women and children, were "raped, sodomized, tortured and murdered" by American soldiers. No witnesses, they thought, and they were probably all Charlie anyway…including the suckling babes. One lieutenant was made the scapegoat.

But to see *him* in action, Tim seemed to remain as upbeat and lighthearted as ever; a real puzzle of counter-intuitive behavior, while I thought Johnny was showing the strain of events in subtle hints of appearance and behavior. This was my observation, and I don't know if anybody else noticed it. There was surging life, too. In the summer of '69, Carol and John had their third child, born in the tipi. The Moon landings were a reality. I went up to the Ranch on one of my periodic trips there. I didn't want to move in, but I couldn't stay away either. John was still expressing high idealism with his usual physically energetic decisiveness. As I was about to drive away back down the mountain after my visit, he came up to the driver's side window of Old Yeller with his eyes beaming that visionary love-light that burned there when he was full of prophecy. He said, with all the thrust of his conviction, "The Golden Age is right around the corner...a thousand years of good livin'!"

I never saw him again.

Several days later I was awakened by the ringing phone before dawn, in my house on the Street of the Blue Lantern in Dana Point. It was Mad Dog prodding me awake with the words, "Go to Laguna and get the antidote! Find Long Drink, and get the antidote! Hurry! Hurry!"

I had no clue what it was all about; that Mad Dog was calling from the hospital in Hemet; that he had rushed pell-mell down the curving mountain road with Johnny chanting "Om" and strangling in the back seat; but there was no missing Mad Dog's urgency. I jumped in Old Yeller and hurried to Laguna, but I couldn't locate Long Drink, nor anybody else who knew what was up, or much gave a damn.

As it happened, I had Johnny's life in my hands for an hour or so, never knew it, and was foiled by Fate. By the time I got back to Dana Point, he had died. He was twenty-six years old.

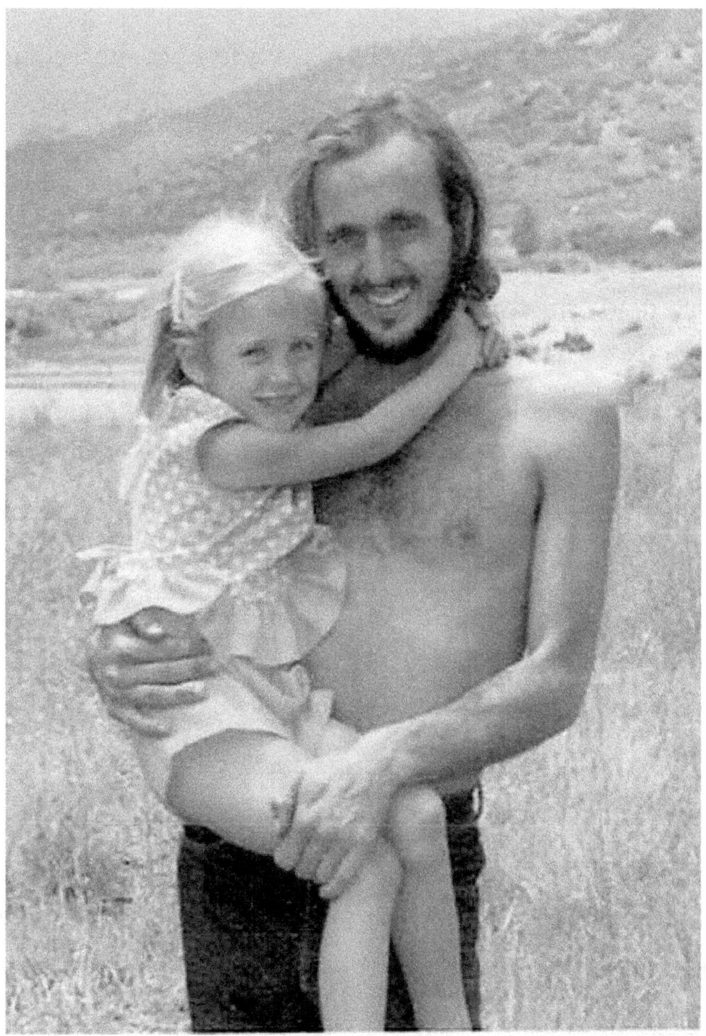

Figure 97: Sissy and John Griggs, just before the sand ran out of the hourglass.

Carol is the only witness. She came by and told us the story a few days later. It had to do with testing a synthetic psychedelic, reportedly psilocybin. Shortly after John took it, he cried out to whosoever could hear him, "It's an O.D.!" None of those within earshot took him seriously. He continued to float away on the tide of chemistry, chanting "OM," sitting in the full lotus in his tipi at the hearth fire.

Carol said that at one point he fell face forward into the flames. She dragged him out, she said, unburned. At last the reality of his mortal danger became convincing enough that Mad Dog bundled him into a car and took off for medical attention, but it was too late.

I've never been able to quite wrap my brain around John's death as being straightforward. It nags at me from my subconscious that there is more to know about it. I guess it will stay a mystery; maybe only a mystery in my mind. If there was foul play involved, what could have been the motive? Professional jealousy? The inconvenience of such a true believer being bad for business, with his interminable prophetic testifying? Revenge for misunderstood events? A Federal mole engineering his death?

Probably it was just reckless behavior, but the incident turned into mythic history so fast that a vacuum of uncertainty was left. My uncertainty...but not mine alone. John's demise continues to trouble me, and I know that it has troubled others as well. Maybe some other, rival "businessman" was able to get into the material and corrupt it.

Maybe Johnny was victimized by a sort of behavioral judo, where somebody *knew* he would overdose because that's how he behaved, providing a compromised substance to him, knowing that he would let his momentum carry him off a cliff. Some say that John was told to mix lemon juice with the synthetic psychedelic chemical to cancel toxins, whether he did or not, and whether that was suggested or not.

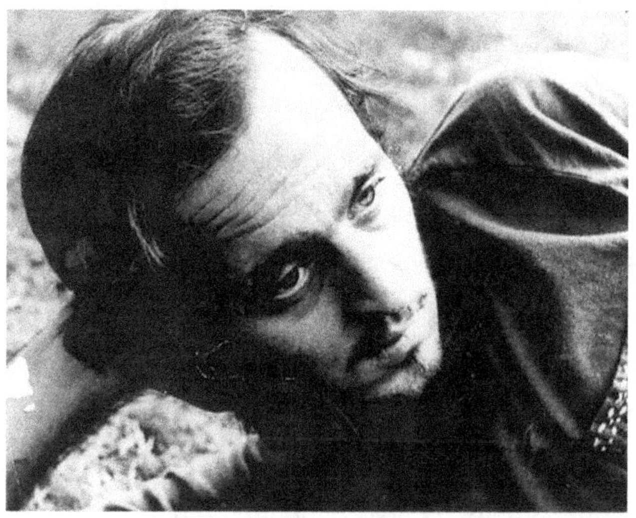

Figure 98: The pensive John Griggs toward the end of his days.

Many years later, Carol said: "He just took too damn much." There is no doubt that John was an intentional high-doser, and thought that it was macho behavior to take a lot of whatever was on the table. Still, psilocybin is a friendly and congenial chemical. Who ever heard of anybody *dying* by psychedelics (except for jumping off a building in paranoia, or something like that)? John overdosed. Let it go at that. Better to just forget about it. It's wrong to mythologize the Happy Farmer, or to make more of him than he was, like some ephemeral Zapata on his white horse in the hills watching, watching. If he is out there watching, he must be damn well discouraged by now.

July 4, 1969, “Give Peace a Chance” by John and Yoko; July 20, Man on the Moon, while US and USSR both continue testing atomic bombs; July 31, Mariner flies by Mars; August 3, John Griggs dies of an overdose of synthetic psilocybin given to him by “a friendly chemist”; August 9, the Tate/La Bianca murders courtesy of Charles Manson; August 18, Woodstock, the last performance at which was the Star Spangled Banner, a solo by Jimi Hendrix, who was John Griggs’ age, and himself dead a year later of uncertain causes. Tough times.

Of all the characters in the Psychedelic Opera, John Griggs was the most deeply enlightened and the most committed to his revelation. He could cause things to be by force of will, carrying what he wanted into reality by charisma and leadership. The Brotherhood of Eternal Love was one such creation, and Mystic Arts World was another. The Ranch manifested through his strength of character as well, although he was largely talked into it by Timothy Leary. Things happened because Johnny decided that it would be so, up to a point. The tsunami of grand events overtook his idealism. Amazing creature that he was, he was only a local phenomenon.

The I Ching refers to "the superior man.” That was John Griggs, certainly more so than Tim, who was formidable, but not superior, in the same karmic sense. John had some power, but I think it was not an addiction, or he wouldn't have given over so much of it to Tim. If anything more than the chemical did him in, it may have been disillusionment. It must have been a heavier and heavier burden to keep expecting something good to come out of what was getting worse and worse and worse.

In the context of the times, Johnny's death was one incident in the ongoing greater catastrophic series of events. On December 6, 1969, a west coast concert that hoped to be "Woodstock II" was produced at Altamont Speedway in the East Bay. "Security" was provided by the Hell's Angels Motorcycle Club, who, whipped into a frenzy by drugs, alcohol and the Rolling Stones, spun out of control and started beating on the pressing crowd. The toll was four dead, without an apology from the Rolling Stones, much less the Hell's Angels.

It wasn't over, the pruning of protest by murderous fiat. At Kent State College on May 4, 1970, President Richard M. Nixon turned loose the National Guard, armed with live ammo, on unarmed peaceful war protesters. An order was given to fire, five students were murdered and more were injured. One of the dead was simply on his way to class, and just happened to be in the wrong place at the wrong time. When informed of the deaths, Nixon dismissed them as "bums." We know who the bum was.

The Brotherhood of Eternal Love paid still more of the butcher bill. The fugitive, "Desert" Chuck Scott was shot in the back in Mill Valley. In Mexico, little Jimmy Dale, the candle-maker, was shot in the lower back, the bullet exiting his chest. The worse horror of it was the beating his face took from the Federales, which made him nigh unrecognizable. Seven more bullets, so they said, were pumped into Jimmy by the savage peace officers. Jimmy and Chuck reprised the bloody death of Peter Amaranthus. They were not innocents. They were casualties of a war. The Flower Children had gradually encountered Ultimate Reality, and discovered that they were just so much meat.

The end of the decade was absurdly punctuated with a blunt period, by the cancellation of the Smothers Brothers, who dared to use humor to tell the truth on television.

The Age of Murder won over the Age of Love with a vengeance. The final, tragic tally of the era inscribed on The Viet Nam Wall was proof: 58,175 killed young Americans who had little or nothing to do with the "Politics of Ecstasy" as Tim Leary called it. They were historical cannon fodder martyred to the myth of the nation, all for the lost honor of the French, the warped misperceptions of the intelligence community, the ego of the Texas Cowboy LBJ, and the dark machinations of Tricky Dick, a sinister but banal politician doing what was good for business.

For the Vietnamese people, who simply and forever just wanted to run their own country, whatever nomenclature was applied to it from outside, the toll was something like a 3,334,000 dead, north and south. In the end, they got their country back, so the Vietnamese were finally the beneficiaries of whatever good came out of the dreadful era.

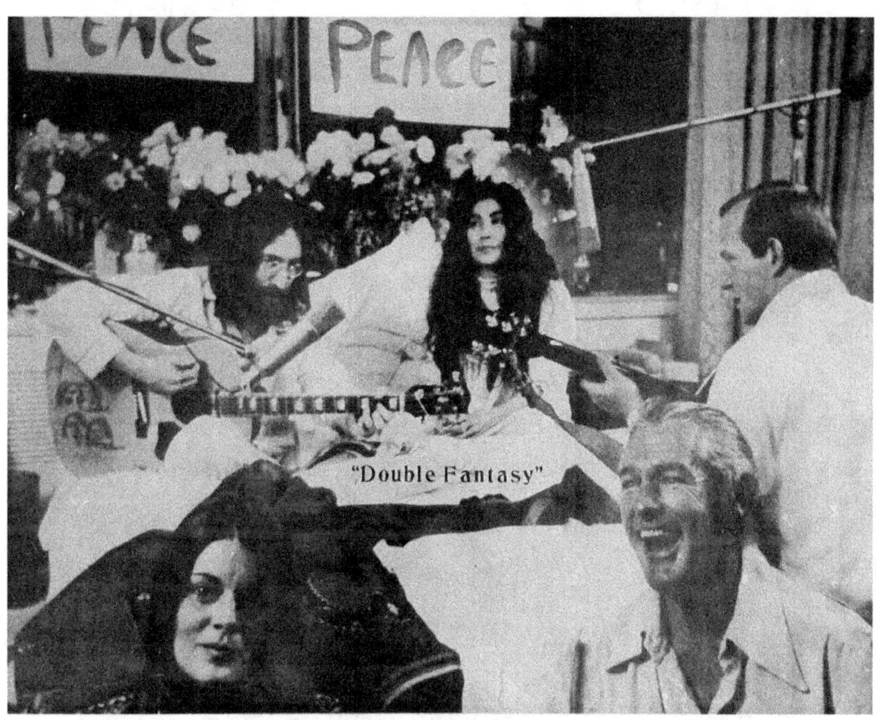

Figure 99: "The Bed-In", in Toronto, ca. 1970. Clockwise from top; John Lennon, Yoko Ono, Tommy Smothers, Timothy Leary, Rosemary Woodruff.

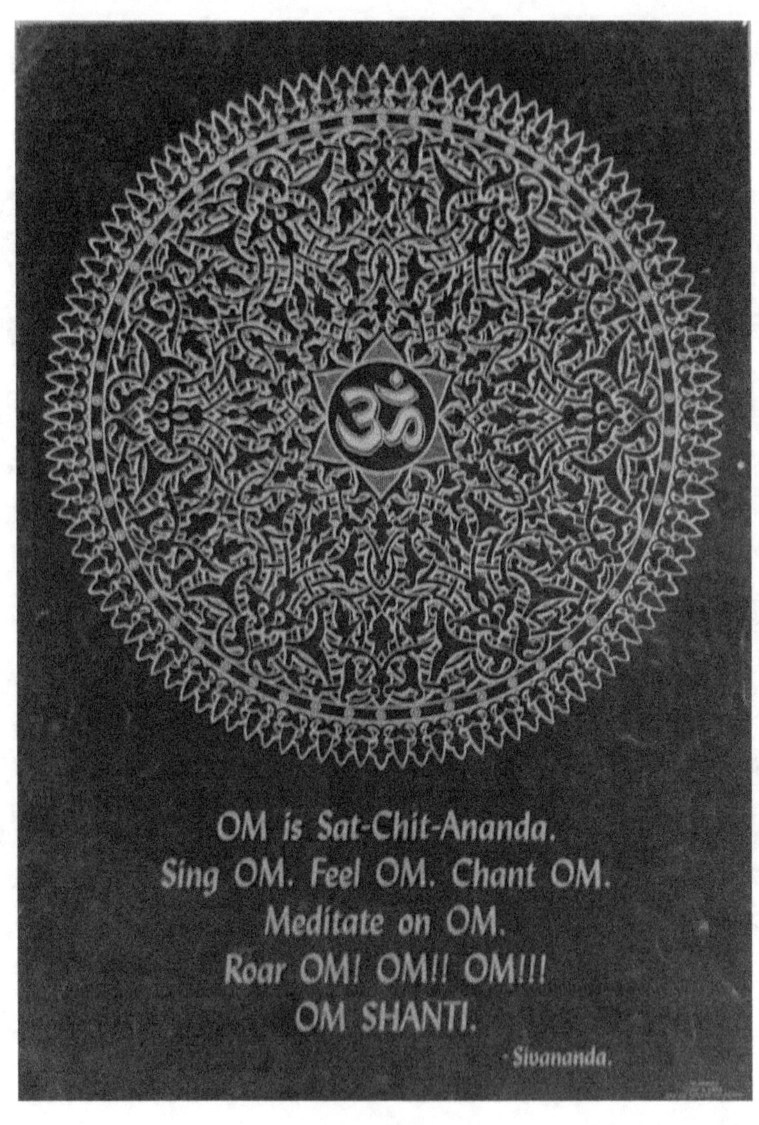

Figure 100: OM

Chapter XXIII

Shiva's Kiss

"Mystic Arts World has burned to the ground," said Norm Babcock to me on the phone at the break of dawn. "You better get down here."

I was awakened in my bed in Dana Point on the Street of the Blue Lantern again with another disaster dropped in my lap. I jumped into my pants and rushed to 670 South Coast Highway in Laguna Beach, where my gallery was a gutted, drenched and smoking ruin. I hurried up to where Detective Norm Babcock was standing behind the yellow tape. A crowd of hippies on the sidewalk across the highway were yelling and cursing poor Norm, and accusing him of being "the son of a bitch who did it."

The roof had fallen in and a ropy trail of melted wax ran across the sidewalk and into the gutter, looking like the entrails of a psychedelic dinosaur, the liquefied stock of the hand-made candle shop that had been at the front of the store. I was amazed to see my Mandala leaning against the wall of the Elks' Club, scorched in the top half, but mostly intact. It was apparently the only object saved from the fire. This was a mystery since it was the biggest object in Mystic Arts World, and the farthest one from the front door. Also, it had been behind a framed wall, leaving the manner in which it had been extricated an unanswered question. I learned that a certain firefighter went in there and carried the thing out on his back, a Herculean effort, as the piece was painted on two five eighth inch slabs of plywood.

The destruction of Mystic Arts World was deemed an electrical fire by the authorities. , but I regarded it symbolically in retrospect, as the final caress of Shiva, the Hindu God of destruction, that brought the era finally and conclusively to an end.

One thing that Mystic Arts World encouraged was a sense of inward searching after spiritual truth. Psychedelic enlightenment, in those days when the chemicals were still the real thing, turned most of the experiencers into Deists of some kind.

John Griggs had immediately shouted out, "It's God! It's all God!", and he never stopped asserting that same thing for the remainder of his short life. After persons' sudden, and often unexpected, introductions to the realities of God, questioning and reevaluation began big-time. It was commonplace for people to embrace some form of religion to assuage their shock. Often these religious conversions were to some other faith than the one in which they were raised. It was common for individuals to feel that they were sold short by their native religions, and to look for a new one.

They had been advised from within, in the most spectacular way, that God was Here and Now, but frequently could not see the connection between this revelation and the religious pabulum of their lukewarm upbringing. So, there was a surge of spiritual searching going on, and Mystic Arts World provided all the texts to go with all the alternatives. This is why there were so many new approaches embraced by so many unexpected people during the '60s, from Hare Krishna, to yoga, to Zen, to mystical Christianity.

All of it was wormwood and gall to the city fathers everywhere. To them, churches were social structures, and not to be shaken up by fervent religiosity, especially as offered by hairy freaks. Far from seeing enlightened searching, the Babbits only saw dangerous boat-rocking. One ancient religion that received new scrutiny was Hinduism, one of the oldest of the world's belief systems, and the one that was quite the farthest from middle-American soporific sensibilities. The philosopher Alan Watts asserted that psychedelic experience had a qualitative Hindu cast to it.

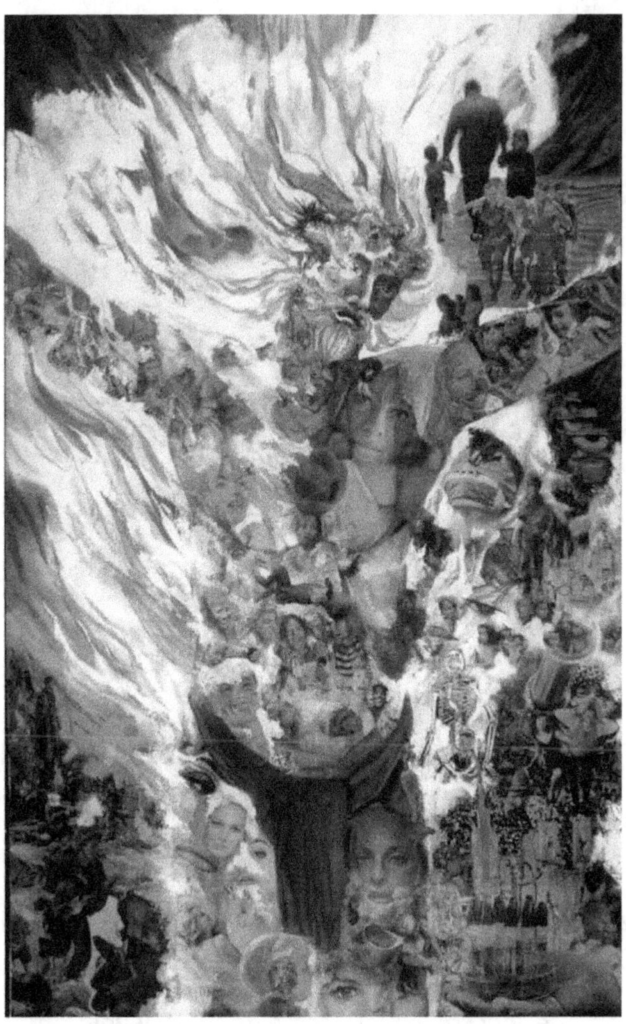

Figure 101: Beth Pewther, "Body of Christ, Body of Man." Collage/painting.

Not to get into any lengthy definition of Hinduism, let it be said that the One God beyond knowledge has three aspects in the world, the Creator, The Preserver, and the Destroyer. All have their groups of worshipers. The destroyer god is Shiva.

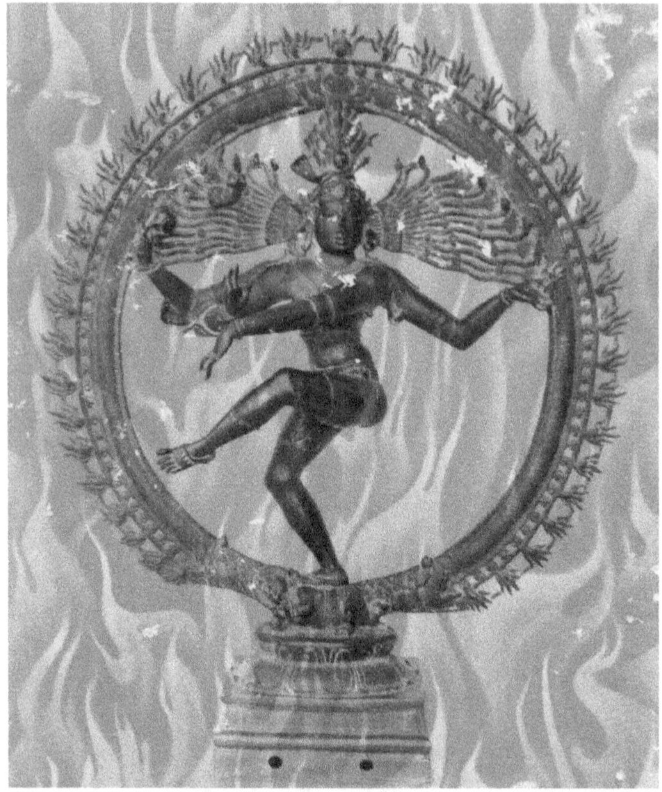

Figure 102: "Nataraja" – Shiva's dance of fire. From back cover, "Psychedelic Review" #10.

Unlike Muslims, Hindus can't seem to get enough of god-images. There are legions of Hindu gods, all of which are rendered ad infinitum in every possible medium. Shiva is executed in painting, textiles and sculpture, traditionally shown in the "Nataraja", the depiction of the god dancing and spinning, poised on one foot, multiple arms extended, within a ring of fire. This is a personifying and objectifying of a constant reality of life:

the folding of manifest physicality into inevitable destruction. One does not have to worship Shiva for this to be happening.

When one does worship Shiva, the question is open as to what sort of energies may be induced by expectation. Tim Leary, who indulged Shiva, came later into the Brotherhood saga, but there was plenty of fire in advance of his appearance, although it is questionable whether any of the bourgeois brothers had ever heard of Shiva in the early days of their enlightenment.

John and the Brotherhood had a long history of brushes with fire, although identifying those with Shiva is only my personal retrospective poetic metaphor. I'm sure the idea never crossed Johnny's mind, although I'm equally sure it did cross Timothy Leary's.

John Griggs was a Leo, for whatever that is worth, a fire sign, and Tim was a Libra, an air sign, and we all know that air makes flame burn hotter. In the absurdly coincidental nature of events within the world of expanded consciousness, it happened that the Griggs Family suffered a home fire at Christmas three years in succession, 1966, 1967 and 1968.

The first fire burned the Brotherhood out of their church/commune in Modjeska Canyon. The second one drove the Griggs Family temporarily out of their house in "Dodge City" at 1220 Roosevelt Lane and into guest residence with Timothy and Rosemary Leary on Gaviota Drive in Laguna Beach, and the third one was the destruction of one of the barns at "The Ranch."

Half the buildings at The Ranch eventually went down to fire. Timothy and Rosemary lived somewhat up the hill and separate from the main Ranch complex, in the old foreman's house. My hair stood on end the day I first saw the large hanging black silk scroll over Tim's desk on which the Nataraja was embroidered in gold thread. The whole symbolic nature of it tried to force my consciousness into the morass of superstition. It's improbable that Tim worshiped Shiva, but he had it there nevertheless, even if it was only an Art object to that cynical man who was quick to evoke all things spiritual, and tardy at their application within his own life. In the aftermath of Johnny's death came the conflagration at Mystic Arts World, and anyone could make what they would of that within the territory of Shiva.

I didn't believe it was an electrical fire, in any case.

Doubts kept itching in my brain about the official version of how Mystic Arts World burned. The new fire chief had doubts of his own, which he revealed on the morning of the fire in a short lecture to Kent Kelly, last manager of Mystic Arts World. "Come here, I want to show you something," said the chief, whereupon he took Kent into the smoking rubble and pointed out where the accelerant that initiated the blaze hit the floor right below where the skylight had been.

"I don't know what the official report is going to say," Kent quotes the chief as saying, "but this was arson." The chief was quickly advised to button his lip, as the official explanation of faulty wiring was released.

As it happens, I was on the scene during the construction of Mystic Arts World every single day between early September and the long-awaited, long-delayed opening. First off, I met John and Carol when they appeared unannounced at my front door one day on Woodland Drive in the spring of 1967, dressed in their most elegant psychedelic finery and asking if they might "experience" in front of my Mandala that they had heard about, and which was hanging in my cloistered and flower-packed back yard. After that, John sold me on the idea of putting the Mandala into the "meditation room" at Mystic Arts World, the new psychedelic emporium which was not yet constructed at 670 S. Coast Highway.

I was to be the Art Director of this extravaganza, having all the walls throughout the multi-business operation on which to show the works that I deemed worthy. In the meantime, I had been offered a one-man show in San Francisco at the Canessa Gallery on Montgomery Street, to run for the whole summer, which also just happened to be “The Summer of Love” in the Haight/Ashbury district of the city.

John and I drove my works up to San Francisco in his pickup truck, "Old Yeller,” and he helped me to hang the show, not failing to display his daredevil derring-do scampering across high beams across two-story falls to hang the Mandala. Then John rushed away back to Laguna to ramrod the renovation of Harry Howard's Pepper Mill factory into its new incarnation as the center of psychedelic culture in Southern California.

I stayed in San Francisco to mind my show, and was given the use of a second-story flat on Shrader Street just off of Haight, where I could sit in the bay window overlooking the terminus of the Golden Gate Park Panhandle, jaw with my endless parade of visitors, and watch that unbelievable street scene unfold before my eyes.

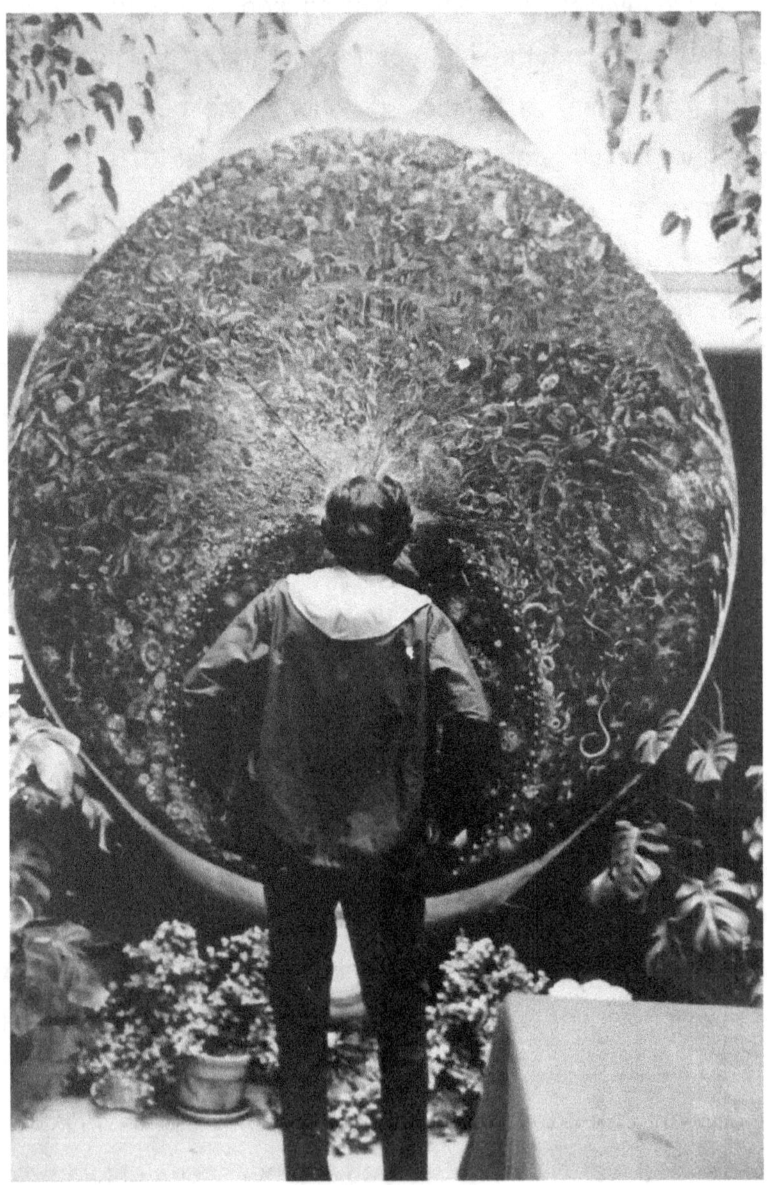

Figure 103: Artist assessing his work in the meditation room at Mystic Arts World.

By the end of the summer, the idealism of June had degenerated into various forms of exploitation, and the Diggers, a hard-nosed practical group of street people trying to serve the hippies and articulate their reality, declared "The Death of Hippie," and had a funeral for the idealism. The news of the end of the game had not been taken seriously back in Laguna Beach, where plans remained plans. John came back and fetched, me, and we returned to Laguna, where basically nothing had been done to turn Mystic Arts World into a reality.

John Griggs found a carpenter named Smitty who claimed he could do all that needed to be done to construct a posh temple where a factory had been. Smitty was a speed freak whose energies, while exaggerated, reached the point where he just vibrated like a tuning fork, hammer in hand and eyes bulging from his face, while he got nothing practical done.

This was the state of affairs when I got back to Laguna around Labor Day, and when the redoubtable Joe Miller appeared on the scene.

Joe was a swarthy and dark-haired Louisiana boy, an ex-Marine artilleryman and jack-of-all-trades who really could do everything, including design structures innovatively. He became excited by every new idea, crossing and uncrossing his legs in an agitated way as his mind raced ahead to envision possibilities on top of possibilities. We saw eye to eye on everything. Joe quickly took matters in hand, and at last, progress began to happen.

It did not happen without the constant and close attention of the building inspectors. I was there every day and saw the way that those inspectors were trying to slow progress via red tags as much as they could. Their critical eyes did indeed slow the progress, but the net result was that each and every aspect of the construction, including the wiring, was held to the maximum adherence to building code. So, there was no faulty wiring.

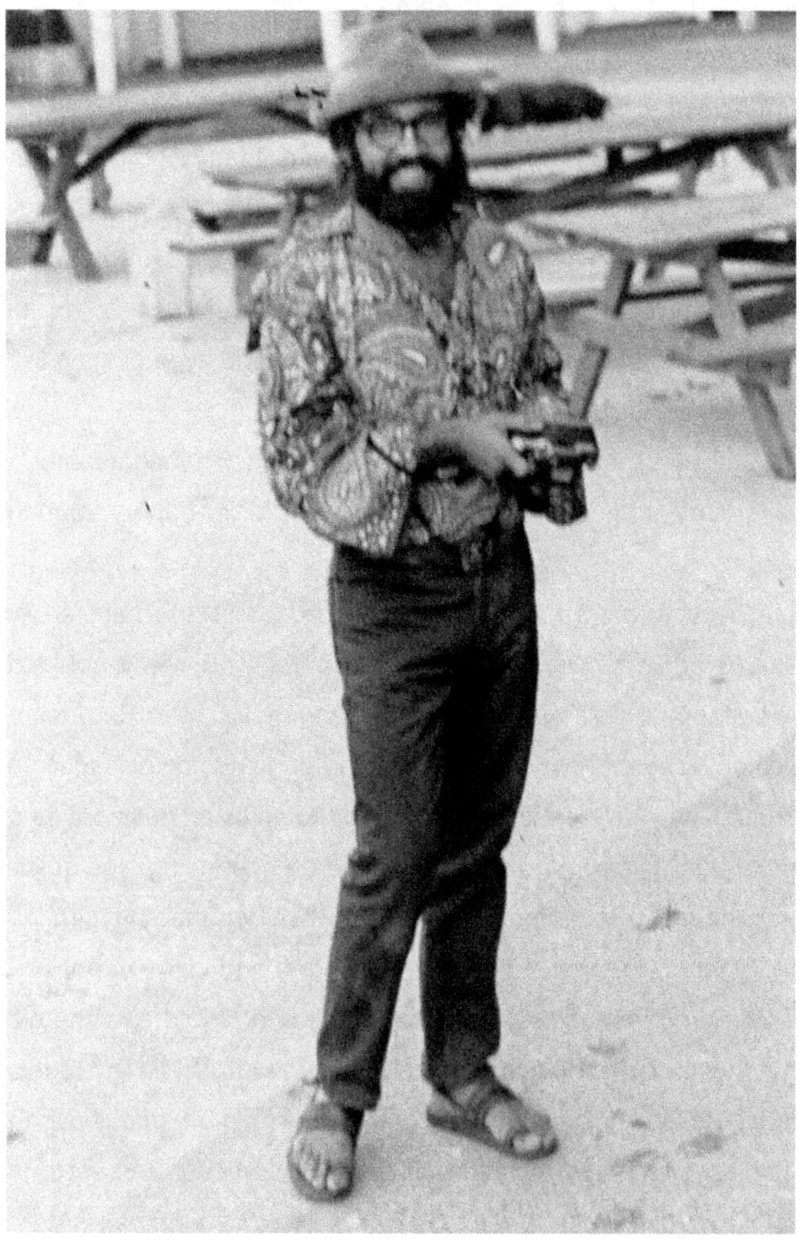

Figure 104: Joe Miller. Photo by Dion Wright.

I was not exactly obsessed with the question of how the arson eventually was contrived, but I picked away at it for years and years, uncovering a bit here and a bit there until the rough outlines of what had occurred began to emerge from the fog of silent discretion. Uncovering the conspiracy to commit arson was not the result of an investigation so much as a gas-bloated corpse slowly rising into view.

The story seems to have been that the most right-wing elements of the community, exemplified by the super-patriotic reactionary John Birch Society, were afraid of Communists in the first place, and regarded avant-garde Art as expressions of Communism. They were doubly alarmed when the psychedelic hippie phenomenon started taking shape, and their very own children began to embrace peace and love, rather than the patriots' own war in SE Asia.

As America polarized between the youth and their parents, the war scaled up, the Civil Rights movement gained steam, and the Women's' Liberation movement invaded their own bedrooms. Black Panthers! Raving bitches! Drug-crazed hippies! It had to be Commies behind all this, opined the reactionaries to each other, detracting from the righteous anti-Commie crusade in Indo-China. When Timothy Leary, the Pied Piper of the youth movement, appeared right in their own town, and took up residence at Mystic Arts World, the tipping point was reached, and the city fathers entered the territory from which vigilantes emerge.

A cartel was formed which bought the building where Mystic Arts World was. They proceeded to try to break the lease, but the lease was cast-iron. When the big shots understood this fact, they turned to arson. Who knows what voices of moderation may have been heard? Some, for sure, but Mr. Big carried the day when he rode over the last objection, that of the businessmen's fear of their own potential loss in property values when the building had been burned out.

Mr. Big covered that problem by pulling strings in government, where he was well connected, and arranging for the taxpayers to foot the bill of restoring the structure, in the understanding that it would be used by bureaucratic government agencies.

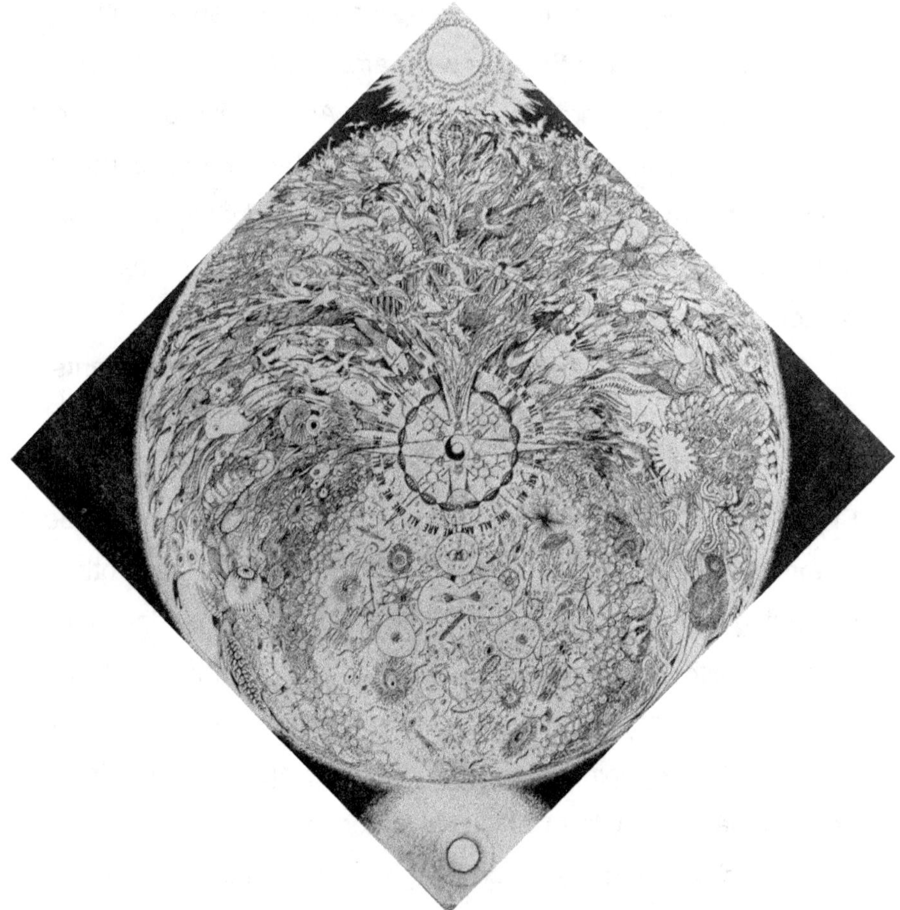

Figure 105: Image used on flyer for my show at the Canessa Gallery on Montgomery Street in SF which serendipitously took place exactly for the two-month period of the Summer of Love.

"Which Boy can we get to throw the cocktail?", they wondered, and such a one turned up.

Casual observers may regard this screenplay as apocryphal sour grapes and invidious mythologizing, save for one thing: Mr. Big, the ringleader of the conspiracy to commit the arson, confessed to me, personally.

He did not seem to know who I was. I was just somebody referred to him by a mutual friend. The mutual friend was Phil Freeman, President of the Festival of Arts in Laguna Beach. Phil and I had known each other since we had both been first-year exhibitors in 1959, and remained close friends over the intervening decades, as our lives took different courses. I was bent on adventure and discovery, believing that an artist needed to accrue experience before articulating meaningfully from a sound foundation. That belief sent me off into the world in pursuit of the Beat Generation and presumably expanded consciousness. Phil Freeman wanted to have a quiet domestic life in which to raise his family, and perfect his craft of crystal-glazed porcelain, at which he was rapidly becoming a master. Phil had a different history from mine. Being some years older, he had been a Marine in the Pacific during WWII, and had borne a flame-thrower in the Battle of Okinawa. He lived the horrors of burning Japanese soldiers in their caves, while a lot of other Japanese soldiers were shooting at him. Phil was an aesthetic and mild man, whose extreme sensitivity must have been tortured by his wartime experience. In any case, he stayed home while I went off careening through mid-century America...but we were in contact often.

One day, many years after the destruction of Mystic Arts World, Phil came to me, knowing of my activities as a writer, and said he had an opportunity for me. One of Laguna Beach's most exalted citizens was looking back over his life, and wanted to write his memoirs, but he had not the skills, and was looking for a ghostwriter.

He and Phil had a mutual background of the War in the Pacific, so he approached Phil to see if he knew of such a possible person. Phil asked me if I wanted to interview for the job. I really didn't want to very much, but, as usual, I was scraping for money, and thought that this might be a way to accumulate some scratch. The interview was scheduled.

I met Mr. Big in his luxurious store, and got the Cooke's Tour. As Mr. Big squired me through his opulent precincts, commenting briefly on this and that item, he maintained a running commentary about himself. He made wide gestures as he extolled all of his many works in the community, planting trees, installing parking meters, boosting athletics, and steering the aesthetics of the Festival of Arts along a path of middle-class respectability. He began to get exercised by the way he and his colleagues suffered the onslaught of degenerate and deteriorating philosophies of Art, and what a struggle it had been to maintain a ceiling on expression at the Festival. The forces of change were unwelcome by Mr. Big, and he proved it to me by bragging how he and his friends "burned out those hippies down on Coast Highway."

Stunned by this revelation, I held my mud and let him prattle on from his juggernaut of braggadocio. Here he was, the ringleader of the arsonists, bragging about his act as if it were a civic virtue, and addressing it to the emblematic victim of the arson.

He dropped a couple of names in the course of the conversation, confirming conclusions I had come to independently about who the malefactors were. I declined the job of being this bird's amanuensis, and went off to nurse my now-full knowledge of the particulars and circumstances of the Mystic Arts World fire.

I had to keep quiet about what I knew, because I had no proof. Mr. Big compounded his folly by telling his fellow-conspirators what he'd said, much to their consternation, as it was reported, and later by writing a sort of confused exculpatory letter to the local newspaper justifying the matter. There is no statute of limitations on arson, but who would have the evidence of it? Who would be willing to testify, and who would prosecute the case against one of their own?

No, I had to keep my trap shut until they all died, which they mostly have now. So, shall their names be revealed?

I have to regard the relative importance of civic good works versus a single Class A felony, but I also have to think about whether it is better to defrock a civic hero or to use the story as an indictment of the general small-mindedness and lack of moral scruples found among the business leaders of any community. Let's go for the latter. Backslapping hypocrites are quite able to put together illegal stratagems and see them through, when the level of their indignation rises higher than their sense of honor. In the intervening years, the property at 670 South Coast Highway, which used to be Mystic Arts World, has had an indifferent history of short-lived and failing enterprises. It is empty as I write these words. It only remains to be told the final irony in this long parade of ironies.

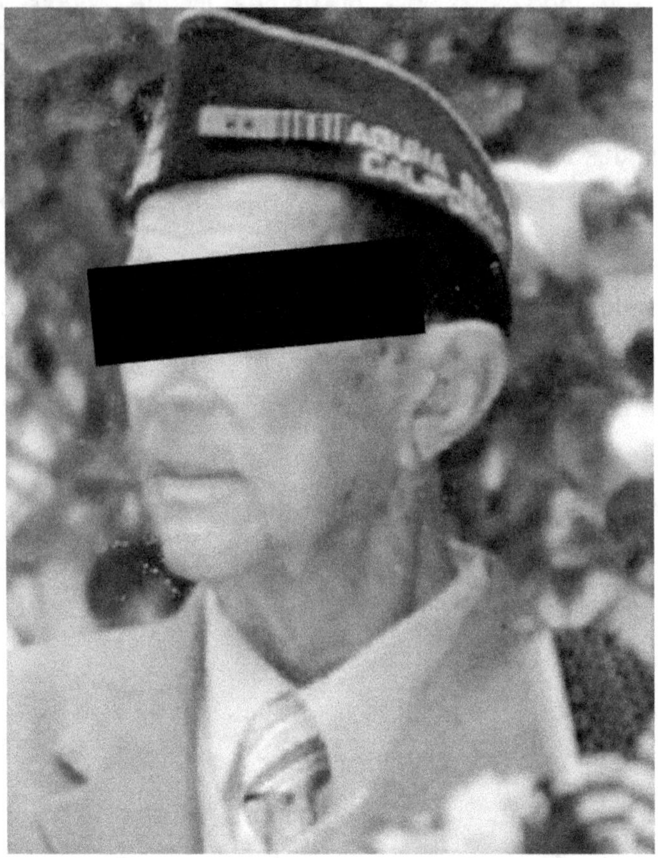

Figure 106: "Mr. Big"

After the destruction of Mystic Arts World, the noose was drawing closed around what remained of the Brotherhood of Eternal Love. Like a covey of startled quail, all the people at the ranch took off at once for parts unknown. After a short while, I made my way up to the abandoned Ranch, a dreary mishmash of suddenly evacuated squalor, where two drunken cowboys and their girls were the only people around.

One of these cowboys' grandfather had started the Ranch in the first place many years before, so I had cause to reflect on dynasties, and their degraded generations. I took down my Mandala from where I had attached it to the ceiling in the front room of the ranch house after the arson, gingerly stepping over unconscious drunks and trying not to drop heavy plywood on them. I left for the last time, Mandala in tow, and sent it off to begin inhabiting another series of interesting locations.

Indictments were coming down, and I felt that prudence dictated I leave Laguna Beach for a while. I really didn't know anything about the nefarious and illegal side of the Brotherhood's activities, but all the same, I was not happy to imagine being subpoenaed to testify about some of my friends, whether I knew anything, or not. So I concocted a way to make a little money so I could go on the road.

Tom Lyster had a glorious A-frame home high up Bluebird Canyon that was one of his partner, Lamont Langworthy's, most elegant designs. I had known both Lamont and Tom for years, so Tom was willing to let me throw a going-away party at his place. I had a two-foot long Stegosaurus dinosaur sculpture in welded steel, and my plan was to sell tickets and to raffle off this piece to finance my meanderings. Things were going along congenially until it was getting late, and the time to draw the winning ticket out of the hat was drawing nigh.

Just then, my old Dana Point pal, Warren Goff, showed up late for the party, dragging his stranger buddy along with him. Good sports that they were, they both bought tickets, and then Tom Lyster drew the winning one out of the hat, after a vigorous shaking. "...and the winner is," said I, reading the ticket, "Stan

Gorgura!" This was Warren Goff's friend who bought the last ticket sold, and was unknown to anybody else at the party beyond Warren.

And here is the final irony: Stan Gorgura was the brother of the fireman who had saved the Mandala from the blaze that destroyed Mystic Arts World.

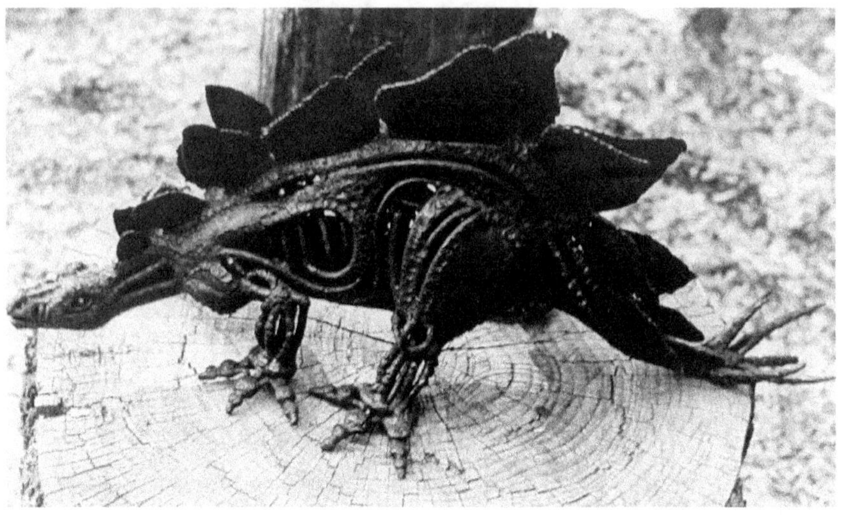

Figure 107: "Stegosaurus" in welded steel by Dion Wright. This is the sculpt that was auctioned off to raise traveling money. Photo by Dion Wright.

Chapter XXIV

Love Animals; Don't Eat Them

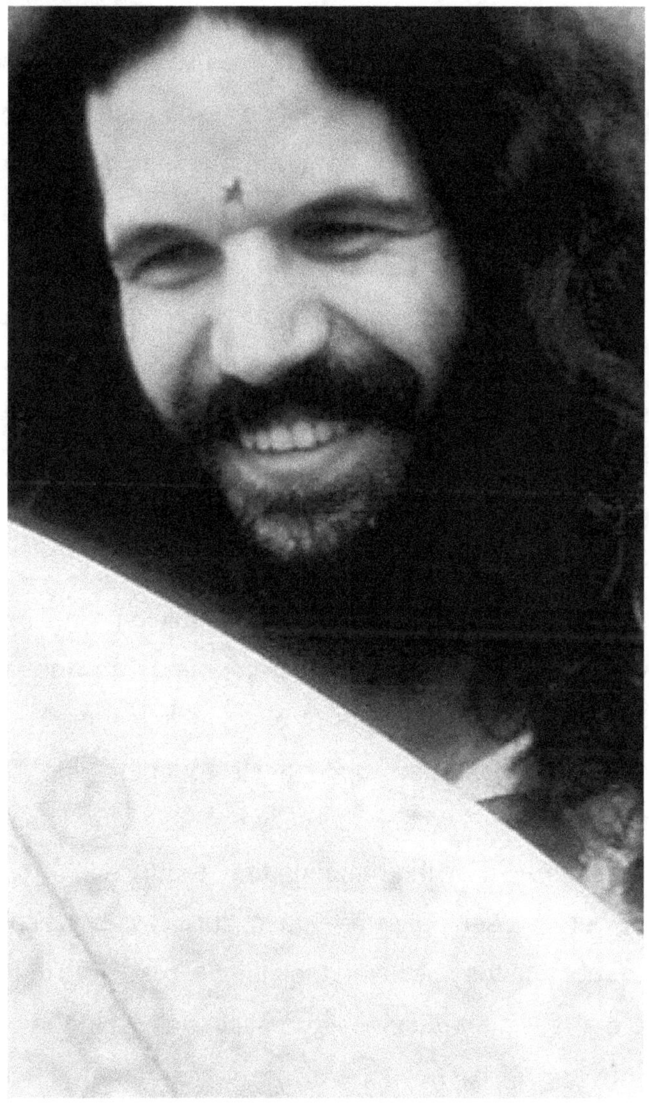

Figure 108: Star Shields ca. 1970.

A Birthday Party for Jesus

Star Shields and Curtis Rainbow were horses of a different color from the buccaneer Brotherhood. These two were pilgrims of a softer order, ultimate flower children who were prophets of vegetarianism. Co-existing in time and locale with the Brotherhood, they were on a separate and less desperate track, which continued beyond the dispersal of the bandit smugglers. They called their movement "Love Animals; Don't Eat Them."

John Griggs was dead, Timothy Leary was captured in Afghanistan and on his way back into the penitentiary, but Love Animals; Don't Eat Them was flourishing. Curt and Star were butterfly-angels whose world was airbrushed in pastel colors. For them, black was not an option, and the possibility of getting shot was never a concern.

Not that Curt and Star were beyond suspicion, if not reproach. They were as devoted to illegal sacraments as anyone, and had the additional suspect behavior of being "a little older" guys who attracted and encouraged 'quite a bit younger' girls into their idealistic precincts, where they were less than altogether innocent, as proved by the offspring they produced.

They were exceedingly smart guys, but not so practical. There was no doubt that they believed their ideals, preached them to the nymphets and waxed passive-aggressive activist in the cause of not killing animals. They opened a vegetarian restaurant on Pacific Coast Highway in Laguna Beach, which caused a furor with the Health Department.

Who knows how the Health Department was alerted to this blooming enterprise? On opening day, there they were. The inspectors were determined to enforce all their regulations, which included prohibiting the honored guests of Love Animals; Don't Eat Them, from staying in the restaurant. This is because those guests were a rooster named Colonel Sanders and a camel named Bony Bananas. Star and Curt tried to keep the inspectors from entering, because they were wearing leather shoes. The inspectors shed their shoes, but forced the departure of the animals.

"Dead animals are welcome in restaurants everywhere," said young flower child Elizabeth Avocado, "but live ones are not."

And so it went, the harmless vegetarians in their riotous pastel colors making copy at the expense of the establishment. Curtis Rainbow, as irresponsible as he was smart, upped the ante. Wouldn't it be nice, thought Curt, if all the hippies in America assembled on Main Beach in Laguna on Christmas? He kicked a pebble, which started a landslide.

Bill Ogden, the illustrator par excellence of the psychedelic surfer set, was dragooned by Curtis to sketch a flier inviting the world's flower children to come to main Beach on Christmas. Curtis showed me this flier on the street one day and I was quick to leverage his effort as best I could into a format that was less fraught with potential riot and disaster.

"Look," I said, "if you get a mob of hippies milling around downtown on the basis of this shallow invitation, you're asking for mayhem. If you are determined to commit this folly, you have to set it in terms of the highest idealism. That will be your only defense against these policemen, who are public servants, but who also are prone to tip over into violence when provoked by un-American eccentrics, which is you, in their terms, at least. You have to cloak your effort in Freedom of Speech and Freedom of Religion, or the cops will bust heads everywhere."

Reluctantly Curtis agreed to allow me to deepen and redefine the invitation in the form of an over-the-top poster, announcing the "event" as a "birthday party for Jesus." I wondered at the time if Curtis might not have preferred a catastrophic clash of hippies and police, for this would achieve a sort of martyrdom for the flower children, and a shameful black eye for law enforcement. Maybe. But if that's what he thought, he was misjudging the tenor of the times, and gambling the skulls of his friends in the interest of a spectacle.

As it happened, Love Animals: Don't Eat Them had a millionaire patron in Malibu who was dazzled by the idealistic rhetoric of Curt and Star, and moved by the nymphets swarming in their wake. This man underwrote the printing and the distribution of the posters. I drew the poster, full of symbols and American and Christian idealism, and handed it over. Curtis and his patron did what they did, and it must have been national and effective, for rumbling through the underground indicated a swell of enthusiasm that was an echo of the Summer of Love. People were coming to Laguna, all right, but who knew how many?

The community mobilized. The City, in a desperate compromise to keep the "event" from blooming downtown, made available a natural setting called Sycamore Flats high up in Laguna Canyon. Dr. Gene Atherton of the Free Clinic undertook to create an ad hoc medical facility; the hippie matrons of the Canyon arranged for a massive vegetarian kitchen effort.

One of the mover-shakers of the soup kitchen effort was Beth Leeds, owner-operator of another health food business in Laguna called Millabee Treats. It turned out that Beth Leeds and Star Shields were "wrestling in the captain's tower" over the direction of culinary affairs. Their points of divergence and struggle for primacy continued unresolved.

A groundswell of talent in many areas rose up; a stage was built for the various musical groups that were anticipated. Porta-potties appeared. Power was run in, and Christmas approached.

Maybe five thousand people showed up at Sycamore Flats before the police shut down the roads and denied access to all

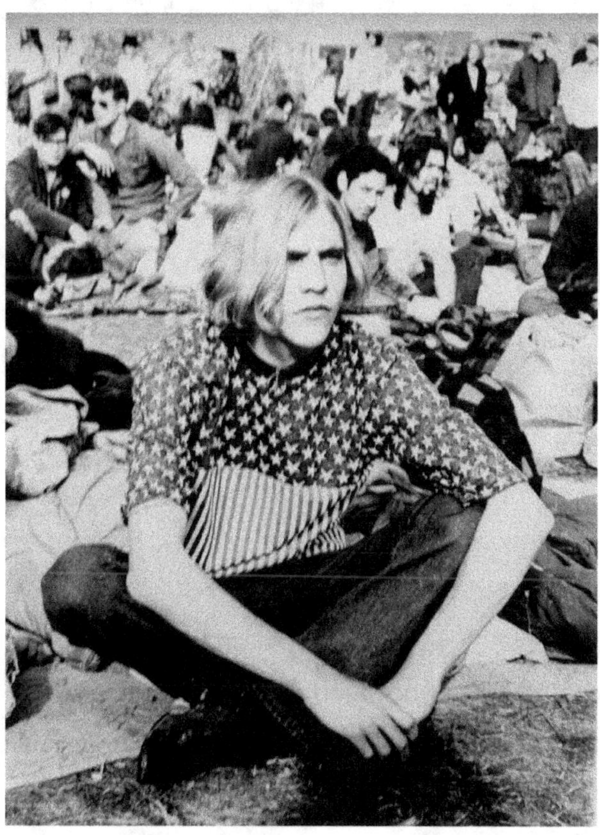

Figure 109: American Pilgrim at Jesus' birthday party.

but emergency traffic. All the same, many more idealists continued to hike in over the hills. The event went on for four days until the Monday morning when we awoke to see a circle of robotic policemen in riot gear on the crest of the ridge above us.

During those four days, society within the enclave of hippies saying Happy Birthday to Jesus was everything one might hope for in the world at large. Music went on constantly. At night, the twinkling campfires stayed under control.

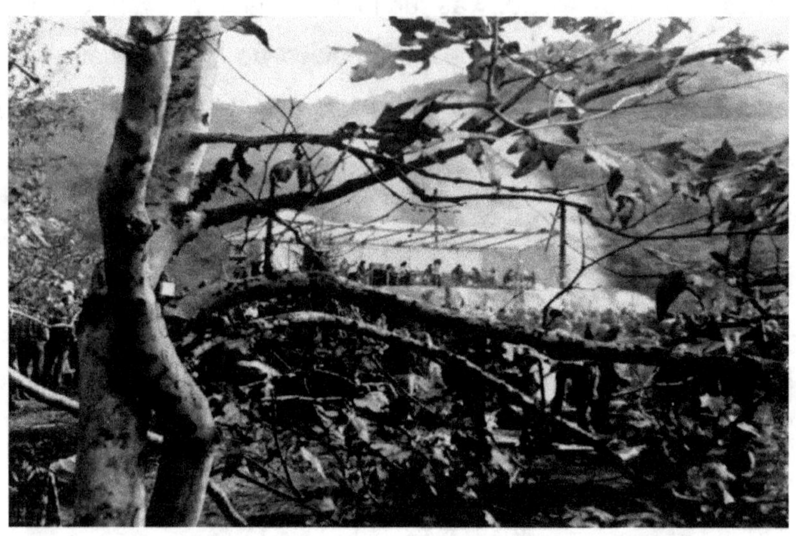

Figure 110: The ad hoc stage at Jesus' birthday party in Laguna Canyon.

At one point Star Shields mounted the podium and gave a passionate oration against eating meat, and had people bringing their hot dogs and hamburger up in front of the stage like Billy Graham converts. There was a solemn funeral for the meat. Two babies were born. Nobody died. Everybody felt blessed by some cosmic agency, despite the repressive way the officials behaved, and the sad way the event ended.

It ended when those helmeted and armed policemen descended the hillside sweeping all before them, herding the pilgrims onto the Canyon Road and into buses to carry them away. A number of people noticed the analogy of the trains to Auschwitz. A bulldozer dug a huge pit and knocked the stage down into it, along with sleeping bags, pots and pans, and God knows what-all. The party was over, leaving a warm glow behind and a graphic commentary on how far American freedom had been both exercised and defrayed.

A subsequent effort to mount an Easter event in Death Valley fizzled, despite the fervent wishes of a few people.

Watergate was right around the corner.

At this point I terminated my involvement with the counter-culture, and went ahead into life with many regrets for what had been lost, but equal resolution to keep the flame alive, which this book as tried to do.

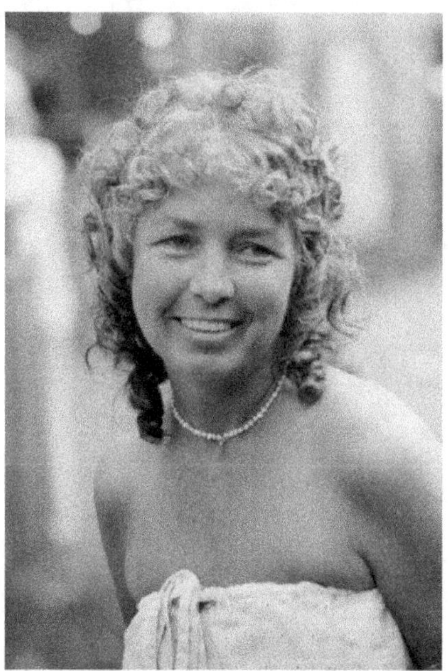

Figure 111: Beth Leeds, at the time of Jesus' birthday party

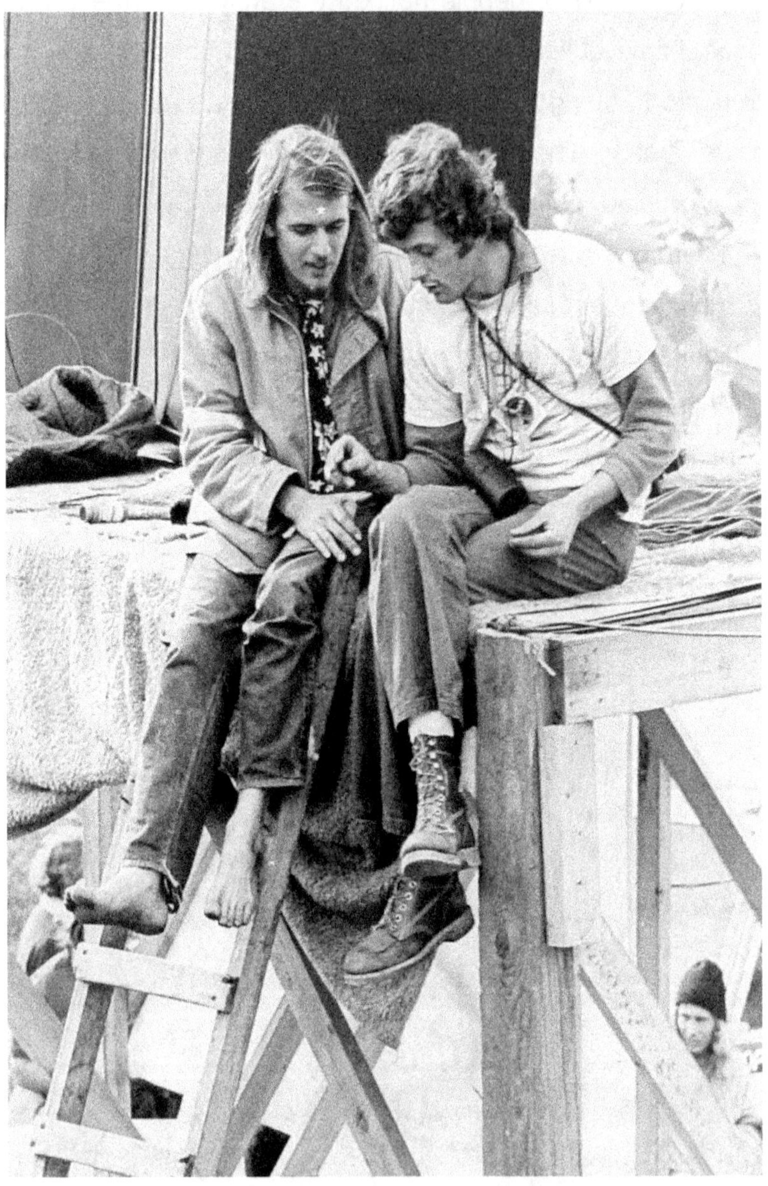

Figure 112: Curtis Rainbow (Love Animals; Don't Eat Them) and Dion Wright, conspiring to throw a birthday party for Jesus. Photo by Mark Chamberlain.

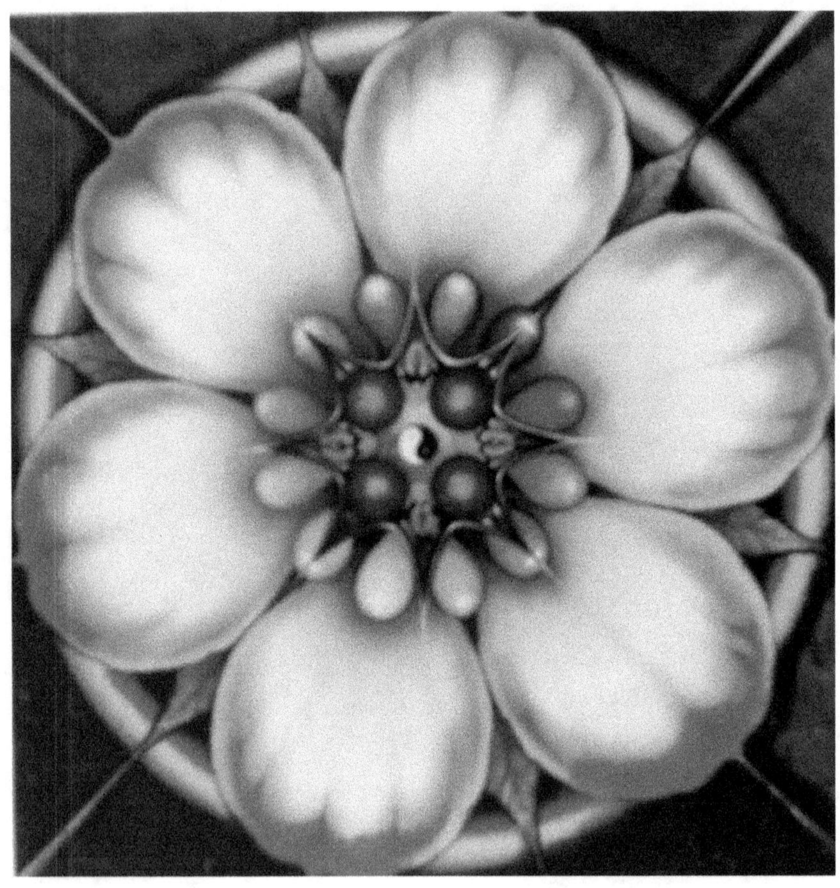

Figure 113: "Starseed," 36" x 36" acrylic on canvas by Dion Wright.

Epilogue

Our Revels now are ended. These our actors

(As I foretold you) are all spirits, and

are melted into Ayre, into thin Ayre,

and like the baseless fabricke of this vision

The Clowd-capt Towres, the gorgeous Pallaces,

The solemne Temples, the great Globe it selfe,

Yea, all which it inherit, shall dissolve,

And like this insubstantial Pageant faded

Leave not a racke behind: we are such stuff

As dreams are made on, and our little life

Is rounded with a sleep.

- William Shakespeare

The Tempest, act IV

We can speculate for a long time about why chemically induced mind-expansion is so controversial, and attended by such legal peril and social repression. In beginning to seek that particular grail of expanded consciousness, we were at first not aware of what it was we were actually doing, "aware" being the operative word. After a while, it was awareness itself we consciously sought. It became clear that awareness was not an either/or condition, but an ascent out of darkness which had no upper limit, as far as random artists like me could tell. The entire business of awareness did have its Academy, which were the esoteric schools, watched over by wise gurus.

In the beginning of our ignorant pilgrimages, however, we knew next to nothing about any of that. We were just artists chasing our flickering horizons like excited hounds.

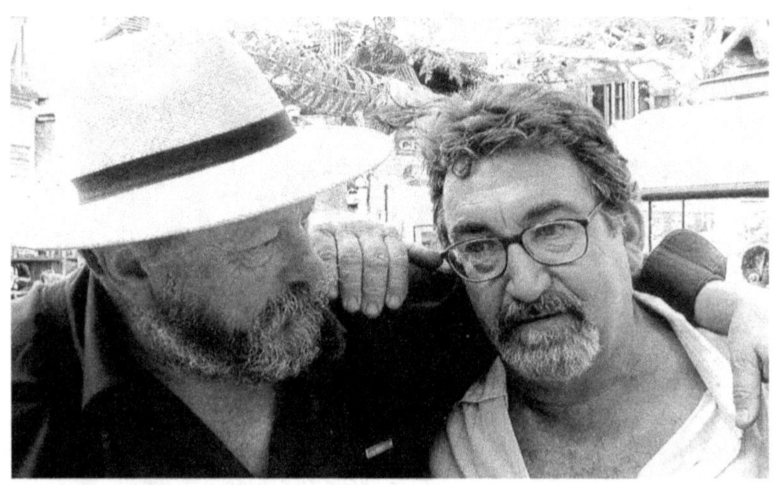

Figure 114: Dion Wright and Noble Richardson at Sawdust. Veterans of Mystic Arts World. Photo by Ruth Wright.

At first, the spark was fanned by good teachers in school, as happens to everybody who is bright. Some people, maybe artists in particular, begin to be introspective, and wonder with growing amazement just what this thing of being aware actually is. It is discovered to be elusive. It seems to be tidal and climatic, in that it's there more at some times than at others, and in that unfolding, daily circumstances can enhance or obscure the purity of such awareness.

It is progressively understood that there are emotional and psychological components to the nature of awareness that are not only unique to the individual; they are also densely tangled, and unwind slowly, and only under diligent application. It was the peculiar fortune of our generation that when we confronted these perennial and timeless questions, we had the spectacular accelerant of psychedelic chemicals to hurl us on our way.

To John Griggs, the whole of revelation burst open with a dazzling flash, and his gift of prophecy immediately took over, and never diminished, even though circumstances piled more and more vicissitudes upon him until he was extinguished by them.

In writing about Johnny, I am not intending to make a mythological character out of him, or even a hero, but we need him as a symbol of idealism. God knows idealism is getting beat up badly nowadays. The mystery arises of who or what it is that is being aware. This question, once asked, never lets go, and never reveals a complete answer either, except maybe to a few philosopher saints after long and rigorous seeking.

Is it ever morally correct to intentionally break the law? The philosopher Alan Watts summed it up with the aphorism: "Citizens will respect Law and Order when Law and Order become respectable." Seen from within the '60s, Law and Order were sliding farther and farther from respectability, while a general mind-expanded sense of righteousness and moral rectitude were becoming more and more obvious to a growing number of awakened people.

Part of the overall problem became clearer as the immoral and repressive aspects of Society were found to be best seen from outside of Society, while the practitioners of repression - too frequently economically motivated - were the least likely individuals to regard themselves as the representatives of the Evil that seemed so obvious to the dropouts. The Viet Nam War was the great escarpment on the moral divide that nobody could avoid, which separated the moralizers from the cynics.

The question of illegality, in personal terms, came in somewhat sideways. It seemed that the law was bent on banning substances which enhanced expanded consciousness as fast as they appeared. Why was this? A carry-over of Prohibition, in which the social mechanics of repression, which still existed, were turned to a new purpose? One thing seems obvious, and that is repressing other substances was good for the liquor industry.

Aldous Huxley knew very well that only a few people are ready to get psychedelically expanded, and able to survive it in a responsible way. Wholesale broadcasting of the chemicals, courtesy of Ken Kesey, trusted to Fate, and failed in every way to try to discriminate between seekers of wisdom and seekers of kicks. Aldous also knew that America was and had been a puritanical country, where nothing agitated the populace more than sex and free love practices.

Huxley, as an English gentleman, had been raised to be perfectly discreet and well-knew how to stay within social forms in a manner that didn't kick the kettle over: a mode of behavior the opposite of Timothy Leary's, the Irish brat who wore his irresponsibility as if it were a flag of independence.

Tim Leary was so charming and intelligent, and so dazzlingly full of wind, that I suspected he had feet of clay from the first, without being able to see them clearly. The first time I looked into his crinkly narrow eyes, there seemed to be no bottom there. He was probably the single most destructive person to the psychedelic cause, excepting maybe Ken Kesey. He used the idealism of the cause to get social perquisites, letting people scramble for high ground as best they could in the wake of his irresponsible behavior, as if they were only window dressing for his personal soap opera. He was one Irishman who'd kissed the Blarney Stone for sure. That Shiva worship of his was pointed. People kept dying in his neighborhood.

Personally, for years and years I've regarded my own survivor's life as a salvage operation, trying to save fragments of that time of such great promise that was torn apart. I often speculate pointlessly about how it might have gone if Dr. Timothy Leary had only stayed in New York. But, we were all in the grip of forces far greater than ourselves. Johnny Griggs was the prophet more on fire than anybody else, but I have to admit that his judgment was pretty shaky a lot of the time. I always felt like Eeyore when talking to him. He was so mercurial and effervescent that I felt as if I were made of lead when in his presence: an old stick-in-the-mud advocating a conservatism that was not only dismissed by John; but also uncharacteristic of *me*, who, in other circumstances, was the radical, compared to those around me.

I suppose the charisma of a leader has little to do with the leader's common sense. John's faith was sterling, and he always left everything in God's hands. What are we left to infer from that? Maybe something like the old joke that ends with God telling the man who prayed to win the lottery, but never did, "Charlie, you had to buy a ticket!"

Today we are looking at the pieces, and wondering if Humpty Dumpty CAN be put back together again. Maybe he can, in a newer and better form, even, recycling the pieces of what was sound in the first rush of surmise. So, this recollection of Johnny Griggs, scratched on the rock of eternity, to disappear in the end another fleeting memory, and maybe also one of yours truly, a tempus fugitive.

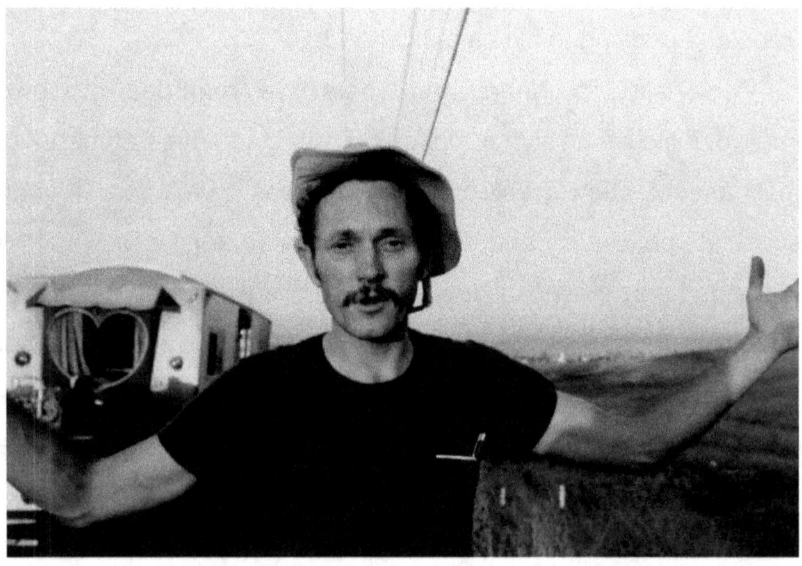

Figure 115: Now What? Leaving Laguna in a homemade camper. ca. 1972.

Index

www.ingramcontent.com/pod-product-compliance
Lightning Source LLC
LaVergne TN
LVHW020655110826
845149LV00012B/2013
9780997334210